*CALLED & COMMITTED:*
World-Changing Discipleship

# Called & Committed:

## World-Changing Discipleship

## David Watson

Harold Shaw Publishers
Wheaton, Illinois

A British edition of this book, titled *Discipleship*, is pub-
lished by Hodder & Stoughton, © 1981 by The Shalom
Trust. References in footnotes may refer to the British
edition of a title. When an American edition could be
found, it is listed in the bibliography at the back of the
book.


ISBN 978-0-87788-101-8

Printed in the United States of America

---

Library of Congress Cataloging in Publication Data
Watson, David C. K., 1933-
    Called & committed.

    1. Christian life—1960-        I. Title.
II. Title: Called and committed.
BV4501.2.W377        248.4        82-824
ISBN 978-0-87788-101-8    AACR2

---

01 99 98

14 13 12 11 10 9

To the various members of the team
who have worked with me in Christian
missions and festivals throughout the
world, who have shared with me,
encouraged me, been patient with me,
and have shown me more of Christ.

# CONTENTS

# FOREWORD

A jolly saint of the recent past (was it William Temple? I can't be sure) confessed to praying, "God who made me simple, make me simpler yet." Surely the very thought of such a prayer will jangle nerves in the modern West, where middle-class respectability, worldly wisdom and—let us say it straight out—spinelessness have muddled up and watered down our Christianity. But in 2 Corinthians 11:3, simplicity appears as a virtue to be jealously guarded. "I fear," writes Paul, "lest... your minds should be corrupted from the simplicity that is in Christ." From Conybeare's rendering of the Greek word as "singleminded faithfulness," Goodspeed's as "single-hearted fidelity," and the *Jerusalem Bible's* as "simple devotion," we see what Christian simplicity is, not naivety or dim-wittedness, but sincerity and straightforwardness in facing the moral and spiritual demands of being Christ's person.

Sin in our hearts, by making us complicated and devious, foments spiritual apathy and moral dishonesty; sophistication in our culture, which makes values relative and encourages detachment as a mental attitude, reinforces sin's effects. However, God's grace—by which I really mean our Lord Jesus Christ, who is grace incarnate—reverses the process, making us increasingly honest, straightforward and childlike in our life with God: in other words, simple in the sense defined above. Study of Scripture is the highway to this supernatural simplicity. Psalm 19:7 celebrates the Word of God as "sure, making wise the simple [those who lack wisdom]," but God's gift of wisdom from the Word, while banishing that kind of simplicity, leads us ever deeper into the sort of simplicity that I have described. The rule is, the wiser the simpler. Simplicity was seen supremely in Jesus, and is a mark of stature in his followers. If ever you have met a genuinely holy person, you know that already.

David Watson's writings seem to me to be shining examples of this kind of simplicity. They are transparently clear, and ruthlessly straightforward in facing up to the Bible's often upsetting and bewildering practical challenges. David Watson takes God at his word! So you will find breath-taking, block-busting, Bible-based simplicity on every page of this book.

He writes out of wide experience of ministry and leadership in the world of charismatic renewal, and his vision of discipleship reflects what is central in that movement. No bad thing! Charismatic emphases have proved infinitely enriching and animating to literally millions in our time. David knows what is going on around him, and every chapter here focuses on razor-sharp issues in following Christ today.

During the years he was God's instrument of new life in the once-dying Anglican parish of St. Michael-le-Belfrey, York, he became one of the best-known clergymen in England, and widely known elsewhere. It is the tested insights from a very fruitful ministry that he dispenses in these pages. You do not have to agree with every single statement to appreciate the authority and power of his vision of life in Christ, and to be made most uncomfortable as the search-light of Watsonian simplicity swings your way.

I am not surprised that David Watson by his own confession found the book hard to write; vivid, searching books often are, and I can well believe that the Devil did not want this one written and tried all he could to stop it. But I am glad and grateful that David persevered till it was done. Now we may all receive the benefit.

This is an important book. Who should read it? Anyone who wants to be a simple follower of Jesus Christ. But be prepared to discover that you are being courteously dynamited! You have been warned.

*James I. Packer*

## ACKNOWLEDGMENTS

During the writing of this book, I discussed its theme with Christian leaders in different parts of the world, and I have a growing conviction that the subject of *Discipleship* is of crucial importance for today. The Christian church has largely neglected the thrust of the Great Commission: *to make disciples*. The result is that other more aggressive religions and political groups have pulled ahead of Christians, and we see the worldwide effects of this. Further, some Christians, in an attempt to correct the church's failure to disciple its members, have swung to extremes, using methods that have aroused suspicion and have brought the name of Christ into disrepute.

I am most grateful to Edward England, whose wisdom as a literary agent is enormously valuable, for suggesting the theme to me in the first place. I have personally benefitted from the reading and study that have been necessary to prepare this book.

Helpful ideas have come from many sources, but I am especially grateful to Liz Attwood, a present member of my mission team, for her perceptive, honest, and invaluable comments throughout the painful period of writing which had to be squeezed in between Christian missions and festivals through the year.

For the main task of typing I am deeply grateful to Jeni Farnhill, together with Bridget Hunt who helped with the first few chapters, to Jennie Lunn and Shirley Anderson who checked the final manuscript and to Janet Lunt for her diagrams.

The writing of this book took place during an exceptionally busy year, which included some tense problems in our church in York (which have sharpened my understanding of certain sections of this book). I have deeply appreciated the patient encouragement given by my wife, Anne, during this time.

Biblical quotations, unless otherwise stated, are from the *Revised Standard Version*.

# INTRODUCTION

IT IS WIDELY HELD that the battle of the century will be between Marxism, Islam, and Third-world Christianity. Western Christianity is considered too weak and ineffective to contribute anything significant to this universal struggle.

## The Battle Between Marxism, Islam, and Christianity

The ruthless determination of Marxism has been proved, sometimes in horrifying proportions, ever since 1917. In a speech to an audience of American Trade Unionists in 1975, Alexander Solzhenitsyn said, "During the 80 years before the revolution... about 17 persons a year were executed. In 1918 and 1919 the Cheka executed, without trial, more than a thousand persons a month... At the height of Stalin's terror in 1937-38... there were more than 40,000 persons shot per month." Stalin was the greatest mass murderer in human history. The militant fanaticism of Islam has likewise been demonstrated in many Muslim countries in the world. The life of any convert from Islam to Christianity is in danger, even from his own family.

Numerically, Christianity is still the strongest of religions. In a world population approaching four billion, approximately one quarter profess to be Christians. There is no greater good news to be found anywhere than the gospel of Jesus Christ. Who else, in the history of the world, can claim to respond to the deepest cries of the human heart? Everywhere we hear the cry for meaning in a meaningless existence, the cry for caring love in an age of selfishness and violence, the cry for forgiveness in an age when reconciliation is rare, the cry for freedom when human slavery and oppression abound on every side, the cry for hope in the gathering gloom of the world. All these cries are summed up in the cry for God, and the clear, resounding answer to that universal cry is Jesus Christ, who, by his living presence among us, has the power to change us to the core of our being.

### The Ineffectiveness of Western Christianity
With such numerical strength, such a relevant message, and such spiritual power, why is the Christian church, especially in the West, so comparatively ineffective? In 1979 the Center for Study of World Evangelization in Nairobi produced a computerized survey, based on an analysis of statistics from the world's 223 countries, 6,270 ethnolinguistic groups, 50 major religions, and more than 9,000 Christian denominations. According to that survey, conducted three years ago, about 1,815,100 adult professing Christians in Europe abandoned the faith to become agnostics, atheists, or adherents of non-Christian religions or cults. North America also registered a decline of 950,000. (These were net figures, after conversions to Christianity had been noted.) However, during the same period, churches in the Third World experienced phenomenal gains: in Africa, 6,152,800, or 16,600 each day; in South Asia, 34,813,000.[1] Why is the church in the West in such sharp decline compared with the church in the poverty-stricken countries of the world?

### Discipleship
Solzhenitsyn said on the BBC program, *Panorama*, in March, 1976: "I wouldn't be surprised at the sudden and imminent fall of the West ... Nuclear war is not even necessary to the Soviet Union. You can be taken simply with bare hands."

Why? Because Christians in the West have largely neglected what it means to be *disciples of Christ*. The vast majority of Western

Christians—church-members, pew-fillers, hymn-singers, sermon-tasters, Bible-readers, even born-again-believers or Spirit-filled-charismatics, are not true disciples of Jesus. If we were willing *to become disciples*, the church in the West would be transformed, and the impact on society would be staggering. And this is no idle claim. In the first century, a tiny handful of inexperienced, timid disciples initiated, in the power of the Spirit, the greatest spiritual revolution the world has ever known. Within three centuries, even the mighty Roman Empire yielded to the power of the gospel of Christ.

All the great revolutionary leaders have struggled with one central, intractable problem—the nature of man. Che Guevara once said, "If our revolution is not aimed at changing people, then I am not interested." Revolutions are aptly named: they revolve. They turn one group of sinners out, and put another lot of sinners in. But the trouble with most revolutions is that they cannot change the human heart. Until human nature is changed, nothing else can be significantly different. It is by the inward power of his Spirit that Christ offers a revolution of love that can transform every one of us from the inside out.

The impact of Christ's revolution can be clearly seen in the history of the Christian church up to the present, but only when Christians were willing to pay the costly price of discipleship. That is why Third World Christianity is so vibrant compared to Western Christianity. Though political and sociological factors may be at work as well, it is often in these materially impoverished areas that we see the clearest living examples of whole-hearted New Testament discipleship.

The future prospects of the affluent West are so serious that the Christian church can no longer ignore the plan chosen by Jesus for the renewal of society. He came with no political manifesto. He rejected all thoughts of violence. He himself shunned positions of influence in public life. His plan was astonishingly simple. He drew around him a small band of dedicated disciples. For three years he lived with, shared with, cared for, taught, corrected, trusted, forgave, and loved them. They often failed him, disobeyed him, misunderstood him, hurt him, and disappointed him, yet never did he withdraw his love from them. And later, empowered by the Holy Spirit, this small group of trained disciples turned the world of their day upside down.

A Communist once challenged a Western Christian: "The gospel is a much more powerful weapon for the renewal of society than is our Marxist philosophy, but it is we who will finally beat you... We Communists do not play with words. We are realists, and seeing our object, we know how to obtain the means... We believe in our message, and we are ready to sacrifice everything, even our life... But you people are afraid to soil your hands."

## Christ's Plan to Transform the World

*Discipleship* sums up Christ's plan for the world. Yet for all its brilliant simplicity, it is the one approach that most Western churches have ignored or neglected. With all our reports, committees, conferences, seminars, missions, crusades, ecumenism, and liturgical reforms, little attention has been given to the meaning of discipleship.

This book is written that we may see again what it means to follow Jesus, and learn how we may help others to do the same. Together with the continuous renewing power of the Holy Spirit, this is our only real hope for the future. God still wants his church to be the unifying force in a world that is falling apart without him, and to be his agent in the healing of the whole of his creation. It is my strong conviction that Christ is calling to himself those who are willing to dedicate their lives fully to him, to commit themselves to all other true Christians out of love for him, and to present their bodies to him as a living sacrifice for all that he wants to do in his world today.

That is what discipleship is all about, and it is what this book will explain and explore.

# CHAPTER ONE

# CALLED TO DISCIPLESHIP

"WHEN CHRIST CALLS A MAN, he bids him come and die," declared Dietrich Bonhoeffer. In this startling statement we see the radical nature of Christian discipleship. There are different ways in which we may die; not every Christian is called to literal martyrdom, as was Bonhoeffer. But every Christian is called to clear, dedicated discipleship, whatever the personal cost may be.

The concept of discipleship was by no means new when Jesus called men and women to follow him, so it is not surprising that, although the verb "disciple" (*manthano*) occurs only 25 times in the New Testament (6 in the Gospels), the noun "disciple" (*mathetes*) appears no less than 264 times, exclusively in the Gospels and Acts. In secular Greek the word meant an apprentice in some trade, a student of some subject, or a pupil of some teacher. In the New Testament times we find the same primary meaning in the terms "disciples of Moses"[1] (students of the Mosaic law) and "disciples of the Pharisees"[2] (those preoccupied with a detailed knowledge of Jewish tradition as given in the Torah). These disciples would submit themselves entirely to their rabbi, and were not permitted to study the

Scriptures without the guidance of their teacher, although they expected to become teachers themselves after extensive training.

Nearer to the specifically Christian concept of discipleship were the followers of John the Baptist who attached themselves to this New Testament prophet. Following their teacher, they fasted and prayed,[3] confronted the Jewish leaders,[4] and remained loyal to John during his imprisonment[5] and at his death.[6] Unlike the disciples of Moses or of the Pharisees, they were fully committed to their master as well as to his message.

Thus we see that the basic idea of discipleship was widely accepted when Jesus began his ministry. At the same time, when Jesus took the initiative in calling people to follow him, when he called them primarily to himself and not just to his teaching, when he expected from them total obedience, when he taught them to serve and warned them that they would suffer, and when he gathered around him a diverse group of very ordinary people, he was obviously creating a radical and unique pattern of discipleship.

### Called by Jesus
In rabbinical circles, a disciple would choose his own master and voluntarily join his school. But Jesus took the initiative and personally called Simon and Andrew, James and John, Levi, Philip, and others to be his followers. Even when the rich young ruler ran up to Jesus and asked him a leading question, Jesus spelled out the costly and total demands of discipleship, and added "Come, follow me." There may have been some who, attracted by the integrity of his person, by the quality of his teaching, and by the power of his miracles, wanted to attach themselves to Jesus and to his disciples, but always it was *Jesus* who laid down for *them* his exacting conditions. "This is more than we can stomach!" some said. "Why listen to such words?"[7] And they departed, leaving only the twelve whom he had called to himself after spending a whole night in prayer. These were the ones whom God had given him.[8] Yet although there is a uniqueness about the twelve apostles, God's initiative and Christ's calling are true for all those who are his disciples. "You did not choose me, but I chose you and appointed you that you should go and bear fruit and that your fruit should abide; so that whatever you ask the Father in my name, he may give it to you. This I command you, to love one another."[9] Two points of interest arise from that cogent statement.

*Choosing or being chosen.* First, our view of ourselves, as disciples who have been personally chosen by Jesus, should alter our whole attitude towards him and motivate us strongly for the work which he has given us to do. If an athlete is chosen to represent his country for the Olympics, his attitude to this event will be different from someone who has decided on his own to go as a spectator to the Olympics. With the competitor, there will be a total dedication to the task, largely because of the honor of being chosen. He will have a sense of responsibility to his team and country which even the most enthusiastic tourist will clearly not have. The Christian church today suffers because so many of its members feel that *they* have "made a decision for Christ," or that *they* have chosen to join a certain church. Such man-centered notions spell spiritual weakness and imbalance. It is only when we see ourselves as chosen, called, and commissioned *by Christ* that we will want to present our bodies to him "as a living sacrifice, holy and acceptable to God."

The apostles never escaped from this awareness of divine constraint. "As men of sincerity, as commissioned by God, in the sight of God we speak in Christ";[10] "Therefore, having this ministry by the mercy of God, we do not lose heart";[11] "Paul, a servant of Jesus Christ, called to be an apostle, set apart for the gospel of God . . . To all God's beloved in Rome, who are called to be saints";[12] "We know, brethren beloved by God, that he has chosen you";[13] "You are not your own; you were bought with a price. So glorify God in your body."[14] Such biblical examples could be multiplied. It was this strong sense of God's calling, of Christ's initiative, of the Spirit's sovereign work, that enabled them to be bold in their witness, to hold fast in their suffering, and to lead lives "worthy of the calling" to which they had been called.[15]

*No solitary disciples.* The second point of interest in John 15:16 is that Christ calls us to a common discipleship, to share our lives and our love both with him and with each other. That is why his statement "you did not choose me, but I chose you" is directly followed by his command "to love one another." It is by this love that we are known to be his disciples,[16] fruitful in his service and effective in our prayers.[17] Discipleship is never easy; often it involves pain and tears, when we shall have to re-think our values and our ambition to follow Christ. But we are not called to face this challenge on our own. As well as the inward power of the Holy Spirit, God provides us with the supportive love of other disciples of Jesus. In the strength of our relationships together in Christ we can win battles and help each other in the task that God has given us.

## Called to Jesus

This again was something unique in Jesus' day. The call *by* Jesus was also a call *to* Jesus. Both the Jewish rabbi and the Greek philosopher expected new disciples to commit themselves to a specific teaching or cause. But the call of Jesus was personal: he called his disciples to follow *him*, to be with *him*, and to commit themselves wholeheartedly to *him*. They could become disciples only by repenting of their sin and by believing in him. For example, in the gospel record of the call of Simon Peter and Nathanael, it was their response to the person of Jesus that was the all-important factor. When Simon saw something of Jesus' authority, "he fell down at Jesus' knees, saying, 'Depart from me, for I am a sinful man, O Lord.' "[18] When Nathanael saw the perceptive knowledge of Jesus, he said, "Rabbi, you are the Son of God! You are the King of Israel!"[19]

In Kittel's *Theological Dictionary of the New Testament*, the writer makes the following comment: "The personal allegiance of the disciples to Jesus is confirmed by their conduct in the days between the crucifixion and the resurrection. The reason for the deep depression which marks these days is to be found in the fate which has befallen the person of Jesus. No matter what view we take of the story of the walk to Emmaus, the fact that 'He' is the theme of their conversation on the way (Luke 24:19ff.) corresponds in every sense to the relation of the disciples to Jesus before his arrest and execution. On the other hand, it is nowhere stated or even hinted that after the death of Jesus his teaching was a source of strength to his followers, or that they had the impression of having a valuable legacy in the word of Jesus. This is a point of considerable importance for a true understanding of the *mathetes* [disciple] of Jesus."[20]

When Jesus called individuals to be his disciples, he shared his life with them. By his incarnation he identified himself fully with them, and he made himself vulnerable by opening his heart to them. Part of his great attraction lay in the fact that his love was so real and open that others sensed intuitively that they could trust him. There was no duplicity about him. His transparent openness and integrity drew others into a quality of loving that they had not known before.

That is why they were all so shattered when Jesus' perfect life of love was smashed on a cross. After the horrifying events of the crucifixion it took time for Jesus to restore the faith of his disciples. He could do this only by leading them gently back into a renewed relationship with him. Thus, after Peter's threefold denial came Jesus' threefold question: "Simon, son of John, do you love me?" In his resurrection appearances he came to his disciples, individually and corporately, to reassure them of his living presence, and of his love and forgiveness. They were to become witnesses *to him*—not masters of his teaching.

When Buddha was dying, his disciples asked how they could best remember him. He told them not to bother; it was his teaching, not his person, that counted. With Jesus it is altogether different. Everything centers around him, his *person*. Discipleship means knowing *him*, loving *him*, believing in *him*, being committed to *him*.

## Called to Obey

The disciples of a Jewish rabbi would submit themselves as slaves to their master until the time when they had finished their schooling and had become masters or rabbis themselves. But Jesus calls his disciples to unconditional, lifelong obedience. We shall never graduate this side of heaven. To obey God's will is to find the fulfillment of our lives. "Not every one who says to me, 'Lord, Lord,' shall enter the kingdom of heaven, but he who does the will of my Father who is in heaven."[21] "Why do you call me 'Lord, Lord,' and not do what I tell you?"[22] To be a disciple of Jesus means to follow him, to go the way that he goes, to accept his plan for our lives. "If any man would come after me, let him deny himself and take up his cross and follow me."[23] It is a call to say *no* to the old life of sin, and to say *yes* to Jesus. Inward belief must be accompanied by outward obedience. Søren Kierkegaard once rightly remarked, "It is so hard to believe because it is so hard to obey." There is no true faith and no true discipleship without obedience.

*Radical obedience: an example.* The world of today is being increasingly influenced by disciples of another kind who understand obedience more clearly than the average Christian. A BBC radio program about women terrorists showed that they were intensely loyal, totally ruthless, and willing to go to any lengths for their cause. Bernadette Devlin declared, "Before, there came a time when one

said, 'This I can't do!' Now there comes a time when one says, 'This I
must do!' "[24]

How can we expect anything less than this kind of total commitment if we are to see Christ's revolution of love changing the world
of today? To say "No, Lord!" is a contradiction in terms, yet many
within the Christian church want the comfortable compromise of
conditional discipleship. The bottom line is our wish to have the
final word, to decide when to say *yes* and when to say *no*. But the
truth is uncomfortably clear: if Christ is not Lord of all, he is not
Lord at all. It is impossible to be a partial disciple of Jesus. Malcolm
Muggeridge vividly comments: "I have a longing past conveying...
to use whatever gifts of persuasion I may have to induce others to
see that they must at all costs hold on to that reality (the reality of
Christ); lash themselves to it, as in the old days of sail, sailors would
lash themselves to the mast when storms blew up and the seas were
rough."[25] In the church today we need urgently true disciples who
will bind themselves to Jesus Christ in unswerving obedience and
loyalty. "The great tragedy of modern evangelism," writes Jim
Wallis, "is in calling many to belief but few to obedience."[26]

*Family reinforcement.* In this painful but liberating life of obedience, however, we do not enter the battle on our own. We are to
exhort and encourage one another "every day," that none of us may
be "hardened by the deceitfulness of sin. For we share in Christ."[27]
We are to "stand firm in one spirit, with one mind striving side by
side for the faith of the gospel."[28] Once again we may have to learn
humbling lessons from fighting groups of today. The leader of Al
Fatah, a Palestinian liberation movement, summarized the strength
of his movement in these words: "I can always fall out with my
comrade ... but my brother is always my brother." Strong and
binding though other human relationships may be, none is
unbreakable except the bonds of family. Within the family of God
we are eternally united to one another. If this union leads to
qualities of love and trust which transcend human relationships, the
resulting corporate strength will be immense. The Spirit of God who
enables us to call Almighty God "Abba! Father!" is the same Spirit
who helps us to see *every* true Christian as a brother or sister. Jesus
can call us to absolute obedience because he has first laid down his
life for us, placed his Spirit in our hearts, and given us to each other
in love.

## Called to Serve

Although Jesus called the disciples to be with him, they were also commissioned to go and preach and to "heal the sick, raise the dead, cleanse lepers, cast out demons."[29] As soon as Jesus called Simon and Andrew, he told them that he would change them into fishers of men.[30] The seventy were sent out in the name of Jesus as messengers of peace: "Heal the sick... and say to them, 'the kingdom of God has come near to you.' "[31] Jesus had come to lay down his life for the sake of others, and his disciples were to do exactly the same.

Yet they did not always understand this. Jesus repeatedly found that his disciples fell into two equal and opposite temptations which crippled their spirit of service. Their first temptation was *to be ambitious.* Several times they were found arguing about who was the greatest. When James and John asked for the places of highest honor in the kingdom of heaven, they demonstrated the spirit of the world that seeks status instead of service. Jesus rebuked them: "Whoever would be great among you must be your servant, and whoever would be first among you must be your slave; even as the Son of man came not to be served but to serve, and to give his life as a ransom for many."[32] He later demonstrated this spirit of service in a way they never forgot; wrapping a towel around his waist and kneeling, he himself washed his disciples' feet.

Their second temptation was *to feel self-pity.* "Lo, we have left our homes and followed you," protested Simon Peter. But Jesus assured him that he would "receive manifold more in this time, and in the age to come eternal life."[33] Though we need to be honest about our own weakness, the moment we fall into self-pity we hinder God's working in our lives. It is only when we accept our human frailty, knowing God's grace to be sufficient, ambitious for God's kingdom alone, that we shall be able to serve others with the loving, gracious and humble spirit of Jesus Christ. The servant should not demand certain conditions of service. He has given up his rights, and may well have to forgo normal comforts and rewards. As we grow in years it is easy to look for privileges, position, and respect. This was not the way of Jesus.

In this advertising age it is easy to present Christ as the one who will meet all *your* needs. Are you anxious? Christ will bring you peace! Are you lost? Christ will help you find your true direction! Are you depressed? Christ will fill your life with joy! All this is part

of the good news of Christ; he longs to meet our deepest needs. But
that is only half the story. In practice many of our needs will be met
as we give ourselves in service to Jesus and to others. Those who are
willing to lose their lives will find them. It is as we give that God will
give to us—"good measure, pressed down, shaken together, running over, will be put into your lap. For the measure you give will
be the measure you get back."[34] When the seventy went out to
preach and heal they returned filled with joy because of all that they
had experienced.

The needs of the world are vast. God longs to reach out to all
those who are crying out for help; but he has chosen to work primarily through his disciples. If we are taken up with our own personal needs, or if we are looking for position and status in the
church, we shall be of little use to God.

## Called to Live Simply

A disciple of a rabbi might give up many material benefits in order
to study the Torah, but he would know that such sacrifice was for a
limited time. He would be rewarded financially for his diligence
when he himself assumed the role of a teacher. It was altogether
different with Jesus. He laid aside all earthly security and material
comfort. Often he had nowhere to lay his head. He also called his
disciples to a life of humility and poverty. Although it was the
Father's good pleasure to give them the kingdom, they were to sell
their possessions, and give to charity. Jesus told them, "Take no
gold, nor silver, nor copper in your belts, no bag for your journey,
nor two tunics, nor sandals, nor a staff; for the labourer deserves his
food." Like their Master, they had to be willing to leave their
homes, their families, their occupations, and their security—for the
sake of the kingdom of God. But as they made his kingdom their
highest goal, all that they needed would be provided for them.

It is fair to point out that such radical discipleship applied primarily to those who were called into a life of full community with
him. Other disciples who were not drawn into such close-knit fellowship seemed to have kept some of their material possessions, and
helped to provide for Jesus and the twelve. Nevertheless, New
Testament disciples were encouraged to live a simple life in which
they held their possessions "in common."[35]

The comparative affluence of many Christians today, especially those in the West, is almost certainly a stumbling-block to effective discipleship. It is unlikely that God will entrust us with true spiritual riches until he sees that we are genuinely serving him, not mammon. It is when we can learn to live on the New Testament principle of contentedness[36] that God will entrust us with the gifts of his Spirit that will enrich our own lives as well as those we serve.

## Called to Suffer

When Jesus called his disciples to follow him, they had to be willing to walk the way of the cross. If they were to share their lives together, they must share pain as well as joy. "For it has been granted to you that for the sake of Christ you should not only believe in him but also suffer for his sake."[37]

Jesus tried to prepare them for this by speaking plainly about his own sufferings and those which his followers must experience. But they could not, or would not, understand his warnings. We read in Matthew 16 that "from that time Jesus began to show his disciples that he must go to Jerusalem and suffer many things from the elders and chief priests and scribes, and be killed..." Peter at once protested, "Heaven forbid! No, Lord, this shall never happen to you." For this he received a stinging rebuke, "Away with you, Satan; you are a stumbling-block to me. You think as men think, not as God thinks." And in case the disciples were under any further illusions, Jesus began to speak plainly about their sufferings, too. "If any man would come after me, let him deny himself and take up his cross and follow me. For whoever would save his life will lose it, and whoever loses his life for my sake will find it..." Life for the Master ended with rejection, pain, and agonizing death. The disciple should never be surprised if following Jesus leads the same way.

*Physical suffering.* Many suffered from physical persecution. Peter and John were imprisoned and beaten for their boldness; Stephen was stoned to death; James was killed with the sword. Before long "a great persecution arose against the church in Jerusalem, and they were all scattered."[38] Paul later wrote about being beaten five times with the 39 lashes of the Jewish whip, three times with rods, and also being stoned. Most of the apostles suffered martyrdom in one form or another. During those early years of the church appalling persecution came from a succession of Roman emperors: Nero, Domitian, Trajan, Pliny, Marcus Aurelius, Decius and Diocletian. In various degrees of ferocity this persecution continued on through the history of the Christian church. In recent years, and even today, thousands of Christians around the world have been imprisoned and tortured for their faith. It is estimated that there have been more martyrdoms for Christ during this century than during the rest of the church's history.

None of this should come as a surprise. Jesus warned his disciples about the physical dangers that lay ahead: "Beware of men; for they will deliver you up to councils, and flog you in their synagogues, and you will be dragged before governors and kings for my sake... Brother will deliver up brother to death, and the father his child, and children will rise against parents and have them put to death; and you will be hated by all for my name's sake..."[39]

*Mental and emotional pain.* It is not hard for us to feel something of Paul's sadness when he wrote, "Demas, in love with this present world, has deserted me... Crescens has gone to Galatia, Titus to Dalmatia... Alexander the coppersmith did me great harm..."[40] We too are often hurt and disappointed in each other since we are, at best, a fellowship of sinners. We often need to forgive and forgiveness is always painful. It cost Jesus his death on the cross. For us, too, it may be a crucifying experience to forgive someone who has hurt us.

*Spiritual grief.* Paul once wrote concerning his overwhelming burden for fellow Jews who did not believe in Jesus as their Messiah: "I have great sorrow and unceasing anguish in my heart. For I could wish that I myself were accursed and cut off from Christ for the sake of my brethren."[41] And during his ministry in Ephesus he said that "for three years I did not cease night or day to admonish every one with tears."[42] God, in his great compassion, "spreads out (his) hands all the day to a rebellious people." Having made us in his image, he longs that we should share in his love. Since love will never force itself on unwilling people, God watches us fall away from him and from each other; he sees us resenting, hating, killing one another. He sent his Son to bring peace on earth, but because we will not have this man to reign over us, mistrust, confusion, bitterness, and war pollute the face of this earth.

Is it surprising that a loving God is grieved? When Jesus weeps for his body, the torn, wounded, broken church, can we be unmoved? When Jesus weeps, as he once did by the grave of Lazarus, when he sees today the ravages caused by man's sin, can we be apathetic? The more we love Jesus, the nearer we come to his great heart of love, the less we should be surprised if we feel his pain.

Suffering is inescapably woven into the fabric of discipleship— "joy and woe are woven fine," wrote William Blake. But it is in suffering that God is working most profoundly in our lives. Those with the greatest spiritual sensitivity and depth are those who have experienced the most suffering. One Christian who spent ten years in a Communist prison in Czechoslovakia said that his torturers broke his bones but not his spirit. He referred to those years as the richest years of his life. "We must pray," he said later, "not that persecution will not come, but that we may be worthy of it, open to the blessings God offers through it."

### Called Irrespective of Qualifications
Whereas the rabbis would accept disciples only from the ceremonially "clean," from those considered righteous according to the law, and from those with the intelligence to study the Torah and become rabbis themselves, Jesus called to himself a curious cross-section of contemporary society. Some were down-to-earth fishermen; James and John were sons of a Zealot; the second Simon was certainly a Zealot; there was despised Levi, a traitor to his countrymen; and among the twelve we find Greek and Semitic names, and probably a Judean, as well as Galileans. "The circle of the disciples is in fact a microcosm of the Judaism of the time. In it we find all the powers and thoughts of the people, even in their divergence."[43]

Most interesting of all, among those called as disciples was Judas who betrayed Jesus. Since Jesus knew in advance what Judas would do (Jesus called him "the son of perdition" in John 17), it was a strange choice, except for two supreme facts. First, Jesus loved Judas, even to the end. Second, Jesus had come to fulfill all the Old Testament messianic prophecies. He therefore knew his role as the suffering Servant, and he also knew Judas' role as betrayer, even to the detail of the thirty pieces of silver. Humanly speaking, we might have chosen for the special band of apostles men with far greater qualifications than these twelve. But God's ways are not our ways, and his thoughts are not our thoughts. In his obedience to the Father, Jesus called those who later failed and disappointed him, but never once did he withdraw his love from them. He loved them to the end.

*Profile of discipleship.* With this thoroughly mixed and fallible band of disciples, Jesus set the pattern for the rest of the Christian church. "For consider your call, brethren; not many of you were wise according to worldly standards, not many were powerful, not many were of noble birth; but God chose what is foolish in the world to shame the wise, God chose what is weak in the world to shame the strong, God chose what is low and despised in the world, even things that are not, to bring to nothing things that are, so that no human being might boast in the presence of God."[44] This unique concept of discipleship, introduced by Jesus, includes all those who hear the call of Jesus and who turn to follow him as Savior and Lord. Although there was a unique relationship between Jesus and the Twelve, we cannot evade the strong demands made on Christian disciples by saying that these applied only to the apostles. The call to obey, to serve, to live a simple lifestyle, to suffer and, if need be, to die, is common to all followers of Jesus. Above all, we are to commit our lives unreservedly to him and to one another as members of his body. The Christian church is not a club that we belong to so that our needs will be met; it is a body, a building, a family, an army— word-pictures used to show us that, by accepting the call of Christ, we take on responsibilities that we cannot avoid if we are to be his disciples. It is not a question of personal feelings and choices as much as it is taking seriously the conditions and demands that Jesus lays upon us. We are no longer our own. We have been chosen by him, called by him, bought by him; therefore we now belong to him, and by virtue of this fact, we also belong to one another, however easy or difficult, joyful or painful, we find this to be.

If the cost is great, the aims, privileges and rewards are infinitely greater. "The glory which thou hast given me I have given to them, that they may be one even as we are one, I in them and thou in me, that they may become perfectly one, so that the world may know that thou hast sent me and hast loved them even as thou hast loved me. Father, I desire that they also, whom thou hast given me, may be with me where I am, to behold my glory which thou hast given me in thy love for me before the foundation of the world."[45] To be a part of the fulfillment of such a profound and magnificent prayer is surely worth the sacrifice of every part of our lives.

# CHAPTER TWO

# CALLED INTO GOD'S FAMILY

IN AN AGE WHEN THE INDIVIDUAL seems increasingly redundant and insignificant, it is a vital part of the good news of Jesus Christ that every single person matters to God. He knows each of us and calls us by name. He has a personal love for each one of us. "Zacchaeus!" called Jesus to the startled tax collector hiding high in his sycamore tree. It was this direct, personal approach that so quickly captured the hearts of many who were lost and alone. Here, at last, was someone who really cared for them as individual persons.

It is equally striking that Jesus calls individuals, not to stay in isolation, but to join the new community of God's people. He called the Twelve to share their lives, with him and with each other. They were to live every day in a rich and diverse fellowship, losing independence, learning interdependence, gaining from each other new riches and strength. They were to share everything—joys, sorrows, pains and possessions—to become the community of Christ the King. Several women, too, joined the small band and helped to support them financially. Indeed all the disciples were called, on different levels, into a depth of sharing that they had never known before.

What excited John, the reality of the shared life the apostles enjoyed with Jesus, was now available to all believers: "That which we have seen and heard we proclaim also to you, so that you may have fellowship with us; and our fellowship is with the Father and with his Son Jesus Christ."[1]

### The Priority of Community

We live in an age of personal insignificance, and great loneliness. More than ever the church needs to recapture the priority of community in Christian discipleship. In his three years of intimate relationship with his disciples, Jesus gave us the model for the church. He loved his disciples, cared for their needs, taught them, corrected them, stimulated their faith, instructed them concerning the kingdom of God, sent them out in his name, encouraged them, listened to them, watched them, guided them; and he told them to do the same for each other. The church which rediscovers something of the God-given quality of such a sharing community will speak with great relevance, credibility, and spiritual power to the world of today. The church, wrote Paul, is "built upon the foundation of the apostles and prophets, Christ Jesus himself being the chief cornerstone."[2] Although Jesus taught his disciples many truths concerning the kingdom of God, he wanted them most of all to know *him*. This is the meaning of eternal life.[3] In their corporate life together they came to know him who is the life, and only with that background were they able to share that life—his life—with others. The word "know" that is used for phrases like "knowing God" or "knowing Jesus Christ" is the same word that is used for a man *knowing* his wife. It speaks of the intimacy of a deep, personal union. For them to achieve such intimate knowledge, Jesus called his disciples into a living, loving community. He saw this as a top priority as he began building his church.

This pattern of commonality that Jesus lived out with his own disciples was clearly continued in the early church and was one of its outstanding features. "All who believed were together and had all things in common."[4] They worshiped, prayed, worked and witnessed together, and shared their possessions as various needs arose. The reality of their mutual love was a rich expression of the joy of their individual conversions and certainly made an enormous impact on the world around them. Jesus had said that love was to be the hallmark of his disciples, and he had prayed that the loving unity of their lives together would bring others to belief in and about him. This is exactly what happened, and it is not surprising that God added to their number day by day those who were being saved. In their commitment to Christ and to one another they became the visible manifestation of his body on earth, and experienced the power of his resurrection. God's power is meant for God's people, not just for individual believers. It is "when brothers dwell in unity" that the Lord commands his blessing.[5]

### God's Plan to Unite All Things in Himself

The forming of the church into the new community of God's people is, however, only the means towards the fulfillment of God's much wider purpose which can best be summed up in Ephesians 1:9-10, where Paul writes: "For he has made known to us ... the mystery of his will, according to his purpose which he set forth in Christ as a plan for the fulness of time, *to unite all things in him,* things in heaven and things on earth." Today it seems clear that our society is sick, that without God it is falling apart. Every part and particle of this world has been polluted by the sin of man and is in the power of the Evil One. Creation itself is "in bondage to decay."[6] For this reason, Christ came to usher in the kingdom of God, and "God's kingdom," to quote a memorable expression of Hans Küng, "is creation healed."

God has chosen the church as his agent to accomplish this great plan. But the church can accomplish this healing, reconciling ministry effectively only if it has first experienced its reality within its own ranks. The existence of over 9,000 Christian denominations throughout the world is an insult to Christ, and a hindrance to the spread of the kingdom of God. It is only when Christians deeply repent for tearing the body of Christ into thousands of separate pieces and pray earnestly for the healing, unifying power of the Holy Spirit, that the church can ever be God's agent in reconciling all things in Christ. Until then creation itself will remain broken, "groaning in travail" and waiting "with eager longing for the revealing of the sons of God."[5]

To be both biblical and realistic, we must realize that there is always both a "now" and a "not yet" about the kingdom of God. To the extent that Christ is reigning over those people and structures that have submitted to his lordship, the kingdom of God is already manifest. "But we do not yet see everything in subjection to him."[7] Christians are no more than redeemed sinners who still live in a fallen world. We shall not see the glory of God's kingdom until Christ comes again in triumph to "put all his enemies under his feet."

A biblical balance is therefore important. As the church becomes a united and caring community of God's people marked by love, there will be substantial healing within God's creation, even if we have to wait until the coming of Christ for a more complete restoration. God in Christ has entrusted to us both the message and ministry of reconciliation, but when a sick church attempts to bring about the healing of a sick world, it should not be surprised at the cynical response, "Physician, heal yourself!" It is crucial that all true disciples of Jesus repent of the negative, unloving attitudes that divide us from one another, and renew our commitment to be totally committed to one another in love.

Once we see that the church is to be God's agent for the redemption of his world, we can understand why the New Testament writers were so persistent and emphatic about the need for believers to be reconciled, to put away all bitterness and slander, to forgive one another, and to walk in love as Christ loved us. In the Epistles we find the repeated emphasis on restoring or maintaining authentic Christian community. Until the kingdom of God can be demonstrated in our relationships of love with one another, we have nothing credible to say to an unbelieving and broken world.

## The Unity of God's People

What is the burden of Jesus in his great High Priestly Prayer in John 17? Notice his repeated plea to his Father, made all the more powerful, perhaps, because of his often painful experiences with his own disciples: "Keep them in thy name . . . that they may be one, even as we are one . . . that they may all be one; even as thou, Father, art in me, and I in thee, that they also may be in us, so that the world may believe that thou hast sent me. The glory which thou hast given me I have given to them, that they may be one even as we are one, I in them and thou in me, that they may become perfectly one, so that the world may know that thou hast sent me . . ." Since the nature of the Trinity may be described as a community of perfect love, the reality of God among us will be seen not primarily in right doctrines (important though these are), but in the church herself becoming a community of love. Instead of allowing herself to be divided by sin, the church must seek seriously to maintain the unity of the Spirit in the bond of peace, however difficult the process may be. In no other way will God's reality and his rule be seen.

*Love—the universal language.* Our unity in Christ is, or should be, an expression of the life of God. The church is, or should be, "the word made flesh" for today. Others should be able to look at our fellowship of love and say, *"That* is what God is like!" Though that will not be the total truth about an infinite God, of course, it may be the most meaningful truth that can touch the minds and hearts of people of all races, backgrounds, cultures, and languages. Love is a universal language. God's love among God's people is the most convincing of arguments for the truth of the gospel. The most fruitful church-based mission I have ever led was effective for precisely this reason. There was such an obvious demonstration of the love of God within the church and flowing out into the community, that all I had to say, in effect, was "This is what you have seen and heard . . . !" No wonder the people flocked into the kingdom of God, for it was right there among them!

When the early church visibly demonstrated that all racial and social barriers had been broken down by the cross of Christ, and that, through the power of the Spirit, people from every background were now one in Christ, there could have been no greater evidence for the truth of the gospel in that ancient world. Today, when I have seen the reconciling power of Christ draw together into a deep, loving fellowship political extremists previously bitterly opposed to one another, terrorists, conservatives, Marxists, blacks and whites, oppressor and oppressed, I could offer no more powerful proof concerning the reality of Christ to an unbeliever. If relationships such as these can be healed, creation itself can be healed.

That is why discipleship, lived out in community, is essential for effective witness. A purely individualistic approach is unbiblical. The New Testament makes it clear that, although every Christian is inescapably a witness to Christ, not every Christian is called to be an evangelist. Committed to evangelism as it should be, the church as the body of Christ has many members with diverse gifts, and only when these gifts of the Spirit are allowed to develop "as he wills" can the body of Christ function properly, and the church fulfill its commission to evangelize.

## Evangelism and Community

Missiologists, such as Peter Wagner, have stressed the "3 P's" of evangelism. *Presence Evangelism* is where the church by its worship, life, and witness brings to the world the sense of God's presence. It is the present-day absence of this, due to the moral and spiritual sickness of the church, that makes evangelism virtually impossible in many places. *Proclamation Evangelism* is when the truths of the gospel are proclaimed at every level to those who have already sensed the presence of God among his people. *Persuasion Evangelism* is when the evangelist endeavors to turn men and women to Jesus Christ in repentance and faith, on the basis of what they have by now sensed of God's presence and understood of the proclamation of his message. They are now being persuaded to respond. Howard Snyder adds a fourth—*Propagation Evangelism*. In his view, the ultimate goal of evangelism is not to see people converted to Christ, nor even made into disciples. "To do justice to the biblical understanding of the church we must go one step further and say that *the goal of evangelism is the formation of Christian community . . .*"[9] If disciples are not formed into the community of God's people, God's plan for the healing of creation cannot begin to be fulfilled.

Elsewhere Snyder makes this important comment: "Many churches do not share the gospel effectively because their communal experience of the gospel is too weak and tasteless to be worth sharing. It does not excite the believer to the point where he wants to witness, and (as the believer uncomfortably suspects) it is not all that attractive to the unbeliever. But where Christian fellowship demonstrates the gospel, believers become alive and sinners get curious and want to know what the secret is. So true Christian community (*koinonia*) becomes both the basis and the goal of evangelism."[10]

Most evangelists and church leaders will say that though training in evangelism is important, the most crucial factor is motivation. Many Christians know what to say; few are enthusiastic about saying it because of the low level of Christian experience in the church itself. But when the church becomes renewed in the Spirit, the life of

Jesus will spill out to others. If we are genuinely excited because Christ is alive within us, and if we are able to say to others "Come and see" because our church manifests the life of Christ, evangelism will happen naturally.

## God's Alternative Society

When the church commits itself to a pattern of corporate life based on radical biblical principles, it will immediately challenge the moral, political, economic, and social structures of the world around it. Thus by its very existence, the church becomes both prophetic and evangelistic, and only in this way will the proclamation of the gospel make much impact among the vast majority of people who, at this moment, are thoroughly disillusioned with the church as an institution. For this reason it is impossible to separate the call to discipleship, the call to community, and the call to mission. Without a strong commitment to discipleship, there can be no authentic Christian community; and without such a community, there can be no effective mission.

For Christians in many churches, however, fellowship means little more than casual acquaintance, or a working relationship because we happen to belong to the same group, which exists for some specific purpose. When Jesus drew men and women into discipleship he required a depth of relationship that was much more demanding than that and, as a result, grew to be much more enriching and powerful. It is hard for a rich man to enter the kingdom of God because his identity and security will almost certainly be in his riches, together with the status and power that these bring. But what Jesus promised his disciples, who nervously protested that they had left everything to follow him, was that "there is no one who has left house or brothers or sisters or mother or father or children or lands, for my sake and for the gospel, who will not receive a hundredfold now in this time, houses and brothers and sisters and mothers and children and lands, with persecutions, and in the age to come eternal life."[11]

The phrase "with persecutions" is significant. Christ's calling is to a radical alternative society which will, by its existence and values, profoundly challenge the existing society. "The church should consist of communities of loving defiance. Instead it consists largely of comfortable clubs of conformity."[12] No one bothers to persecute dull conformity. But as soon as we adopt a lifestyle of "loving defiance" which challenges the status quo concerning covetousness, oppression or self-centeredness, there is likely to be strong opposition. Fellowship for those first Christians "meant unconditional availability to and unlimited liability for the other brothers and sisters—emotionally, financially and spiritually."[13] This striking statement exposes the superficiality of many church fellowships today. It is interesting that the word for fellowship (*koinonia*) in the New Testament occurs in the context of the sharing of money or possessions more frequently than in any other. If the church is to become a community of God's people (as Christ demonstrated with his own disciples), it means much more than singing the same hymns, praying the same prayers, taking the same sacraments, and joining in the same services. It will involve the full commitment of our lives, and of all that we have, to one another. It is only as we lose our lives that we find them, so bringing the life of Jesus to others.

*Polarized Christians.* If the church is to be effective as God's agent of reconciliation, it must be *in* the world, but not *of* the world. On this issue many evangelicals and ecumenicals today have taken largely polarized positions, neither of which is biblical.

Evangelicals have frequently perceived the church as a religious ghetto, separated from the world, preoccupied with its own doctrinal and moral purity, and regarding itself as the special object of God's favor and blessing. As such, Christians go out to the world, in the style of spiritual commandos, aiming to destroy its strongholds, weaken its defenses, and generally prepare the way for the gospel, while living essentially apart from the world. In such a context, social and political involvements in the world are viewed with suspicion and classified as "liberal."

Ecumenicals, reacting strongly to this, and aware that God loves the whole world, not just the church, have all too often secularized the gospel, and, in allowing the world to set the agenda, have abandoned the distinctive profile of the church in the world.

The church, however, is "God's experimental garden in the world. She is a sign of the coming age."[14] Gospel proclamation and social action are equally important. They are like two blades of a pair of scissors. If either is missing, the power to cut is lost.

It is far from easy to maintain the distinctive qualities of salt and light in a rotten and shadowed society. To withstand the pressures of the world, while offering it the love and life of Jesus, Christians urgently need the strength and support of other committed disciples. It is all very well for Paul to say, "Don't let the world around you squeeze you into its own mold";[15] if you are on your own it is frankly impossible to defy the materialistic and humanistic pressures of society on every side. Ronald Sider writes, "The values of our affluent society seep slowly and subtly into our hearts and minds. The only way to defy them is to immerse ourselves deeply into Christian fellowship so that God can fundamentally remold our thinking, as we find our primary identity with other brothers and sisters who are also unconditionally committed to biblical values."[16] On our own we can never stand against the principalities and powers that wage war against us. If circumstances leave us with literally no alternative—in the home, at work, in prison, or wherever—God's promise is clear; there is always "grace to help in time of need."[17] In normal circumstances, however, we are able to overcome in spiritual warfare only when we are strongly united with other Christians.

### Time to Act

Jesus' training of his disciples was a crash course; in less than three years he set out to win their hearts, instruct their minds, bend their wills, bind them together into his new society, and equip them with the power and gifts of his Spirit. He knew that his time with them was short and that he must send them out into a hostile world which would oppose them, persecute them, and destroy them. There was no time to lose. Although he had come to bring them "life in all its fulness," and to fill their empty hearts with his love and joy, he warned them of times of suffering: "The hour is coming... when you will be scattered... In the world you have tribulation... They will lay their hands upon you and persecute you, delivering you up to the synagogues and prisons... You will be hated by all for my name's sake... Many will fall away, and betray one another, and hate one another... And because wickedness is multiplied, most men's love will grow cold..."[18] Such words were not a manipulative device, an empty threat. The persecution of the early church was appalling in its severity and cruelty. Only the love of Christ controlling them enabled them to conquer in his name. In their hearts, God's grace welled up so that they were able to praise him with inexpressible joy in the midst of appalling trials.

Only a fool could fail to see the parallels of all this to this present time. Throughout this century, countless millions of Christians have been imprisoned, tortured, beaten, and killed for the sake of Christ. Vast numbers suffer today. Yet in many Communist countries, where the going has been the toughest, God's grace is so evident that the disciples of Jesus, who are patiently enduring such trials with considerable faith and love, are often a strong rebuke to the coldness, apathy and complacency of the church in the West. And there are many signs that even if we live in comparatively safe surroundings we need to be alert to the sufferings that almost surely lie ahead, the result of the restlessness and aggression increasing everywhere, the vast nuclear stockpile, the population explosion, the dwindling of the earth's resources, the continuing economic recession, and the militancy of Marxism and Islam.

## Preparing for Future Shock

"Strengthen yourselves in the time of peace" is a line of a song we often sing in our church. It is essential that we prepare ourselves *now*, in every way, for the battles we shall have to fight later. We must deepen our personal knowledge and love of the Lord Jesus; we must increase our faith in our heavenly Father; we must learn how to be continuously filled with the Holy Spirit; above all, we must resolve our differences, forgive and be forgiven, and renew our commitment to one another out of love for Christ. It was the Christian *community* that withstood the persecution of the first century, and it is Christian communities around the world today that overcome the increasing pressures. When Christians come together in the name of Jesus he promises to be with them with special power. Together we can lift up the shield of faith to quench the fiery darts of the Evil One. Now is the time to act.

Carlos Mantica, a leader of the City of God Christian community in Managua, Nicaragua, wrote in 1978: "Since 1973 we had been warned through prophecy that a period of trial would be coming soon, and we began to take this seriously. When the time of testing came we were not fully prepared but strong enough to withstand its first impact." Christians in that country went through severe testings through the genocide, torture, and terrorism that flared up in 1977. *Those who were deeply committed to one another in true Christian community were, however, largely able to stand fast in the midst of suffering.* Mantica shared some of the vital lessons that he and his people learned:

1. In war, the most important time is preparation time. For all of us the most important time is *now.* When the time of real trial arrives, preparation is over: you are either ready or unprepared. If you are not prepared, you will suffer the consequences.

2. In times of trial, spiritual warfare becomes twice as intense. The world, the flesh and the devil work against you very powerfully. Being as strong as usual is not enough... It is important to have some kind of fortress or stronghold.

3. This fortress is built with deep conviction, firm decisions, and strong relationships... Our firm decision must be to choose God's kingdom and reject any other. To accept Jesus as our absolute and only Lord. The Lord of our time. The Owner of our money and possessions. The Lord of our thoughts, emotions and acts...

Jesus decided that community should come before suffering so that we could assist each other and many others when necessity arose. Now we understand the importance of it and feel the need to strengthen our relationships. In addition to God's covenant with us, a covenant with our brothers and sisters is the best insurance we can get for times of hardship.[19]

The superficial fellowship of many church groups is not enough. We need to see ourselves as members of one family, one body, eternally united in Christ. We must make that unity real now, in strong, loving, mutual commitment.

*Guard your circle, brothers,*
*Clasp your hand in hand.*
*Satan cannot break*
*The bond in which we stand.*

*Joy is the food we share.*
*Love is our home, brothers.*
*Praise God for the Body;*
*Shalom, shalom.*[20]

# CHAPTER THREE

# CALLED TO COMMUNITY

DISCIPLESHIP INVOLVES SHARING and realism. We are called to
share our lives both with Jesus and with other disciples, but we cannot share what we do not really know. "Know thyself" is an ancient
maxim, but amid the pressures of today many people face identity
crises. This is partly due to today's emphasis on *doing* rather then on
*being*. In Western society what seems to matter is what we do, how
much we achieve, what we accomplish. While we may see our suc-
cesses clearly, we may be left wondering who we really are; and
until we have some insight and assurance about our own identity,
purpose and make up, we cannot share ourselves with others.

**Facing Reality**
Another reason for this lack of personal identity is the fantasy world
in which many people live—a dream world encouraged by television, advertising, and the press, and further emphasized by contrast with the hopelessness of much of the real world around us. Because most individuals cannot face the complexity and enormity of
today's crises, the natural defense mechanisms are either a dazed

apathy, a denial that such problems exist, or a retreat into a world of fantasy and illusion.

Of course, no Christian is immune from personal conflicts. But being a disciple of Jesus means not an escape *from* reality, as some critics suppose, but rather an entrance *into* reality. Jesus was a total realist. Born into the real world of sin and pain, he fully shared the struggles, temptations, joys, and problems of humanity. He tackled man's last enemy—death—head-on; and by dying and rising again from the grave gave man his only solid, realistic hope in the face of death. Unlike the false prophets, he did not say "peace, peace" when there was no peace. He warned the people of his day of the coming judgment of God upon Jerusalem. Straightforwardly, he told us all to expect wars, famines, earthquakes, and much tribulation before his coming again. He was also honest and direct with people. Sometimes gently, sometimes ruthlessly, he went straight to their greatest needs, whether the individuals concerned knew them or not.

Jesus calls his disciples today to a life of realism, openness and honesty. Only when we take off our masks, when we are real with one another, when we walk in the light, as he is in the light, can we have true fellowship with him and with each other. And if that light of Christ exposes sin, the blood of Christ goes on cleansing us.

*Meeting face to face.* There is probably nothing which so shatters our fantasy dream world, helps us to come to terms with our true identity, and enables us to be real with each other, as genuine Christian community. I am not referring only to one particular life-style—Christians living together under one roof (although that arrangement may often speed up the necessary process of coming to terms with ourselves and with others). I am including all expressions of Christian community, especially those that may be found in the local church. Some people, of course, join a fellowship with a fantasy dream about Christian community, expecting to find there a heaven upon earth, marked by perfect love, joy, and praise. Such balloons need to be burst, and the disillusionment is likely to be soon. Bonhoeffer comments: "God's grace speedily shatters such dreams. Just as surely God desires to lead us to a knowledge of genuine Christian fellowship, so surely must we be overwhelmed by a great disillusionment with others, with Christians in general, and, if we are fortunate, with ourselves... God is not a God of the emotions but

the God of truth. Only that fellowship which faces such disillusionment, with all its unhappy and ugly aspects, begins to be what it
should be in God's sight... When the morning mists of dreams
vanish, then dawns the bright day of Christian fellowship.[1]

In open and frequent fellowship with other Christians we can be
sure that we are being real in following Jesus, and not just playing
religious games, however correct our theology may be. Christianity
is all about relationships: with God and with others. But such is the
nature of sin, and so powerful are the forces of darkness, that we can
easily be both deceived and deceitful in our relationships. Jesus re-
served his sternest judgments for the religious phonies of his day.
Many of them were, no doubt, startled and offended by his charge
of hypocrisy. Were they not devout, moral and upright, highly respectable members of their religious society? Yet they didn't see
that their relationship with God was mere play-acting. "This people
honors me with their lips, but their heart is far from me."[2]

This sense of Christian community for all disciples was so strong
and fundamental in the first century that salvation apart from the
church was considered impossible. When individuals were added to
the Lord, they were added to the church. When they belonged to
Christ, they belonged equally to his body. The severest punishment
for gross sin was to be excluded from church fellowship. This was
tantamount to delivering the offender over to Satan, since God's
grace was to be experienced especially in the church. And since the
New Testament concept of the church is neither a building, an institution, nor an organization, but the people of God, the disciples of
Jesus were meant to gain great strength from belonging to one
another. Bonhoeffer once wrote, "He who looks upon his brother
should know that he will be eternally united with him in Jesus
Christ."[3]

## Community and the Cross

The true basis for all fellowship is when two or more persons kneel
at the foot of Christ's cross, trusting only in his mercy and love. At
that point of reality, we come to see how our sins crucified Christ
and how they wound his body, the church, today. Once we really
face that, nothing that we can say or do should surprise us concerning the image we have about ourselves. Also, as I turn towards
my brother, nothing he may say or do should surprise me about

him. I can no longer be critical or judgmental, since there, at the cross, I have discovered the state of my own sinful heart.

*Level ground.* The cross is the heart of all fellowship, and it is only through the cross that fellowship is deepened and matured. This will involve the frequent and painful crucifixion of self in all its forms—self-seeking, self-centeredness, self-righteousness—and the willingness to remain vulnerable in open fellowship with other Christians. Often we try to encounter each other from positions of strength. We talk about our gifts, blessings, and achievements. Mutual encouragement along these lines is often necessary and helpful, but it must be balanced with true fellowship, which begins when we meet at the point of weakness and which binds our hearts together in love. When I am willing to be open to you about my personal needs, risking your shock or rejection, and when I am willing for you to be equally open with me, we find ourselves both on level ground, at the foot of the cross, the place of God's healing and grace.

John Powell expresses the fears we have of being open with one another in these words: "I am afraid to tell you who I am, because, if I tell you who I am, you may not like who I am, and it's all that I have."[4] We find it safer to maintain an image, to put on a mask, to hide our real selves. This explains why many churches never demonstrate the quality of community life that Jesus wants us to experience, and why there are so few (if any) real disciples. Keith Miller described the predicament like this: "Our churches are filled with people who outwardly look contented and at peace but inwardly are crying out for someone to love them... just as they are—confused, frustrated, often frightened, guilty, and often unable to communicate even within their own families. But the *other* people in the church *look* so happy and contented that one seldom has the courage to admit his own deep needs before such a self-sufficient group as the average church meeting appears to be."[5]

*The masked congregation.* Genuine fellowship comes when Christians stop relating to one another as righteous saints, and accept one another as unrighteous sinners. A pious fellowship makes no room for the sinner. Everyone *must* wear a mask. We dare not admit who we really are. If the true facts about any of us were exposed, the shock to the system would destroy the system; so sin remains concealed beneath hypocrisy. It is only when we are encouraged to say honestly who and what we are that we discover the reality of free-

dom as children of God. In God's presence we are at liberty to admit
our sin, since we know from his Word that he loves us and accepts us
even though he knows the worst about us. Until we come to that
same point of honesty with one another we shall never experience
how deep is God's love, never know the reality of that accepting,
forgiving and caring love as it is expressed tangibly through each
other.

When we close our hearts to one another, we close our hearts to
God. We need to learn to recognize the Spirit of Christ in our
brothers and sisters. As we love and serve each other, we are loving
and serving him. Paul wrote that "we regard no one from a human
point of view," because "if any one is in Christ, he is a new creation;
the old has passed away, behold, the new has come."[6] We should
try to see one another not as we are naturally, but as what we are
and can become in Christ.

## Community and Confession
We live today in a sick church that desperately needs God's healing.
In his epistle, James guides us to an important remedy: "Confess
your sins to one another, and pray for one another, that you may be
healed."[7] Unconfessed sin holds us in the darkness, and breaks our
fellowship both with God and with each other. It tears apart the
body of Christ. It robs both the believer and the community of
God's *shalom*. "When I declared not my sin," records David, "my
body wasted away through my groaning all day long. For day and
night thy hand was heavy upon me; my strength was dried up as by
the heat of summer."[8] Christian fellowship, likewise, is infected
through the sin of any one of its members. Fellowship is restored
and the body healed only when that sin is openly confessed, brought
into the light, and forgiven.

This acknowledgement of sin in the presence of another brother
or sister is a safeguard against self-deception. Curiously, it is easier
to confess our sins privately to a holy and sinless God than openly to
another unholy and sinful friend. If that is true, "we must ask ourselves whether we have not often been deceiving ourselves with our
confession of sin to God, whether we have not rather been confessing our sins to ourselves and also granting ourselves absolution.
And is not the reason perhaps for our countless relapses and the
feebleness of our Christian obedience to be found precisely in the

fact that we are living on self-forgiveness and not a real forgiveness?"[9]
James, in the context of open confession to another brother, gives
the assurance that any sin committed will surely be forgiven. Its
power has been broken. It can no longer hold the believer in bondage, nor tear the fellowship apart. The sinner can honestly be a
sinner, and still experience the grace of God and the love of the
family of God. Fellowship in Christ becomes a profound reality. "In
confession the Christian gives up all and follows. Confession is discipleship. Life with Jesus Christ and his community has begun."[10]

*Confession with discretion.* Wisdom may be needed in knowing
how much to confess in any given group. Explicit confession may
not always be expedient or healthy for some in the group. For example, if a leader is totally honest about all his failures with a young and
immature group of Christians such frankness may hinder rather than
help them. But each Christian should have a peer group, or a coun-
sellor, in whose presence he or she can *say anything.* Because of
certain abuses in the Catholic confessional system, many evangelical
groups virtually deny the value of confession. But, wisely used, the
practice is both biblical and healthy. A common feature in many of
the great revivals in the church has been this open confession of sin
to one another. As concealed sin is brought out of the darkness, the
light of Christ is able to shine as never before, fellowship and unity
are restored and the Spirit is free to move once again with power.

## Bearing with One Another

Paradoxically, the more deeply we commit ourselves to loving fellowship with others, the more we shall be hurt; as sinners we shall
fail one another again and again. Yet as we accept, with love and
understanding, the foibles and frailties of others, the irritating habits
that try our patience, the sins that we have to forgive, we shall be
fulfilling the law of Christ, the law of love. Jesus had to bear all this
from his disciples; if we want to follow him we must do the same.
That is why Paul urges the Christians at Philippi to have the mind of
Christ. Just as Jesus humbled himself and became a servant for our
sake, so we must humble ourselves and serve one another out of
love for him. We are to be concerned not only about our own interests, but also about the interests of others. We are not to judge or
criticize but to love and forgive. We are not to dominate or exploit
others, nor use them for some selfish advantage, nor mold them into

our own image; instead we are to see in others the image of God to be honored and respected.

*Truth hurts.* A Christian leader with some experience of community once asked me, "Have you come to that point in your relationships where you *have* to depend on the Holy Spirit?" He knew that we had gone through some difficulties in our extended household. Once the honeymoon period—the Christian fantasy—was over, various aspects of our individual discipleship were being strongly challenged. We were surprised by the degrees of selfishness and covetousness still active in our hearts. Through guile and deceit we tried in vain to conceal these areas of darkness. We were startled to find that such areas still existed, depressed to discover our natural deceitful reactions to them. In self-defense we became suspicious and critical. Mutual love and trust wore thin. Unexpectedly, we found ourselves to be spiritually bankrupt. The moment of disillusionment—and of reality—had arrived.

In any true community in Christ all darkness will sooner or later be exposed to the light. Human love, for all its powerful out-flow of emotions, is basically self-centered and self-seeking. It desires to have, to possess, to capture; it does not serve and give. Human love is reluctant to release the object of that love for the good of the whole. Human love manipulates people and situations to achieve its end. It is restless, insatiable, and destructive of true fellowship. "If we say that we have fellowship with him (or with others) while we walk in darkness, we lie and do not live according to the truth."[11]

Once we confess our total inadequacy to build up the community, we can know the joy of God's complete forgiveness, and then ask that *his* love be poured into our hearts each day by the Holy Spirit. His love cares for people as people. When we are controlled by his love we will be able to go on forgiving. We will care for the needs of others, laying down our lives for them, giving to those in need, sacrificing time and money for them, listening to them as God speaks to us through them. God's love is concerned with maintaining unbroken fellowship, walking fully in the light with him and others.

## Loving One Another—*Agape*

William Barclay describes Christian love like this: "*Agape* is the spirit which says: 'No matter what any man does to me, I will never seek to do harm to him; I will never set out for revenge; I will always seek nothing but his highest good.' That is to say, Christian love, *agape*, is *unconquerable benevolence, invincible good will*. It is not simply a wave of emotion; it is a deliberate conviction of the mind issuing in a deliberate policy of the life . . ."[12] Such love is, of course, perfectly revealed within the Trinity; it is seen in the love God has for the whole world; it is marked by the motivation of the life and ministry of Jesus; it is measured by his total self-sacrifice on the cross; it takes the initiative towards man in his sin; it calls for a response of love towards the great Lover; it is to be found among those who are his disciples; it is the supreme mark of the Christian and of the Christian church in the world.

It may be helpful to examine first God's love for man, next man's love for God, then man's love for man, and finally the characteristics of love itself.

*Love: God's for man.* The essential nature of God is love.[13] It is *all-embracing* love, since God desires that all should be saved.[14] It is *unmerited* love, in that while we were still sinners Christ died for us.[15] It is *sacrificial* love, marked by God's gift of his Son, whom he even made sin for us.[16] It is *merciful* love, since God longs to put away and forget our sins; he does not keep his anger for ever.[17] It is *conquering* love, that enables us to overcome the trials and temptations that God in his wisdom, allows us to experience for growth into full maturity.[18] It is *indissoluble* love, which nothing can ever break—neither depression, disease, demonic forces, nor death itself.[19] It is *chastening* love, since discipline is necessary for our "highest good."[20] It is *everlasting* love; the Scriptures remind us of that 180 times! It is also *jealous* love, in that God expects and demands the total devotion of our lives to him who has given himself unreservedly to us.[21]

*Love: man's for God.* In response to this, our love for God should be *exclusive* (since our hearts have room for only one supreme devotion),[22] *obedient* (the ultimate proof of our love),[23] *responsive* to his initiative,[24] the primary sign of the fruit of the Spirit.[25]

*Love: man's for man.* The Bible, however, emphasizes that our love for God, though intensely personal, is not to be private. It is also expressed in our love for one another. The Christian is to love his own *family*,[26] or else he is disqualified as a leader of the household of God.[27]

The breakdown of family life has reached devastating proportions and threatens immense problems for tomorrow's world. Christian homes, especially those of Christian leaders, seem under special attack. More than ever we need to help each other to work at our marriages, to love, to repent, to forgive, and to strengthen our marriage vows. Quality time with our children is equally important, particularly for the active Christian worker. To express Christian love between husband and wife, parent and child, we deeply need the help of the Spirit of God.[28]

This nuclear family unit, although special and sacred in God's eyes, is not to be exclusive. Christian love encourages us all to form strong brother-sister relationships with the wider *family of God.*[29] If we fail here, we have nothing to offer the lonely, the single, the divorced, and the widowed members of the church, together with single parents and numerous others who need a genuine, tangible expression of God's love. "See how they love one another!" should be the outstanding impression of the outsider who is watching the Christian church.

*Agape* love also reaches out to *neighbors;*[30] Jesus made it clear that anyone in need is our neighbor, regardless of differences of race, color, creed, or class. Barclay comments: "More people have been brought into the church by the kindness of real Christian love than by all the theological arguments in the world; and more people have been driven from the church by the hardness and ugliness of so-called Christianity than by all the doubts in the world."[31]

Christian love encircles *enemies* as well[32]—one of the most striking aspects of God's love as shown to us by Jesus Christ. The one who prayed "Father, forgive them; for they know not what they do" is the same one who, by his Spirit, can help us to forgive anyone, anything, always. Love overcomes evil with good. It can soften the hardest heart. It stays steady through the worst of storms. It changes the negative into the positive, pain into joy, darkness into light. "The Christian's only method of destroying his enemies is to love them into his friends."[33]

*Love's essence.* How, then, can we summarize the nature of this extraordinary quality of love? Jesus-love is *sincere;*[34] it has an open heart, an open hand, and knows nothing of manipulation and deceit. It is *generous,*[35] marked by the sacrificial giving of time, money, energy, and gifts to anyone in need. It *is active,*[36] backing verbal expressions of love with loving acts. It is *forbearing and forgiving,*[37] turning a blind eye and a deaf ear to the faults of others. It is *unifying*,[38] always working to make peace and heal divisions. It is *positive*,[39] believing the best about others, not expecting or fearing the worst. It is *sensitive*,[40] careful not to say or do anything that will cause another to stumble. It is *upbuilding*;[41] the truth may wound, but "speaking the truth in love" will heal and edify. Jesus-love summarizes all that we believe and do as Christians.[42]

Does that leave you somewhat breathless? It is meant to! To strive for such qualities in our own strength would be humanly impossible. But when we are forced to depend on the Holy Spirit, God's grace will be sufficient for us. Anyone who is willing to be a disciple in the context of community will often know tears, depression, even despair. But through the ashes of our failures can emerge the phoenix of a fresh, new quality of love, God's love, which assures us of his constant forgiveness and lifts us out of darkness into his marvelous light.

Bonhoeffer rightly stresses the impossibility of Christian community without *agape*, the love of God, and the destruction of such community if the inadequacy of human love is not clearly recognized. "The existence of any Christian life together depends on whether it succeeds at the right time in bringing out the ability to distinguish between a human ideal and God's reality, between spiritual and human community."[43] Many fellowships run into difficulties through failing to distinguish clearly between these two. When Christians open their hearts to one another, and love and serve one another in their human strength, the result is that natural desires are awakened, vulnerability and emotional entanglements soon follow, and suspicion, jealousy and resentment are aroused. What may have begun as a genuine work of the Spirit ends in the flesh, bringing confusion and disaster. Unfortunately, the natural reaction from those who have been hurt, is to back away from deep relationships altogether, to withdraw to a safe distance, to erect defenses to prevent further wounds. This fleshly reaction is another way of destroying the community of love that Christ longs to see in his church.

## Covenant Love

Remember, Jesus knows all about our human desires and reactions. He saw them in his own self-seeking disciples when they schemed for positions of influence in the kingdom of God, when they argued as to who was the greatest, when they were jealous, critical, and resentful with one another. Later, the risen Christ saw human desires manifesting themselves in all the churches. We sometimes single out the Corinthian church as being carnal; but perhaps no New Testament letters would have been written apart from natural, human problems arising within each church fellowship. *But never once did Jesus withdraw his love from his disciples whose lives were not perfectly under the control of the Spirit.* Had he done so, how could any of us have confidence in our relationship with him? As he binds himself to us in covenant love, he calls us to do the same for each other, so that we will help each other to grow up into Christ, with his love pervading our fellowship.

The basis of covenant love is commitment, not natural feelings and desires. We commit ourselves to our brothers and sisters because of Christ in them. We give ourselves to them in loving service, laying down our lives for them, thinking of their needs and interests above our own. "Community demands great personal sacrifice. Real community will not function without covenant love, the nature of which is to love others more than oneself and to give one's life for them. Without a doubt, the practical experience of life in community will sorely test and stretch the love of anyone who attempts it."[44] Only God's love, given to us by his Spirit, will ever make community possible. That is why love, more than anything else, should be the unique feature among Christ's disciples.

### Community as a Means of Growth

We have seen that community is clearly a major factor in spiritual growth. God gives various gifts to his church "to equip the saints [all Christians together] for the work of ministry, for building up the body of Christ."[45] In fact, all the gifts of the Spirit have this specific purpose—the building up of the whole community, not just of the individual. The only exception to this is the private gift of tongues, given to help the believer in his personal communion with God and thus, indirectly, to strengthen the body of Christ; when I am personally edified I will want to edify others.

God's purpose in this is that we should "all attain to the unity of the faith and of the knowledge of the Son of God, to mature manhood, to the measure of the stature of the fulness of Christ."[46] As we seek *together* to deepen our knowledge of the Son of God, we will grow into spiritual unity and maturity, and thus reveal something of the glory of the fullness of Christ. No individual Christian can do this on his own. Paul here, and in other passages, is showing that as the body grows, the individual members will naturally grow, but each member needs the life and gifts of the rest of the body before there can be true development. For this to happen we need to submit to one another, learn from one another, listen to what God may be saying through others, and count others better than ourselves.[47] It is with all the saints, whatever our age, maturity, or tradition, that we shall be able to know the breadth and length and height and depth of the love of God.[48]

There is an important place for solitude, private prayer, and meditation, of course. But in the Western church the emphasis has been excessively on the individual Christian, and this is not a biblical emphasis. The instructions given in the New Testament epistles were almost all for the churches, not for individuals. The common word for Christian, *saint*, occurs sixty-two times and of its uses sixty-one are plural. "Greet every saint" is its only use in the singular! The overwhelming emphasis is on our corporate life together in Christ.

*Mutual edification.* The more we live as members of the body of Christ, the more we shall experience the gifts of the Spirit to edify that body. The manifestation of the Spirit is given only "for the common good." As we live together in love, the Spirit will give his gifts as an expression of his love within his body, the church. No one member can say to another, "I don't need you." In humility and love, we must be willing to bring God's word or a spiritual gift to another member, whoever that might be. Those who are more mature in the faith must realize that they may need help, encouragement, forgiveness, and even rebuke from someone who is much younger. Regardless of our maturity, we are all sinners in constant need of God's mercy and grace, which may come through *any* member of the body. We must continuously be reminded of our interdependence, as we grow together into Christ.

I am grateful to those who are willing to speak the truth to me in love, even when it hurts. I am even more grateful when the truth comes from those who are young enough to be my children. Naturally, by virtue of greater knowledge or experience, one member may have more to contribute than another. But essentially Christ is the Discipler, the Shepherd of the flock, the Teacher in our midst.

## Holy Communion

The clearest expression of Christian community is to be found in Holy Communion, the Lord's Supper, the Eucharist. Here, uniquely, we thank God for the basis of all our fellowship—the cross of Jesus Christ. Although once we were "separated from Christ, alienated from the commonwealth of Israel, strangers to the covenants of promise, having no hope and without God in the world," we celebrate the fact that "in Christ Jesus we who once were far off have been brought near in the blood of Christ." We also rejoice that all human barriers have been broken down through the cross, "for he is our peace, who has made us [all] one, and has broken down the dividing wall of hostility."[49] We all come to the cross as sinners, and God accepts us as children. We look up to him with confidence saying, "Abba! Father!" We turn to one another in love saying, "My brother! My sister!" Here, at this fellowship meal, we are struck by the truth that we are "no longer strangers... but members of the household of God." Being members of one body, we eat of one bread and drink of one cup, the solemn guarantee of our eternal relationships with God and with one another. We praise and worship God who has joined us together through the death of his own Son. No one can tear us apart.

*Sinners welcome.* It is in the Eucharist that we remember the matchless, measureless grace of God. We openly acknowledge that we have sinned against him and each other "through ignorance, through weakness, through our own deliberate fault." This meal is for sinners only. We are present at the Table of the Lord simply because we need his forgiveness, and in the symbols of the bread and wine we have the solemn pledge that, as we confess our sins, God will remember them no more. In this Eucharist we thank God that our fellowship with him and with each other is restored. Because the body of Christ was once broken on the cross, the body of Christ on earth today can be healed. We come therefore with expectant faith, knowing that the risen Christ is with us. As we lift up our hearts to him, we can also expect spiritual gifts to be given to edify his body: gifts of prophecy, healing, faith, and love. In turning to one another, we can bring each other the peace and love of Christ.

It is here that we must sort out our relationships with one another. If we fail to do that, we shall be "guilty of profaning the body and blood of the Lord," thus bringing judgment upon ourselves.[50] It is interesting to note that the context in which Paul wrote those words is partly division within the church at Corinth, and partly the material inequality of its members: "For in eating, each one goes ahead with his own meal, and one is hungry and another is drunk." Had they really loved each other, they would have shared their food together, as well as repenting of the divisions within their fellowship. Because they had come, divided and unrepentant, to the one meal which spoke so powerfully of their unity in Christ, they were experiencing God's chastening in the form of physical sickness and even death. This fellowship meal is both a means of grace and a form of discipline for all who follow him today.

At this meal we are also spiritually strengthened in order to serve God in the world. The focus on the death of Christ reminds us to take up our cross and follow him. We are to walk with Christ into this alien world, willing to suffer for his sake in order to reconcile the world through Christ.

Finally this fellowship meal should be a foretaste of heaven. We remember that at best it is only a shadow of the marriage feast of the Lamb. With our hopes fixed on the glory that is waiting for us, we will not lose heart because of the slight momentary afflictions of this present time. If our joys are mingled with tears, this fellowship meal encourages us that one day God will wipe away all our tears. Until then, we remain a community of God's people, members of his family, his household, encouraging and serving one another, renewed daily by God's love, as we work together for his kingdom.

# CHAPTER FOUR

# CALLED TO MAKING DISCIPLES

THE CHRISTIAN GOSPEL IS God's good news for the whole world. The startling truth that shook those first Christian Jews was that "God shows no partiality, but in every nation... every one who believes in [Jesus] receives forgiveness of sins through his name,"[1] and the last words of Jesus before his ascension into heaven had been, "Go therefore and make disciples of all nations."[2] This was his master plan for the salvation of the world, brilliant in its simplicity but strangely ignored by much of the church through many generations. His disciples were to make disciples who would make disciples, ad infinitum.

A disciple is a follower. A Christian disciple has committed himself to Christ, to walking Christ's way, to living Christ's life, and to sharing Christ's love and truth with others. The verb *to disciple* describes the process by which we encourage another person to be such a follower of Jesus and the means we use to help that person to grow up in Christ to the point where he or she can disciple someone else. Since *every* Christian is a disciple of Christ we must be careful not to develop "discipling programs" so specialized and stereotyped that they develop into almost another denomination, or at least a faction within the church.

In recent years there has been a strong emphasis by a number of Christian leaders in different countries on "shepherding, discipling, and submitting." Much of this has been disturbing and divisive, for reasons that we shall see later. Nevertheless, unfortunate extremes are nearly always the result of protests to weaknesses in the church. In rediscovering a neglected emphasis, it is all too easy to push it so strongly and so far that it becomes unbalanced, contentious, and even heretical. The New Testament word "heresy" originally referred to a divisive party that was not necessarily linked with major doctrinal errors at all. Such a group became a heresy or faction[3] simply because of the strong personality of its leader or the overemphasis of what at base was a biblical truth.

So we must be careful not to throw out the baby with the bath water! While we need to be wary of overstressing certain aspects of discipleship, we must be equally wary of underestimating the importance of a vital biblical principle that the church has neglected to its own peril.

### The Need for Discipling
Certain failures in the church have made the shepherding movement, with all its excesses, inevitable.

First, many Christians, especially in some of the mainline churches, have been deeply disturbed by *the lack of doctrinal and moral discipline* within the church. An article in *The Times* [London][4] on the Church of England's Doctrine Commission Report recently reported, "What the 18 theologians hold in common is a belief in the likelihood of God, and reverence for Jesus. They disagree about everything else." When ordained clergymen openly deny Christ's divinity or reject his bodily resurrection or permit sexual immorality, clear discipline is needed. Given the need for compassion when any Christian, including a leader, is wrestling with honest doubts, we need also the courage to stop such a theologian or teacher from exercising a public ministry while working through his other personal uncertainties.

Second, there is a desperate *lack of commitment* among professing Christians, and a corresponding reluctance to preach about the cost of following Jesus. Little reference today is made to self-denial and the cross. We rejoice that Jesus died on the cross for us;

but do we take up our cross daily to follow him? The church has endorsed the "club" mentality of church membership. A good church member, complains Juan Carlos Ortiz, is "like a good club member: he attends the club, pays his dues, and tries not to embarrass the club." But where does the New Testament mention church membership? Nowhere! We are members of Christ, and members of one another, both ideas stressing total commitment. But our shallow fellowship, flabby evangelism, lack of body ministry, neglect of spiritual gifts, sterile worship, feeble prayer, and general lack of love attest only to lack of commitment.

Who wants to belong to such an ailing body? In our meaningless world, increasing numbers of people are looking for something to live for, perhaps even to die for. Why are the cults increasing in numbers, when the established churches are declining? The cults call for total commitment! So do the revolutionary and terrorist groups that are capturing so much of the world today. The "shepherding movement" is an understandable protest of the failure of the church to take seriously the radical demands of Jesus.

Third, in numerous churches there is a depressing *lack of direction.* Many of the debates and activities in the church are as appropriate as playing bridge on the *Titanic* after it has hit the iceberg. Most people are profoundly aware of the uncertainty of this present age. Everywhere there is a sense that time is running out fast. Large numbers of Christians are looking for leaders who have the courage to give a clear prophetic call, who will train and mobilize the church for the tasks that are obviously relevant for today. Yes, many Christians are willing and wanting to be discipled.

Fourth, with the renewed biblical emphasis on every Christian being involved in the ministry of the church, and with increased openness to the gifts of the Spirit, there is often *confusion and excess* where there is not firm leadership and wise pastoral control. The sad fact is that many clergy and ministers are cautious and suspicious of spiritual renewal. The laity are often eager to move forward, but the clergy drag their feet. Consequently, new life in the Spirit is frequently sought and found not in churches but in home-based "renewal fellowships" that may lack experienced leadership. When the gifts of the Spirit are not carefully tested and controlled, some excesses and fleshly self-display are almost inevitable.

Fifth, depending on the tradition of the church, there has been either *gross neglect of evangelism,* or an *over-dependence on the big-time evangelist* to do the church's job. Neither is biblical. Although some are called to be evangelists for the benefit of the whole church, the New Testament clearly lays the emphasis on the witness of every Christian. Dr. James Kennedy has given a graphic illustration to underline this truth. If a gifted evangelist with an international reputation could win 1,000 persons for Christ every night of the year, it would take him over 10,000 years to win the whole world for Christ (ignoring the population explosion). But if one true disciple of Christ were able under God to win just one person each year and train that person to win one other person each year, it would take only 32 years to win the whole world for Christ! In churches where discipling is taken seriously, there are few, if any, specifically evangelistic services with a gifted evangelistic preacher, but many are being won for Christ through personal witness.

The need for some discipling or shepherding program should now be apparent. "Unless disciples are adequately built, there will not be enough competent leadership to carry on the work of the church."[5] If the church does not take this need seriously, it has only itself to blame for unhelpful and divisive alternatives.

## The Dangers of Shepherding

There are many biblical references to the leader of a church in the role of a shepherd. "Take heed to yourselves and to all the flock," said Paul to the Ephesian elders.[6] "Tend the flock of God that is in your charge," wrote Peter.[7] "Feed my lambs... Tend my sheep... Feed my sheep," said Jesus when he re-instated Simon Peter as a leader of the church.[8] Why, then, do many churches view the whole concept of shepherding with suspicion and dismay? There are some obvious pitfalls to be avoided.

First, *serious discipling is often legalistic and authoritarian.* Regulations covering a wide range of behavior (not all spelled out in the Bible) have become the norm, often marked by narrowness, legalism and a self-conscious spirituality that lacks the spontaneous love and joy characterized by the early church. I have seen Christians who once were relaxed and radiant, looking cowed, anxious, and fearful again, because they have come into the bondage of strict human shepherding. The pressures are often emotional. Those under the constant care of mature Christian couples, especially single girls, will feel strong, emotional ties that are hard to break. Similar pressures are exerted through a single-sex discipleship. Such strong loyalties are established that any deviation seems like rebellion. If you show signs of thinking for yourself or personal initiative, there will be a major confrontation. Only as you conform will the fragile security of your submissive relationships with other Christians remain intact.

Similar dangers were known in New Testament times. Paul once urged the Colossian Christians not to "submit to regulations, 'Do not handle, do not taste, do not touch'... according to human precepts and doctrines." Paul commented that such "rigor of devotion" may seem godly and wise, "but in actual practice they do honor not to God, but to man's own pride."[9] The Galatian Christians had fallen into a similar trap. Paul wrote, "O foolish Galatians! Who has bewitched you?" Some of them had followed Peter, who "drew back and separated himself, fearing the circumcision party." (Yielding to the Judaizers, Peter and others had slipped from Christian liberty into religious legalism.) Paul urged them, "For freedom Christ has set us free; stand fast therefore, and do not submit again to a yoke of slavery."[10] Legalism and license are the two main dangers which rob us of our true freedom in Christ.

Yes, there must be leadership and discipline within every church; but when this effectively quenches the Spirit in people's lives, and causes Christians to draw back from one another, becoming critical and fearful, Paul's teaching is highly relevant.

Second, *strong shepherding can develop into a new priesthood.* In some cases, every disciple submits virtually every area of his or her life to a shepherd, and every shepherd (with not more than twelve disciples under him) submits his life to another shepherd— a pyramidal structure. Submission is often practiced across the miles rather than within the fellowship of a local church. For example, the leaders of one church might submit their lives to the leaders of another church many miles away. They, in turn, might submit to international leaders in another country. Such submission may involve tithing and detailed accountability to a shepherd, and obedience in matters such as marriage, family, housing, work, finance, lifestyle, and so on.

Such a system produces a "new priesthood." How can I hear the voice of God if I must listen only to my shepherd? What is the will of

God for my life? My shepherd will tell me. What is the right interpretation of this passage of Scripture? My shepherd will explain it
all. One woman, trying to describe the blessings of all this to me,
said, "It is such a relief not to have the responsibility for making
such decisions yourself." That, however, is the point of danger.
When a shepherd assumes detailed control over the lives of others,
there will be a serious loss in their personal responsibility, maturity,
and even significance. Almost all of us find guidance difficult, so
initially it may be a relief to let someone else make our decisions for
us. In the long run, however, this produces an unhealthy dependence on a human shepherd instead of a healthy dependence on the
Great Shepherd. Pastors and teachers are God's gift to the church.
As they teach us the biblical principles involved in decision making,
they help us think through complex issues more objectively; but we
must each give an account of ourselves to God. Responsibility and
maturity go together. Paul and the writer to the Hebrews lamented
the immaturity of those who should have become teachers and
leaders themselves but still needed others to feed and care for
them.[11]

Carl Wilson comments that in certain groups the leaders "are
beginning to claim the right to speak for Christ in telling people
what to do, without having any clear scriptural authority for what
they say. Some ... are claiming an authority that actually puts them
between Christ and the people. They tell them when to marry, divorce, go to school, and the like ... If the people of the churches
concede to clergy the right to make decisions of life and doctrine
apart from the clear teaching of Scripture, it will inflict the death-
blow to disciple building in the churches, even as it did in the early
church."[12] The apostle Peter, for this reason, urged the elders not to
be domineering over the flock.[13]

In the same way, caution needs to be exercised over prophetic
utterances. These may be part of God's word for a church, but when
they are given greater authority than Scripture itself, serious problems can arise. The New Testament envisages prophecy as a gift of
the Spirit for "upbuilding and encouragement and consolation...
You can all prophesy one by one, so that all may learn and all be
encouraged."[14] Sometimes God may want to speak strongly and
clearly to a church; if so, we should expect it to be confirmed from a
number of quite different sources.

Third, *dominant shepherding inevitably becomes divisive.* When a group of disciples looks too much to one leader, the natural consequence will be a carnally competitive spirit, "I belong to Paul, I belong to Apollos, or I belong to Cephas." Such factions were splitting the Christians at Corinth, and Paul had to point out the damage to God's building, the church. Paul was not rebuking the leaders; he was warning those who were exalting leaders above their God-given role. "What then is Apollos?" Not "who," but *"what"*! "What is Paul? Servants..." The leaders were nothing in themselves; the growth and life came entirely from God. If the Corinthian believers continued to group themselves around various leaders (or shepherds) they would destroy God's temple; and "if any one destroys God's temple, God will destroy him."[15]

Unfortunate emphases on shepherding, discipling, and submission have been the cause of sharp controversy within the charismatic renewal (in particular) in different parts of the world. In 1976 a measure of reconciliation over this very issue was reached between prominent leaders in North America. The leaders of the Christian Growth Ministries in Fort Lauderdale, Florida—associated with the "shepherding movement"—issued a statement which began: "We realize that controversies and problems have arisen among Christians in various areas as a result of our teaching in relation to subjects such as submission, authority, discipling, shepherding. We deeply regret these problems and insofar as they are due to fault on our part, we ask forgiveness from our fellow believers whom we have offended." The signatories were Don Basham, Ern Baxter, Bob Mumford, John Poole, Derek Prince, and Charles Simpson.[16]

Bob Mumford later expressed the situation like this: "In the past, we taught people to act as they 'felt led.' The result in many places was chaos. In an effort to help people more accurately interpret the leading of the Holy Spirit we asked people to 'check out' their guidance with a pastor or shepherd for a confirming word. The result in many cases was a bureaucratic system which squashed spontaneity and removed the joy of seeing God work... Without question, there have been situations where leaders have "played the Holy Spirit" to believers under their care, requiring a type of allegiance that only the Lord has the right to demand... As leaders we must become secure enough in our people to allow them to make mistakes in learning to hear the voice of the Holy Spirit..."[17]

One of the great needs of today is to keep discipling high on the church's list of priorities, fully aware of the dangers of excesses, always seeking to maintain the unity of the Spirit in the bond of peace.

## Disciples and Leaders

The disciples of Jesus were very ordinary people, with all the human faults and failings that we often see in ourselves. Because of the integrity of the Gospels, we see the disciples as ambitious, selfish, argumentative, weak in faith, anxious, fearful, impulsive, immature in words and actions, proud in the face of temptation, lethargic in prayer, impatient with the children, weary of crowds, bewildered and depressed by the events leading to the crucifixion. We notice how slow they were to learn, how quickly they forgot even the most dramatic spiritual lessons. In other words, they were just like most of us! Yet these were the men that Jesus chose to be disciples and trained to be leaders.

Many ministers complain to me about the lack of leaders in their congregations and see this as a hindrance to their work. Naturally those churches with many natural leaders seem to have a potential for growth which leaderless churches do not. In the vast majority of cases I doubt if this is true. We have simply missed the way in which Jesus first made disciples, and then trained leaders, out of very raw material. How he did it we shall see later in this chapter. But notice first that *the marks of a disciple* and *the marks of a leader* are very nearly identical. True, a spiritual leader will have the God-given *charisma* of leadership as well; but most of the other characteristics will be the same, since every true leader must first learn to be led. If we take seriously the responsibility of making disciples, we shall also be providing the church with the leaders that are so urgently needed

## The Marks of a Disciple

What do we want to produce in a disciple? Let me mention some characteristics that I have observed over the years. I am not claiming that this list is complete, or that every disciple will display the full range of qualities. But we should know what we are hoping and praying to achieve. A disciple:

1. *Is willing to serve.* This was a lesson that Jesus repeatedly had to teach his status-seeking disciples, as in the dramatic foot-washing of John 13 (cf. Mark 10:35-45).

2. *Is learning to listen.* Simon Peter was full of bright ideas on the Mount of Transfiguration, but God told him to listen to his Son (Luke 9:35). Martha, impatiently bustling around preparing a meal while Jesus was talking, was gently rebuked for not being like quiet Mary who was sitting listening to him (Luke 10:38-42).

3. *Is willing to learn.* When Jesus spoke about his coming sufferings and death, Peter blurted out, "God forbid, Lord! This shall never happen to you." The stinging reply was something that Peter never forgot (Matt. 16:22-23).

4. *Is teachable,* accepting honest criticism when others speak the truth in love (Matt. 18:15).

5. *Is submissive to authority* even when he does not understand or enjoy what he is being asked to do (1 Thess. 5:12; Heb. 13:17).

6. *Is willing to share the faith with others,* in open and honest fellowship (1 John 1:1-3).

7. *Is learning humility,* glad when others are blessed (Phil. 2:3-4).

8. *Examines his own life* before criticizing others (Matt. 7:1-5).

9. *Knows his own weaknesses* and allows God's grace to work through them (2 Cor. 12:9).

10. *Is not a perfectionist* and is therefore not a prey to self-righteousness, self-condemnation, self-pity, or a judgmental spirit. "We all make many mistakes" (James 3:2; 1 John 1:8-10).

11. *Is forgiving* (Matt. 18:21f).

12. *Is persistent, courageous,* not easily discouraged (Eph. 6:10-18; 2 Cor. 4:8-11).

13. *Is trustworthy, responsible* (1 Cor. 4:2).

14. *Is not a busybody* or a gossip (John 21:21-22; 1 Tim. 5:13).

15. *Does things well,* whether great or small (Col. 3:17).

16. *Uses time wisely,* as a gift of God (Eph. 5:15-17).

17. *Aims to please God* most of all (Gal. 1:10; 2 Cor. 5:9).

18. *Is quick to obey* when God speaks. When Peter heard Jesus' instructions on the Sea of Galilee, how foolish they may have seemed; but he obeyed, with astonishing results (Luke 5:4-9).

19. *Has faith in God,* though there may be nothing visible to encourage his faith (Mark 11:20-22).

20. *Is willing to trust* the love and faithfulness of God, even without temporal and material security (Matt. 6:25-34).

21. *Is willing to follow the Spirit's leading,* to make adjustments

and changes, as the Lord requires them.
22. *Has a clear understanding* of God's priorities (Acts 6:2-4).

## Making Disciples

The golden rule is—start small. Although Jesus often mingled with
crowds, and on one occasion, at least, sent out seventy disciples on a
specific mission, it is clear that he spent most of his ministry on this
earth with the Twelve. Of those twelve, he concentrated especially
on three, James, Peter, and John, who were with him in the sick
room of Jairus' daughter, on the Mount of Transfiguration, and in
the Garden of Gethsemane, perhaps provoking the jealousy of the
other nine. But it is impossible to disciple more than a small group
at any given time. On those twelve depended the whole future of
the Christian church. One failed completely, and from time to time
all the others were disappointments. But as Jesus persisted with
them, loving them to the end, he was laying a firm foundation for
the whole church of God.

Any wise leader will likewise concentrate his time with a small
group of committed Christians, the fewer the better, twelve probably being the maximum number for effective discipling. Paul clearly
spent much time with Timothy, Luke, Titus, Silvanus and a few
others and told Timothy to entrust what he had learned "to faithful
men who will be able to teach others also."[18] Concentrating on a few
in depth, so that they in turn will be able to do the same with others,
is in the long run far more effective than the much more superficial
teaching of a larger group. Truly, small is beautiful, and fruitful.

Who is the discipler in any group? The common and natural
answer is—the most mature and experienced leader present. A
much healthier model, however, is to see Christ as the primary
Discipler, so that we all seek to encourage, correct, and build each
other up in love under him. Those with greater knowledge and experience will, of course, give more input than others; but we genuinely need each other if we are to grow up into Christ in every way.
He is the one we are to listen to, learn from, and obey; and he may
well speak to us through any member of the group. The Spirit dis-
tributes gifts as he wills, all for the common good.

Problems are predictable when any Christian leader sees himself,
or is seen by others, as the "guru" of a group. Domineering leadership will hinder individual spiritual growth and development. Also,

every leader needs constant encouragement or even correction, and the Holy Spirit may well use a much younger and less experienced member of the group to speak clearly to that leader. The writer to the Hebrews, while urging the Christians to remember to obey, and to submit to their leaders,[19] also knew the vital importance of mutual ministry: "Exhort one another every day... consider how to stir up one another to love and good works... encouraging one another..."[20]

*The together team.* I work with a small team that travels with me everywhere as we lead Christian missions or festivals in different parts of the world, and naturally we spend much time together, working closely as a team, and praying together. But even at home, between engagements, we meet together at least four times a week. We usually begin with a time of worship and praise, then we share together what God has been saying to us or doing in our lives, nearly always relating this to verses or passages from the Scriptures that we have been reading.

These sharing times are neither pooling our problems, nor just picking out nice devotional thoughts from the Bible. They are times of reality, when we let down our masks, tell what is going on in our thoughts or lives, and link this with what God may be teaching us in our present situation. For example, I might share the pressure I have felt recently of trying to write this book; but when reading Psalm 37 this morning God reminded me to "take delight in the Lord" and to be more aware of his loving presence always with me. Another member of the team might wish to add what he or she had been learning from the Lord recently when under pressures, or to gently "speak the truth in love" to me by showing how I had allowed my work to make me tense and irritable with the team lately. Our one desire is to encourage each other to grow up into Christ in every way, in the atmosphere of God's unchanging love. Occasionally these times are painful; as we face up to where we really are with the Lord and each other, we are brought to deep repentance, even tears. More often we have great fun together, and nearly always these are times of mutual encouragement. We all know the dangers of any public ministry; and that the credibility of what we do on the stage or in the pulpit will depend entirely on the quality of everyday relationships, with God and with each other. On some days we give ourselves to intercession for a forthcoming festival or

tour; on other days we study the Bible carefully together, or tackle
some theme, such as counseling or personal evangelism that may
be relevant. These are learning times, but the learning may be rela-
tional or devotional, not merely cerebral.

Is this concentration of time as a very small group a matter of
spiritual indulgence? Should we not make ourselves more widely
available to a larger number of needy people? I think not. Because
so much of our ministry is in reaching out to numerous people with
all their various needs, our time of mutual discipling is all the more
important, and its spiritual fruit soon becomes apparent. Further,
although the work of this particular team may be specialized, the
principle of sharing, caring, praying, and working in small groups is
vital for every church. A pastor may kill himself trying to attend to
the needs of his whole parish or congregation; but if he can give himself to a small group of disciples, including potential leaders, his
congregation will eventually thank him for conserving his time and
energy during those earlier years.

There is a growing shortage of trained clergy and ministers today.
George Martin, in *Today's Parish*, suggests a practical plan: "Perhaps pastors should imagine that they are going to have three more
years in their parish as pastor—and that there will be no replace-
ment for them when they leave. If they acted as if this were going to
happen, they would put the highest priority on selecting, moti-
vating, and training lay leaders that could carry on as much as possible of the mission of the parish after they left. The results of three
sustained years of such an approach would be quite significant. Even
revolutionary."[21]

## The Shared Life

An ancient proverb says: I hear, I forget; I see, I remember; I do, I
understand. This suggests how Jesus trained his disciples. Luke,
writing to Theophilus said, "I have dealt with all that Jesus began to
*do* and *teach* . . ."[22] The doing came before even the teaching! Jesus
had no formal curriculum, no planned course of instruction, no classroom syllabus. Instead, he called his disciples to be *with him*. Jesus
said to them, "You also are witnesses because you have been with
me from the beginning. . . You are those who have continued with
me in my trials . . . I have given you an example . . ."[23] They watched
him at work, they worked with him, they questioned him, they went

out in pairs to practice what they had learned, they reported back, they asked more questions and received further instruction and slowly but surely they learned about the kingdom of God.

This is discipling at its best, when deep relationships are formed within a small group of Christians who are living, working, and sharing together. According to Moses Aberbach this was also the ideal rabbi-disciple pattern of education at the time of Jesus. The disciple would spend as much time with his teacher as possible, often living in the same house. "Disciples were expected not only to study the law in all its ramifications, but also to acquaint themselves with a specific way of life, which could be done only through constant attendance upon a master . . . The rabbis taught as much by example as by precept. For this reason the disciple needed to take note of his master's daily conversation and habits, as well as his teaching." Following a teacher meant literally "to walk behind him." Yet there was nothing distant about this relationship. The rabbi would try to raise his disciple as his own son, caring for him, providing for him, encouraging him, correcting him, until the day when the disciple would become a teacher himself.[24]

All this was strikingly similar to the pattern of New Testament discipleship. Although Jesus asked more of his disciples than any other rabbi dared to ask, and gave more, by laying down his own life for them, the principles of teaching by example, learning by watching and doing, were much the same. Jesus was the Good Shepherd who cared for his sheep, provided for them, called them by name, knew them, kept them, loved them. The sheep in turn knew the voice of their shepherd and followed him.

*Paul's pattern.* An especially warm and tender relationship developed between the apostle Paul and Timothy, whom he called "my true child in the faith," "my son," "my beloved child."[25] Paul, an experienced leader, took Timothy with him on several missionary journeys, so that Timothy would learn simply from being with him. Later Paul sent Timothy off on his own missions, and then appointed him to look after the large and flourishing church at Ephesus. He wrote Timothy two lengthy pastoral letters, instructing him how to handle various issues that had arisen in that key church. He told him how to pastor both older and younger men and women. He guided him about his personal health. He gently rebuked him for his timidity, and urged him to stir up the gift of the Holy Spirit within him. He cared for Timothy as a loving father would care for his son and, in keeping with the father-son relationship in Hebrew families, he trained Timothy to take over spiritual leadership.

This seems to have been Paul's pattern wherever he went. He wrote to the Christians at Thessalonica: "We were gentle among you, like a nurse taking care of her children. So, being affectionately desirous of you, we were ready to share with you not only the gospel of God but also our own selves, because you had become very dear to us... Like a father with his children, we exhorted each one of you and encouraged you and charged you to lead a life worthy of God..."[26] They were also taking responsibilities for themselves. "The word of the Lord [has] sounded forth from you..."[27] As disciples develop in spiritual maturity, their opportunities for Christian ministry should correspondingly grow.

Most people blossom when given responsibilities. Unless leaders train others to take over their own tasks, the expansion of any church will slow down. "Time multiplication occurs when disciples are trained in evangelism and disciple building. No matter how dynamic the pastor, no matter how financially stable and well organized the church, expansion will not continue if people are not trained to minister."[28] This is Jesus' method: "As the Father has sent me, even so I send you."[29] He sent them out on their own, gently correcting them, instructing them, until he could leave them altogether, knowing that his Spirit within them would continue to be their helper and guide. "Jesus seems to have given his men as much responsibility as they could reasonably assume. He sent them out on their own, allowing them to have a ministry without him. Thus, he was preparing them for the time when he would no longer be present. It is best not to do for a disciple what he can do for himself. He must be given an opportunity to act independently and responsibly."[30]

*Formation or information?* All this means that disciples must be formed—not just informed, as the church has tended to do for so long. Just as God "has predestined us to be conformed to the image of his Son," so Paul was willing to be "in travail until Christ be formed in you."[31] Imparting information is important, but it is not enough. More than that, as we share our lives with one another, God is able to share his life in us and through us, until he forms us into the likeness of his own Son, and until he develops the gifts and ministries he has given us into full maturity. Ultimately God is not concerned with academic and theological knowledge, but with life— his life within us. He wants us not just to know *about* Jesus, but to be *like* Jesus, filled with his Spirit, bearing his fragrance, controlled by his love. Such a quality of life is caught, rather than taught; and however important it may be to "devote ourselves to the apostles' teaching," as did those first Christians, it is even more important that the life of Jesus be manifest among us.

## Teaching
It would be a profound mistake, of course, to put true spiritual life in opposition to good biblical teaching. The words of Jesus are *words of life,* as his disciples clearly appreciated.[32] Jesus spent considerable time teaching his disciples as in the Sermon on the Mount, or his discourse during the Last Supper, or his forty days of teaching about the kingdom of God after his resurrection. Paul and the other apostles also spent much time preaching, teaching, instructing, exhorting, or writing letters. Paul told the Ephesian elders, "I did not shrink from declaring to you anything that was profitable, and teaching you in public and from house to house... the whole counsel of God..."[33] The New Testament epistles are eloquent examples of the importance the early church gave to Christian doctrine and its practical outworking in the various churches. Look how Paul urged Timothy to "attend to the public reading of scripture, to preaching, to teaching," to "follow the pattern of the sound words," to "guard the truth," to "preach the word, be urgent in season and out of season, convince, rebuke, and exhort, be unfailing in patience and in teaching," to become "a workman who has no need to be ashamed, rightly handling the word of truth."[34]

So I do not minimize the enormous value of thorough biblical teaching at every level; the church's failure to take preaching and teaching seriously is one reason for the general spiritual malaise of today. But when the emphasis in many churches is on theological study, Bible courses, seminars and classroom work, it is important to remember that the training of New Testament disciples was along different lines.

## The Marks of a Leader
We have already seen that good discipleship is the best preparation

for good leadership. The charisma of leadership, however, is not given to every disciple, and there are certain key qualities that we need to look for and develop, if we are to produce the dynamic leaders that the church needs. Every natural ability comes from God and can be used in his service. The apostle Paul, for example, used his considerable intellectual gifts to the full, and the theological wealth in his epistles has stretched the minds of the most able scholars ever since. Today we need men and women with the capacity to discern the significant trends in modern philosophy and psychology, politics and sociology, and then interpret these trends for the benefit of the whole church. Unless we understand what the world is saying and doing we cannot speak to the issues with the cutting-edge of a relevant, even prophetic word. We need Christians with academic skills to grapple with the exegesis of biblical passages, to engage in serious theological debate or religious dialogue, to be alert to crises within the church that may cause moral or doctrinal disarray, and to communicate the gospel to secular people through all available media.

*Spiritual power needed.* At the same time, it is interesting to note that the biblical picture of the disciple or leader has no specific reference to academic qualifications. Paul and Luke had plenty; Peter, James and John, very few. Most of the mainline churches place too great an emphasis on academic training, and too little on spiritual renewal and life. The result is that church leadership today is not lacking in intellectual credibility—and in some situations that is necessary and good; but the overwhelming and desperate need of the church almost everywhere is for spiritual renewal. A. W. Tozer remarked that "the only power God recognizes in his church is the power of his Spirit; whereas the only power recognized today by the majority of evangelicals is the power of man. God does his work by the operation of the Spirit, while Christian leaders attempt to do theirs by the power of trained and devoted intellect. Bright personality has taken the place of the divine afflatus. Only what is done through the Eternal Spirit will abide eternally." People are hungry for life, and no church can share life it does not possess.

It is also a mistake for churches to be on the watch *only* for natural leaders—those who would rise to the top in any walk of life. A natural flair for leadership does not necessarily make a good spiritual leader; his natural strength may well have to be broken until he comes to genuine dependence upon God for resources that he does not possess on his own. We see a hint of this when Jesus said, "You know that the rulers of the Gentiles lord it over them, and their great men exercise authority over them. It shall not be so among you; but whoever would be great among you must be your servant, and whoever would be first among you must be your slave."[35] Paul, too, with all his intellectual ability, natural strength, and spiritual experience, had to learn through a painful thorn in the flesh (some physical handicap?) that God's power is made perfect in weakness. He went on to say, "I will all the more gladly boast of my weaknesses, that the power of Christ may rest upon me."[36] Spiritual leaders, like disciples, are *made*, not born, and since it took Jesus, the master-trainer, three full years to produce his leaders (not entirely successfully, from a human point of view), we can hardly expect to do the job ourselves in a shorter time. Nor is a course of lectures on Christian leadership a substitute for imitating the way in which Jesus shared his life with the Twelve, guiding them, loving them, correcting them, encouraging them, forgiving them, and praying for them.

What especially are we to work and pray for, in order to grow a leader from a disciple? Together with the qualities mentioned earlier, there are several in particular that we need to encourage.

First, a Christian leader must have *the spirit of service*. A ruler *tells* people what to do, but a leader *shows* people by his own example. Jesus first washed the feet of his disciples, and then said, "I have given you an example, that you should do as I have done for you."[37] Paul was able to write to the Philippians, "What you have learned and received and heard and seen in me, do."[38] He rejoiced that the Thessalonians "became imitators of us and of the Lord";[39] and he urged Timothy to "set the believers an example in speech and conduct, in love, in faith, in purity."[40]

Moreover, a true leader will serve another Christian in a way that develops the other's full potential. As the disciple grows into maturity, the true leader will increasingly step back to allow the disciple to step forward. The coach of a football team is not the star performer; he does not score the goals; he does not steal the limelight. His task is behind the scenes, enabling his players to come into their own. A Christian who is ambitious to be a star disqualifies himself as a leader. "A true and safe leader is likely to be the one who has no desire to lead, but is forced into a position of leadership by the inward pressure of the Holy Spirit and the press of the external situation... The true leader will have no desire to lord it over God's heritage, but will be humble, gentle, self-sacrificing and altogether as ready to follow as to lead, when the Spirit makes it clear that a wiser and more gifted man than himself has appeared."[41] John the elder had trouble with Diotrephes, "who likes to put himself first."[42]

Second, a leader must possess *spiritual authority* which has nothing to do with status, but with obedience to God and being filled with his Spirit. The seven helpers in Acts 6, who were chosen by the congregation and appointed by the elders, were marked out as being "of good repute, full of the Spirit and of wisdom." Their spiritual authority was evident. Stephen, for example, was described as a man "full of faith and of the Holy Spirit... full of grace and power." He did "great wonders and signs among the people,"[43] and spoke fearlessly when on trial for his life.

Bob Mumford once wrote: "Real authority is never taken, it is given. No leader should ever take more authority in the life of one of his charges than he is given by that believer."[44] The danger comes when the believer gives too much authority to the leader, either to avoid personal responsibility or because of the requirements of that particular fellowship. Exercising a healthy and balanced authority within a church is not easy; the balance comes only from walking constantly with Jesus, being controlled by his Spirit, sensitive to his people, and equipped with his spiritual gifts.

Such a leader is quick to take advantage of momentum. When the Spirit seems to be moving in a certain direction, he must be willing to hoist his sails and go with the wind of the Spirit. He therefore needs to make clear decisions. Though he may need time to wait on God and seek the counsel of other Christians, a good leader will take decisive action even though sometimes he may humbly have to acknowledge that he was wrong. He must also have vision. He must learn to hear from the Lord, to see where he is going, to impart the vision to others, and to inspire them to go with him.

Although spiritual authority is given to a leader by those he seeks to lead, ultimately it comes from God to those who are concerned to "obey God rather than men."[45] When Jesus, the perfect model, walked this earth, he was Son of man as well as Son of God, and he showed us a life of absolute obedience. In John's gospel we see this especially clearly. "I can do nothing on my own authority";[46] "I have come down from heaven, not to do my own will, but the will of him who sent me";[47] "I have not spoken on my own authority; the Father who sent me has himself given me commandment what to say and what to speak."[48] In his perfect submission Jesus found his spiritual authority and power. That is why he was so impressed with the faith of the centurion who came to him about his sick slave. As the soldier explained, "I am a man *set under authority,* with soldiers under me: and I say to one 'Go,' and he goes; and to another 'Come,' and he comes; and to my slave 'Do this,' and he does it." When we are willing to be "set under authority" we shall find we have spiritual authority over others.[49] As an immediate consequence of being filled with the Spirit we will "be subject to one another out of reverence to Christ."[50] "Obey your leaders and submit to them; for they are keeping watch over your souls, as men who will have to give account."[51] Just as the leader must give account for his leadership, so the disciple must give account for his submission. And the wheels of authority and submission are oiled by love. "Outside the context of committed, loving relationships, authority and submission can be incomprehensible or frightening. But we know that we are not called to go it alone. Rather, we are called to community, to the development of meaningful relationships and the sharing of our lives."[52] Within such a context, carefully ordered structures of relationships are vital for the health and harmony both of the church and of the individuals within the church.

In a helpful article called *Where Does Authority Come From?* Stephen Clark, a co-ordinator of The Word of God community in Ann Arbor, Michigan, gives some of the scriptural protections against the abuse of authority.[53] First, authority within a church or community should always come from a group, never from one individual; in New Testament days whenever a church was established, elders (always in the plural) were appointed for the oversight of that church. Second, clear qualifications were given so as to ensure that the right people were in authority; Paul gave full instructions to Timothy and Titus, for example, about the sort of persons who should be chosen as leaders in the church.[54] Third, Jesus made it clear that authority must be marked by humble service, as we have already stressed. Fourth, it is God who ultimately "executes judgment, putting down one and lifting up another."[55] It is he who calls leaders to their position within the church, and the church must recognize those whom God has called. When a leader stumbles, we can trust God to correct and discipline, since he is Lord of his church.

This brings us to the third mark of a leader: the willingness to *exercise discipline*, always "in a spirit of gentleness."[56] A younger Christian, with whom I was working closely, once said, "I've been going through a difficult time for the last few weeks. I know I haven't made it easy for anyone. But I wish you had said something to me. I needed your correction, and it never came." Had I really loved this man, I would have undertaken the necessary gentle discipline before this cry for help. God has given us the responsibility of admonishing one another,[57] not in our own righteousness or spiritual superiority, but as a vital expression of our mutual care within the one body of Christ, and only in humility. If we see a speck in a brother's eye, we must first see if there is a log in our own eye; perhaps that speck in our brother's eye is only a reflection of the beam in our own.[58]

When giving correction, concentrate on important issues, not on trivial matters that happen to irritate us. Always we need to be positive. Paul, in his letters, repeatedly encouraged his readers with the evidence of God's grace in their lives, even when he also had hard things to say. Our world is quick to condemn and slow to encourage; so it is especially important that we speak positively about what is good. Correction should be accompanied by teaching: what went wrong, and why? How can it be avoided the next time? Even if the lesson has been taught before, we must not fight shy of repetition.

The leader needs also to give clear warnings—about false teaching and teachers, about temptations and trials, about the activities of the Evil One. "Warning every man and teaching every man" was Paul's constant concern.[59] Prevention is better than correction. Good church leaders will not be ignorant of Satan's devices.

The pattern of discipline in any church has been given clearly to us by Jesus in Matthew 18:15-17. Discipline within the leadership group will follow the same guidelines, but Paul gives an important principle to Timothy which, if acted upon today, would avoid much of the destructive gossip about Christian leaders that often devastates the church. "Never admit any charge against an elder except on the evidence of two or three witnesses."[60] Stanley Jebb helped me to see the significance of this verse—We should never listen to negative criticism against any Christian, especially a Christian leader, unless the critic is willing to repeat the charge in the elder's presence, even as a witness in court. When there are two or three witnesses, and though we receive the charge, we do not believe it or act upon it without further investigation. False accusation is one of the commonest ways the Devil divides Christians from one another. "Let us then pursue what makes for peace and for mutual up-building."[61]

### Training Leaders

All that has been said already about making disciples will be relevant for the training of leaders. However, one further structural development in the small group pattern for church growth is important.

Howard Snyder once noted, "Virtually every major movement of spiritual renewal in the Christian church has been accompanied by a return to the small group and the proliferation of such groups in private homes for the Bible study, prayer, and the discussion of the faith." John Wesley saw the necessity of this, and it was a powerful factor in the revival which swept England, influencing not only the personal religion of countless individuals, but causing immense social changes as well. Wesley himself was astonished by the effectiveness of the Moravian movement, which was largely due to their constant attention to personal relationships in small groups of 8-12 people called *banden* organized by Count Zinzendorf. These contributed to the spiritual health of the church, and also became the springboard of evangelism. In this century, the extraordinary growth of the church in South America is due first, to the emphasis on the power and filling of the Holy Spirit; and second, to the development of cell groups, with many thousands springing up and multiplying.

However, the leadership of these cell groups is all-important to healthy growth and expansion. In our church in York, we have seen the value of developing a "support group" of all the leaders of house groups in a given area. The leader of this support group will be an elder who has pastoral oversight of all the groups represented. Insofar as this support group of leaders is able to be open to God and to each other, that same openness is likely to happen in the groups they lead.

## Summary

Paul, when writing to the Colossians, declared that it was his aim to "present every man mature in Christ."[62] This is the ultimate goal in making disciples. Since God is the God of all life, his concern is that we should become whole people, not just religious people. Sometimes the Christian church gives the impression that it is interested only in religion. In fact, William Temple once called Christianity the most materialistic of all religions since it affected every area of life: everything was to be redeemed for Christ. Maturity in Christ refers therefore to our relationships at home and at work, our leisure, our use of time and money, our involvement in society—in other words, our whole style of living.

We must never restrict discipleship to religious events. It is the sharing of our lives together. Making disciples is never easy. Always it will mean hard work, coupled with spiritual wisdom and discernment from the Holy Spirit. Few, if any of us, feel qualified for the task; Paul, however, spoke of the mighty inspiration of the Spirit when it came to making others mature in Christ. We must trust the Spirit's resources as we seek to obey Christ's Great Commission.

# CHAPTER FIVE

# LIFE IN
# THE SPIRIT

FOR ABOUT SIXTEEN YEARS I have suffered from asthma. Fellow-sufferers know what a crippling condition this can be, gasping for breath and literally fighting for life, at times unable to talk, walk, work, or do anything but struggle to breathe.

The church in many parts of the world today is in a chronic, asthmatic condition. A century ago, Edwin Hatch wrote the hymn:

*Breathe on me, Breath of God,*
*Fill me with life anew;*
*That I may love what Thou dost love*
*And do what Thou wouldst do.*

We need to pray with our whole heart today that the breath of God's Spirit will bring new life to the whole church, and to every Christian.

Alexander Solzhenitsyn has said that Christianity is the only living spiritual force capable of effecting the spiritual healing of Russia—or of any nation and that the world situation is now so serious that spiritual revival may be essential for our physical survival. Our materialistic society is apathetic, cynical, frustrated, alienated and hopeless. In our spiritually bankrupt generation, people are not looking for religion but for reality. Few people want to recite a meaningless creed in a dreary liturgical service. Unless we become the living, loving, caring body of Christ on earth, why should anyone believe in our Savior?

The call of Jesus to his disciples was absolute: they were to deny themselves, take up their cross and follow him all the way. His commitment to them was also absolute. He gave his life for them on the cross; and he promised to give them his Spirit of life in their hearts. Without either of these supreme gifts of grace, their discipleship would have been hopeless and disastrous, but they started the greatest spiritual revolution the world has ever seen. Nothing could stop them. Despite threats, imprisonments, beatings, and killings, their enraged opponents had to acknowledge that these ordinary men and women had turned the world upside down. Devoid of human resources, they were totally dependent on the power of the Spirit of God. Today, the church has numerous resources: buildings, investments, seminaries, libraries, films, cassettes—the list is long and impressive. But there is little evidence of the Spirit's power.

In the closing hours of his ministry on earth, Jesus several times spoke of the coming of the Holy Spirit, the *Counselor*, who would be with the disciples for ever. All that Jesus had been to them during those three short years, the Spirit would be to them always and everywhere. He would be the *Spirit of truth*, not received or understood by the world, but forever dwelling in all those who followed Jesus. He would teach them all things, and bring to their remembrance all that he had said to them.[1]

Four main aspects of the Spirit's work are important for us to experience today: spiritual birth, spiritual growth, spiritual gifts and spiritual power.

### Spiritual Birth

The wife of an Anglican clergyman wrote to me one day: "You prayed that the Holy Spirit would make my Christian life new, and he did just that... I was filled with new life and joy, and I saw praise and love on every page in my Bible. Now I do not know *about* Jesus; I know *him!*"

In the imparting of new spiritual life, the Holy Spirit is sovereign at every stage. First, he *shows us our need*. "When he comes," said Jesus, "he will convince the world concerning sin and righteousness and judgment."[2] Recently I have had the privilege and joy of seeing a number of terrorists and long-term prisoners find living faith in Christ. In their letters they have almost all used the same words to describe their experience: "For the first time I *feel free.*" The pain of a guilty conscience is relentless. Our conscience, that God-given faculty within us, is constantly vulnerable to the Holy Spirit's action. Suddenly and unexpectedly we feel guilty for something we have done, or not done, in the past. "Nothing is more characteristic of the human sense of guilt than its indelibility, its power of asserting itself with unabated poignancy in spite of all lapse of time and all changes in the self and its environment..."[3] That is why the apostle Paul aimed clearly at "every man's conscience in the sight of God."[4] From experience he knew how the Spirit of God could wield the Word of God, a two-edged sword piercing through all the barriers and defenses to expose a guilty conscience. It is only through an awakened conscience that we are made aware of our spiritual or moral need of God and begin to call on God for his mercy and forgiveness.

Second, the Holy Spirit *brings us new life.* Since God is Spirit, we must be spiritually alive before we can know him. But sin, our natural state, has rendered us spiritually dead; we are in the kingdom of darkness, of Satan. How can we come into the kingdom of God? How can we be born again, born spiritually? Jesus never really answered that question for puzzled Nicodemus, but he pressed home the point firmly: "That which is born of the flesh is flesh, and that which is born of the Spirit is spirit. Do not marvel that I said unto you, 'You must be born anew.' "[5] There is no substitute for this.

Without the new birth we cannot *see* the kingdom of God. Imagine you are visiting York, and I am trying to show you the beauty of the stained glass in York Minster. From the outside, you cannot see it, however accurately and eloquently I describe it to you. Only when we go inside can you see what I am talking about. Until we step into God's kingdom by being born again, we cannot see the spiritual truths—we are blind to them. "I once... was blind, but now I see" is how John Newton expressed the change, in his famous hymn *Amazing Grace.*

Nor, without the new birth, can we *enter* the kingdom of God. Though the air is all around me, I need to breathe it in, in order to live physically. So the Spirit of God is all around me, and I need to breathe him in (or receive him), in order to live spiritually. Malcolm Muggeridge, after a spiritual journey that lasted for much of his life, discovered the reality of Christ, and shortly afterwards described the situation in these words: "I come back to the Christian notion that man's efforts to make himself permanently happy are doomed to failure. He must indeed, as Christ said, be born again... As far as I am concerned, it is Christ or nothing."[6]

Third, the Spirit *assures us of our salvation.* "When we cry 'Abba! Father!' it is the Spirit himself bearing witness with our spirit that we are children of God, and if children, then heirs, heirs of God and fellow heirs with Christ."[7] Once we have this inner assurance, variously called the "witness of the Spirit" or the "sealing of the Spirit,"[8] then we are ready for anything, through Christ who strengthens us. So Paul was able to say, "I consider that the sufferings of this present time are not worth comparing with the glory that is to be revealed to us"; he was absolutely convinced that nothing could "separate us from the love of God in Christ Jesus."[9] Yet, because the level of spiritual experience in much of the church is minimal, Christians today often lack assurance about their relationship with God, or their forgiveness of sins. The result is a weak and uncertain faith that, instead of shaking the world, will easily be shaken by it.

In much evangelistic work I realize that some who "come to Christ" are simply finding assurance of their faith. They already have a true relationship with God. But William Temple used to say that "until a man is converted *and knows it,* he is not the slightest use to God."

## Spiritual Growth

When Jesus spoke of the Holy Spirit as a Counselor, he used a word meaning "one called alongside to help." In the spiritual growth of any Christian or any church, the Spirit's initiative is essential. Some of these areas have been examined elsewhere in this book. However, a quick glance at four other aspects of the Spirit's work may be helpful.

1. **Christ-likeness.** The primary and sovereign work of the Spirit is to glorify Christ.[10] First he opens our blind spiritual eyes to see the glory of Christ ourselves, and then, by working within every part of our lives he reveals, with increasing measure, Christ's glory through us to others: "Now the Lord is the Spirit, and where the

Spirit of the Lord is, there is freedom. And we all, with unveiled face, beholding the glory of the Lord, are being changed into his likeness from one degree of glory to another; for this comes from the Lord who is the Spirit."[11] God's image in us has been marred and sullied by sin. Having redeemed us through the death of his own Son, God sends his Spirit into our hearts to start the repair work. It is a slow, delicate operation, which largely depends on our willingness to cooperate. Our natural self pulls away from the Spirit. "For what our human nature wants is opposed to what the Spirit wants, and what the Spirit wants is opposed to what our human nature wants. These two are enemies, and this means that you cannot do what you want to do . . ."[12] In this passage, Paul goes on to describe the results of depraved human nature, and then contrasts it with the fruit of the Spirit—love, joy, peace, and so forth.

Because there is much confusion about spiritual growth, and many Christians fall into the bondage of trying hard to become what they think they should be, a simple diagram may help.

We know that we ought to be full of love, life, power, faith and wisdom; but for many it seems a hard, long and bewildering struggle. These Christ-like qualities seem to be detached from us. How can we integrate these qualities in our lives? (See figure 5-1)

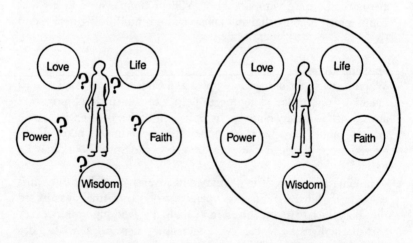

*Figure 5-1*                                    *Figure 5-2*

What we need to realize is that all that we need is in Christ; and once we are truly "in Christ" ourselves, we are complete in him. In figure 5-2, the outer circle represents Christ. In him we already have all the love and life, all the power, faith, and wisdom we need. We simply have to claim it, and begin to enjoy the unsearchable riches God has already given us in Christ. It is important to see the difference between trying to get something that we do not possess, and letting the Spirit release from within us what we already have in Christ. Our responsibility is to abide in him, and then trust his Spirit to work in and through us, as we are obedient to his prompting.

2. Healing. The healing ministry in the church has been, until recently, largely neglected. Biblically, however, Christ's command to the disciples to go and preach the gospel was nearly always linked with the specific instruction to heal the sick. This is a vital part of God's salvation. Indeed, the English word "salvation" is derived from the Latin *salvare*, "to save" and *salus*, "health" or "help." It means deliverance from danger or disease, and implies safety, wholeness, and prosperity. Although in new covenant times the word refers more to the moral and spiritual than the physical, God is still concerned with the "wholeness" of every one of his children. Paul stressed that he worked with all the energy that God mightily inspired within him to "present every man mature (*teleion*) in Christ."[13] The word *teleios* means full-grown, whole, mature, perfect. God's plan is that we should be whole in Christ.

Through sin, we are naturally separated from God, and often from one another. We may also be alienated from ourselves—emotionally fractured, paralyzed, wounded and scarred, and in need of inner healing. Until we are made more whole within ourselves, we shall be trapped by certain negative attitudes and reactions. It was the mark of Jesus that in every situation he reacted in perfect love. God's holy love could blaze forth with righteous anger when confronted by hypocrisy or oppression; but even though he was often sinned against, always he responded in love. God seeks to work in us by his Spirit, so that we too have this positive response of love, regardless of the situation we are in. For this, some inner healing is necessary for every disciple of Christ.

*Stress and growth.* God's original plan for his creation is that every child born into this world should enjoy the protective love of parents and family. As the child begins to develop, the process of maturation allows some limited stress, but the protective love of the family circle guards against more permanent damage. Even Jesus had to learn obedience through suffering; some pain is necessary for healthy growth.[14]

That protective circle of love is partially broken in every family because of sin. Every child experiences some harmful stress that may cause deep wounds. Further, as we are born with sinful tendencies, we wound ourselves by negative reactions to various situations. Thus we all grow up with personalities that are to various degrees aggressive, defensive, critical and hostile, and do not act and react in a Christ-like way towards each other. When the parental circle of love is badly damaged through the breakdown of marriage and family life, the scars will be even more serious. For example, the crime rate from broken homes is much higher than from loving and harmonious homes. Thus we have the problem, not only of "battered babies," but of emotionally battered children, teenagers, and adults.

*The great cover-up.* As we grow, we protect ourselves from further hurts by erecting our own defenses or masks. We keep our distance from others; or we hide our real selves by a veneer of over-confidence, shyness, joking, or aggression. We become experts at cover-up; we do not like to see ourselves as we really are, and we certainly don't want others to know the truth. These masks guard against vulnerability

In many Christian fellowships, therefore, our relationships are superficial: we relate to one another over doctrine or work, but rarely do we know one another deeply; we are frightened of being known. Our society teaches us to deny our own weaknesses; and the church often makes this worse by telling us that we should always be victorious, radiant, loving, peaceful and strong! We may subsequently find ourselves relating to people who will both reinforce our defenses ("don't be too introspective"), and refrain from probing too deeply into those inner areas that are scarred. Even in a Bible study or prayer group we still may not face up to who we really are; we need inner healing;.

God's plan for wholeness is clear. Through Christ we can be reconciled to God, and begin to know the healing of our relationship with him. Through the coming of his Spirit into our hearts, we are reborn and given new life—"Christ in you, the hope of glory."[15]

As we allow Christ to be Lord of our lives, his Spirit begins to change us into his image,[16] and the Spirit makes increasingly visible in our lives love, joy, peace and all his other lovely spirit-fruit. However, it is through our new relationships in the family of God that the work of Christ and the operation of the Spirit effectively work in us. Our salvation, or wholeness, is all there in Christ, but we need to open our lives to God *and to one another* for his Spirit to heal our inner hurts and to renew us in God's love.

*Deep-down healing.* For this healing to be effective, several steps must be taken. First, we must be willing to *take off our protective masks.* In fact, we are so blind that we may well need the help of other Christians to recognize those masks for what they are. It may be only in the security of accepting Christian love that we shall be willing to take them off and admit to our failure, hurt, and need. This is humbling and often painful; it may take sensitive, probing love to get through those barriers.

Second, we must openly *confess to God our real selves,* our deep desires, attitudes and reactions, humbly asking for his forgiveness and for the healing love of his Spirit. God is outside time so we can go back in prayer to those moments of hurt, releasing or forgiving those who hurt us, confessing some wrong done to another, and asking for God's help to put things right, if it is possible. In other words, we are specifically asking for the Holy Spirit to heal those inner hurts that are revealed to us as we take off our masks.

Third, by the open sharing of our lives with one another in love, we must *work out and make real the healing of the spirit.* In a caring Christian fellowship we can speak the truth in love, be honest with one another, pray for each other, and so receive God's healing through the caring fellowship to which we all should belong. It is still God who heals, but his Spirit is able to move more freely through the lives of Christians who are genuinely open to one another in caring and unjudging love. "Confess your sins to one another, and pray for one another, that you may be healed."[17]

All three steps are vital for God's kind of wholeness. My own cultural conditioning has resisted this third step of openness and sharing; I have been reluctant to remove my own masks! In private I could tell God everything, ask for forgiveness, and pray for the transformation of his Spirit. So far, so good. But still my masks and defenses were firmly in place. Gradually, through the gentle love and tenderness of other Christians, I let go some of these defenses. It was shattering to be known as I really am, and I felt sure that I would be both judged and rejected. But in an atmosphere of God's unshakable and compassionate love, shown through my brothers and sisters (who in turn needed all this just as much as I did!), I began to experience in greater depths than ever before God's deep inner healing of my whole personality. God is far from finished with me yet; but I am profoundly aware of much greater wholeness caused by the healing Spirit of Christ, as he works directly in my heart and also reaches me through other Christians, insofar as I keep my life open to them as well as to God.

Other forms of healing are also gifts of the Spirit and expressions of the love of God. Always we must bow to God's sovereignty in salvation, including healing; God will work in us usually through medical means, one of his good gifts. But the same Spirit who worked wonders and signs through Christ and the apostles is still available to us who believe. He longs to release us from physical sickness, from mental disorder, and from satanic bondage. And even if his immediate will does not include physical healing, his Spirit within us can reveal God's strength and beauty in the midst of our felt weakness.

3. Worship. This is the first priority of every Christian. Jesus called it the first and great commandment. It should be our natural response when we first commit our lives to Christ and when we sense his presence. It is the first mark of the Holy Spirit in our hearts. Yet, though nothing is more important than worship, nothing is more impossible without God's help. "God is Spirit," said Jesus, "and only by the power of his Spirit can people worship him as he really is."[19] All the revivals in the history of the church have been accompanied by great singing and praise, and the church that is concerned about spiritual renewal must take seriously this primary matter of worship. Our hearts may be cold and unresponsive, but if we offer to God a sacrifice of praise, the Spirit of God will turn those cold hearts of stone into warm hearts of flesh.

For this to happen, we must *take time* to worship. Many forms of worship keep the congregation at a very cool level of communication with God. We stand up to sing one hymn, then sit down to pray; we stand up to sing again, then sit down to read; we stand up to sing once more, then sit for another reading; so it continues. This pattern discourages intimacy with God, which is what worship needs to be. The commonest word for worship, (*proskueo*), occurring 66 times in the New Testament (the other six words are used only once each), means "I come towards to kiss." This is the language of intimacy and love. Christianity is a love affair with God and with his Son Jesus Christ. If I am to express my love with any feeling towards someone, I must give that person time. So it is with God. A. W. Tozer once said that "worship means 'to feel in the heart.' A person that merely goes through the form and does not feel anything is not worshipping ... Worship also means 'to express in some appropriate manner' what you feel." With the help of the Spirit, we need to bring ourselves to where all that is within us will bless his holy name.[19]

The Spirit gives us "access... to the Father."[20] He comes to pour God's love into our hearts, so that we can love him in response.[21] He always takes the initiative, releasing us from self-consciousness, delivering us from paralyzing inhibitions, making us aware of the presence of the living God. It is he who helps us to express our love in ways that delight and serve our Father, honor his Son, and encourage his family: "O magnify the Lord with me, and let us exalt his name together!"[22]

**4. Generosity.** One remarkable sign of the Spirit's presence after Pentecost was the extraordinary generosity of the early church. They "had all things in common; and they sold their possessions and goods and distributed them to all, as any had need... No one said that any of the things which he possessed was his own... Distribution was made to each as any had need."[23]

Why is the giving of most Western churches so meager compared to this first-century church, or even to many Third-World churches today? The answer is the Holy Spirit. Proportionately, the most sacrificial giving today comes from areas where, like the Macedonian church in the New Testament days, believers experience "extreme poverty."[24] In such circumstances, they are forced to trust God for everything; there is no alternative, and their genuine and active faith in Christ results in miracles, not least the miracle of generosity. Those of us in comparative affluence do not *need* to trust the Spirit, at least for our material needs; because we *have* an alternative, our faith is not so active, and the Spirit is less able to pour God's grace into our lives.

Writing about the early church, Clark Pinnock wrote some time ago in the *Post American* (now *Sojourners*), "This concern for the needy, this willingness to sacrifice one's own possessions did not arise (it seldom does) from a merely human resolution to be less selfish and more ethical. It arose out of an encounter with the Spirit. Perhaps the reason that today we are afraid to risk our property, to dig into our savings, to choose less lucrative careers, is that we are not really yielded to God, not really living in the full unhindered presence of the Spirit. The love of God does not overflow in our hearts, and we fear that God is unable to take care of us."

## Spiritual Gifts

Jesus promised his disciples that they would do the same works that he did during his earthly ministry, and even "greater works."[25] He then went on to speak of the coming of the Holy Spirit, through whose power and gifts this promise was fulfilled.

During this century there has been a world-wide rediscovery of some of the gifts of the Spirit that seemed lost to the church since the first few centuries. There have also been numerous spurious and counterfeit "gifts," sometimes with tragic consequences, which have made some Christian leaders cautious, critical, even antagonistic. But the answer to *misuse* is not *disuse* but *right use*. To discern whether certain manifestations are from the Holy Spirit, we need to look at the scriptural teaching concerning them and our attitudes must be positive. The Scriptures give us several cautionary words:

1. **Don't resist the Holy Spirit.** As Stephen told the Jewish leaders, whenever God does something new there will be those who resist what he is doing.[26] We must be very careful when we speak against some possible activity of the Holy Spirit, for, as Gamaliel once pointed out, we "might even be found opposing God!"[27]

2. **Don't quench the Holy Spirit.** In the church at Thessalonica, some of the younger Christians would not submit to the leaders of the church; Paul told them to respect those who worked among them and to esteem them very highly in love. But to some of the leaders who criticized the enthusiasm of younger members, and objected to their use of certain spiritual gifts, especially prophecy, Paul wrote: "Do not quench the Spirit, do not despise prophesying, but test everything; hold fast what is good."[28] The reason for division in some church fellowships over spiritual gifts is usually that some people push them too hard, while others (often the leadership)

oppose them too rigidly. A wiser approach is to encourage what is good, and gently correct what is wrong.

**3. Don't fear the Holy Spirit.** Someone once said, anxiously, "I hope that nothing supernatural will happen in our church!" Because of fear, it may not! Some of us are frightened by the "risks" of allowing the Holy Spirit full control. We box God up in the narrow limits of our own understanding. We tell him what we want, and don't want. We define the ways we want him to work—ways that are safe and respectable, that will not disturb, that we can easily grasp and keep firmly under control. But God's ways are not our ways. Sometimes the Spirit is a most uncomfortable Comforter, cutting across our preconceived plans and preconceptions. Cardinal Suenens has said, "The Spirit of God can breathe through what is predicted at a human level with a sunshine of surprises." We should never be afraid of the Spirit's renewing power. God is the giver of *good* gifts. Moreover he gives, not a spirit of fear, but a spirit of "power, love and a sound mind."[29]

**4. Don't grieve the Holy Spirit.** Much anger, jealousy, pride, bitterness, and resentment may arise over spiritual gifts. Even when the Holy Spirit comes to unite us in Christ and to fill our hearts with love, we may allow negative attitudes towards one another to dominate our thoughts. How tragic! "It is better to be loving than to be right." Unless we keep our relationships harmonious, we grieve the Spirit of God, no matter how "right" we may be.[30].

**5. Don't ignore the Holy Spirit,** particularly when it comes to his gifts.[31] The fulfillment of the prophecy of Joel at Pentecost referred specifically to the bestowing of gifts upon all who called on the name of the Lord. In particular, gifts of revelation are mentioned, to help us understand the will of God. For example, it was through prophecy that the first great missionary journey of the church was launched, and the gifts as a whole are given to edify the church for service in the world.

What, then, are these gifts? It may be helpful focusing on four main words in 1 Corinthians 12:4-7.

*Gifts.* Paul speaks of "varieties of gifts." The word "varieties" occurs three times in verses 4-6. Certainly there is a rich and wide variety. Nine gifts are mentioned in verses 8-10, three more in verse 28; and there are further lists in Romans 12, Ephesians 4 and 1 Peter 4. And there is nothing to suggest that these lists are complete; they are simply *examples* of spiritual gifts. Moreover, in the New Testament, there is no sharp distinction between "natural" and "supernatural gifts." *All* good gifts are from God, though some—miracles, for example—more clearly demonstrate the unusual action of God in his world. The word *charisma* means a gift of God's love; and Paul refers to many such gifts, including forgiveness, eternal life, fellowship, leadership, marriage, and celibacy.

So we must never despise any of God's gifts. Some Christians scorn the gift of tongues, for example. If you, in love, gave me a gift, and I scornfully refused it, you would be hurt. So is God.

Further, since these gifts come entirely from God, we must depend on his Spirit to direct our exercise of them rightly so that they become true spiritual gifts. Natural gifts, like music, administration, or hospitality may either be expressions of God's love, or opportunities for self-display. If I see a gift as "mine," to be used for self-fulfillment, I rob others of God's intended blessing. But if I see the gift as "his," asking him to control it by his Spirit and use it to his glory, then it will become a true spiritual gift for the building up of the church.

*Service.* The word for service, *diakonia*, implies an eager readiness to serve. God will give us gifts, or use the talents he has already given to us, if we have a genuine desire to serve Christ and to strengthen his body, the church.

It may be important here to stress the relationship between the gifts of the Spirit and the body of Christ, since Paul firmly binds the two together in 1 Corinthians 12-14. The church may have lost certain spiritual gifts because it has so often failed to become, in any real sense, the body of Christ. It is only when we are deeply and lovingly committed to one another as members of the same body that God will entrust his gifts to us as varieties of service within that body.

This truth is also a safeguard against an independent use of certain gifts. All should be weighed and tested within the community of God's people. For example, a man may think that he is called to preach and teach, but any such calling must first be proved within the church where he is a member. The recognition of our gifts by the congregation, and especially by the leaders of that church, is an extremely important protection against the abuse of spiritual gifts. Warning lights should flash if anyone is not willing for his or her gifts to be tested.

However, once we see that these gifts are for "service," we need to use them. As Paul wrote, "Having gifts that differ according to the grace given to us, let us use them."[32]

*Working.* Spiritual gifts are ways in which God works in and through his church today. Someone is healed or converted—God at work! A generous gift of money is given—God at work! A new atmosphere of joy and love is experienced in a church—God at work!

It is vital that we should *always* keep our hearts wide open to the fresh working of the Holy Spirit, because God is always wanting to do a new thing among his people. He is the God of today. He speaks today, acts today, saves today. We may look back with thanksgiving at all that he has done in the past, but we need to develop an expectant faith, believing that God wants to do something new and fresh for us today.

*Manifestation.* Spiritual gifts are given to manifest, or to make visible, the invisible God. We may not be able to hear God very easily, but through prophecy or exposition of the Scriptures, God may speak. We may not see God, but when we love one another God shows himself to us.

Further, such manifestation of the Spirit is continuously being given (*didotai*—present tense in the Greek) to each Christian if we are open to God and willing to serve. Our gifts and ministries may change in the course of time, but every person is vitally important within the body. Those who seem to be "weaker" are in fact "indispensable."[33] In his most helpful book, *Fire in the Fireplace*, Charles Hummel writes: "Suppose you are walking near a lake and hear a cry for help. As you turn toward the water you see that a child has fallen in, whereupon you run to the spot and pull the youngster out. It is obviously absurd to argue about which member of the body was most important to the rescue—ears, eyes, feet or hands—since each met a specific need. If any of them had not functioned at the right time the child would not have been saved."[34] Every gift is vital within the body of Christ; each needs the other. It may often be through the combined use of several different gifts that a person is literally saved—rescued from the kingdom of Satan to the kingdom of God's Son.

When spiritual gifts are exercised in an atmosphere of God's love (Paul's great chapter on love is sandwiched between two major chapters about gifts) they will be "for the common good." The Greek word, *sumpheron,* means literally "for the bringing together," "for the healing, restoring, renewing, or strengthening" of the body of Christ. Love controls the gifts. Love ensures that they are always used to edify the body of Christ, never to display self or to manipulate others. Love protects the fellowship from the misuse of gifts. Love encourages what is good, and gently corrects what is not so good. Love cares about the needs of others, so that spiritual gifts become genuine expressions of the love of Christ for members of his body. We should make love our foremost aim *and* earnestly desire the spiritual gifts.[35]

## Spiritual Power

Cardinal Newman once said that the church is like an equestrian statue: the front legs are lifted up ready to leap forward, every muscle of the back legs is standing out and throbbing with life. We expect it to spring forward at any moment. Unfortunately, when we come back twenty years later, it has not moved an inch. Yet look at the early church twenty years after the outpouring of the Spirit; they had moved forward by astonishing leaps and bounds for one reason: the power of the Spirit was with them.

How can we have this inward power? The answer, said Jesus, is to ask our heavenly Father for it. "If you then, who are evil, know how to give good gifts to your children, how much more will the heavenly Father give the Holy Spirit to those who ask him!"[36] However, there are several reasons why we neither ask for nor receive the renewing power of God's Spirit.

*1. Lack of personal commitment.* Jesus gave the promise of the Spirit to those who were already committed to him as disciples. They had left all to follow him. Peter later said that God gives the Spirit "to those who obey him."[37] A woman wrote to me after a service in our church: "On Sunday I yielded all my life to Jesus, problems and all, praised him for everything and told him I was happy to accept whatever he planned for me. I was suddenly filled with the Holy Spirit, and my life since then has been transformed."

*2. Unconfessed sin.* The third person of the Trinity is the *Holy* Spirit who will not fill a vessel that is not clean. We cannot make ourselves clean, but we can repent of every known sin, trusting in the blood of Jesus to thoroughly cleanse us. Ask the Spirit to search every part of your life, in order to show you anything that is displeasing to God. Only when you have done this, humbly and honestly, and have dealt with everything that he has revealed, can you ask God to fill you with his Spirit.

3. *Complacency*. Jesus sets the promise of the Spirit in the context of the story of a man who was disturbed at midnight by a friend banging on the door, asking for some food to give to a late-night visitor. Because the friend was so persistent, the man eventually got out of bed and gave him what he needed. Jesus often taught by contrast; if a grumpy man at midnight will give someone what he needs, how much more will our loving heavenly Father give us whatever we need, especially the power of his Spirit.

Some years ago I was studying the Beatitudes in Matthew 5. For two or three months, God showed me, through my own experience, the meaning of the first four Beatitudes. As his Spirit moved gently in my life, I began to see how spiritually poor I really was: alone, on my knees before God, I was bankrupt—in my heart I knew it, though I had often tried to cover it up with active Christian ministry. Then God caused me to mourn about my spiritual poverty. I became genuinely concerned at my lack of love for Jesus, my low level of faith, my disobedience in various areas in life. That was how God made me meek, or humble, before him. I saw myself at the foot of the cross, silently weeping for my spiritual poverty. Then I became very hungry and thirsty for righteousness, for a life that would truly glorify God and please him in every way. Pride and complacency had been stripped away. It had been a painful and humbling experience, but God was preparing me to be filled with his Spirit.

Lack of physical hunger is usually a sign of sickness. Similarly, if we are not hungry for God, something is wrong with our spiritual health and we need God to break that hard shell of complacency within our hearts.

4. *Unbelief*. What if we do not believe that God will do anything new in our lives? We may have asked him often to do it but nothing seems to have happened. Here Jesus encourages our faith by saying, "Ask, and it shall be given you; seek, and you will find; knock, and it will be opened to you..." By repeating the same idea in different forms he is effectively saying to us, six times, "It will happen, it will happen, it will happen..." As soon as we believe this, we need to express our faith in him in praise. Feelings and experiences vary considerably: they come in God's way, at God's time. It is always a

mistake to expect a certain experience that someone else may have had. The vital thing is to trust God's promise, claim it for ourselves, start praising God that it is now true, and let the fulfillment of that promise work out in God's way and in God's time.

5. *Fear.* Do you ask yourself: What am I letting myself in for? What changes will there be? What will God do in my life? Jesus understood this natural human reaction to something new, so he reassures us, "What father among you, if his son asks for a fish, will instead of a fish give him a serpent; or if he asks for an egg, will give him a scorpion?" There is no sting-in-the-tail with God. He never plays tricks on his children. And if we, who are evil, know how to give good gifts to our children, "how much more will the heavenly Father give the Holy Spirit to those who ask him?"

It is important to stress that this is not a once-for-all experience. We may well ask anyone who claims to have been baptized or filled with the Holy Spirit, "Well, where is he?" The inward renewing of the Spirit may bring about a release, a fresh experience of the love of God, or a leap in spiritual reality. Something may certainly happen, however we describe it or explain it. But the scriptural command is to go on being filled with the Spirit (Eph. 5:18—the Greek present imperative). Every day we need to come to Jesus for fresh cleansing of our sins, and the fresh filling of his Holy Spirit. Several times after Pentecost we read that the disciples were filled (again) with the Holy Spirit. There may also be times of anointing for some specific work.

Whatever the experiences may be, we should never be afraid of opening our hearts wide to the Spirit of God and his love. James K. Baxter puts it beautifully: "Can we say it more simply? Lovers have many ways of expressing their love, but especially two. One is the words, 'I love you.' The other is the kiss. God's word to me, reduced to essence, is 'I love you.' His Spirit, as the mystics long ago observed, is his kiss. And the baptism in the Holy Spirit? That's simply allowing myself to be kissed."[38]

It was once said of John Wesley that he had a strangely warmed heart allied to a strangely cool head. The latter on its own will always find deeply convincing reasons for playing it safe, remaining open-ended, instituting a dialogue, setting up a commission, running a pilot scheme, circulating a paper, doing some research—in fact anything rather than going out onto the streets of Jerusalem drunk with the Spirit, and showing others how to find God. We urgently need to recapture the vision of daring living for the Lord, throwing ourselves totally upon the power of his Spirit, without whom we are nothing. This is the church's greatest and most pressing need. Everything else we do is like trying to set sail in a boat when the tide is out and the wind is still.

"The crisis of the church is not at its deepest level a crisis of authority or a crisis of dogmatic theology. It is a crisis of powerlessness in which our sole recourse is to call on the help and inward power of the Holy Spirit."[39] Nothing less than that will save the church from senile decay and death, and the world itself from plunging headlong into self-destruction. God has never withdrawn his promise. He still gives the Holy Spirit to those who ask him. The next step is up to us.

# CHAPTER SIX

# *PRAYER*

JESUS WAS ALONE with his disciples. Deep in prayer, he revealed an intimacy with his Father that was unknown to them. Amazed at his total concentration and restful communion with his Father in heaven, they addressed him when he had finished and rejoined them. "Lord," they asked, "teach *us* to pray..."

The Gospels show that Jesus constantly encouraged and inspired his disciples to pray. Prayer was the breath that he breathed, the driving force of his life, the secret of his astonishing ministry. Later, it was the same with the apostles ("I bow my knees before the Father ... always... making my prayer with joy... we have not ceased to pray for you... constantly mentioning you in our prayers..."[1]) and with saints of God in every generation of the church. George Whitefield, who retired at ten o'clock every night, rose at four o'clock in order to pray. John Wesley spent two hours daily in prayer, and often said that "God does nothing but in answer to prayer." Martin Luther commented, "If I fail to spend two hours in prayer each morning, the devil gets the victory through the day. I have so much business I cannot get on without spending three hours daily in prayer." The leaders of the Clapham Sect of British social reformers such as William Wilberforce, daily gave themselves to three hours of prayer and organized Christians throughout the country to unite in special prayer before critical debates in Parliament. William Temple replied to his critics who regarded answered prayer as no more than coincidence, "When I pray, coincidences happen; when I don't, they don't."

With such examples we may feel like crushing failures! Most of us are ashamed at the poverty of our prayer life. In our activist Western society we have lost the prayerful meditation of our Eastern brethren. The prayer of those first disciples, then, is highly relevant for us: "Lord, teach us to pray..."

### The Example of Jesus

If Jesus was God, equal with his Father, why did he spend so much time in prayer? Was it really necessary for him? The answer is twofold.

First, *Jesus was not only God; he was also man.* And man, created in the image of God, is meant to live in dependence upon his Creator. The essential nature of sin is independence: as I live my own life my own way, doing my own thing, God's image in me is blurred. For that image to be restored, I must turn from my sins, trust Jesus as my Savior, and live in total dependence upon God— a dependence marked by prayer.

Second, *Jesus was also the perfect man.* Only as he remained blameless and sinless could he become our sinbearer. We are expressly told that he was in every way tempted as we are, yet without sinning.[2] How did he win this constant battle against temptation? Simply through continuous prayer. "Pray," he told his disciples, "that you may not enter into temptation."[3]

If Jesus found prayer essential, how much more should we. "Prayer—secret, fervent, believing prayer—lies at the root of all personal godliness," wrote William Carey. Prayer keeps us trusting God for everything, opens the way for the Holy Spirit to transform us into the image of Jesus, and enables God to touch the lives of others whom we meet.

### Our Approach

God knows that the natural self recoils from prayer, seeking to hide from the presence of God. "No one [naturally] seeks for God."4 It is at this point that we urgently need the help of the Holy Spirit: "The Spirit helps us in our weakness; for we do not know how to pray as we ought, but the Spirit himself intercedes for us with sighs too deep for words."5 When we do not know God's will, or when we stumble for the right words, the Holy Spirit is there to help us in our prayers. Since he is the Spirit of God, he knows the mind of God. He can put within us the longings of God's heart, and interpret our own stuttering prayers to make them effective and powerful.

Similar to these "sighs too deep for words," yet distinct from them, is "speaking in tongues," a valid form of communication from the human spirit to the Holy Spirit. It is not so much irrational as supra-rational. We need not always use perfect English to communicate with someone we know and love. "If I pray in a tongue, my spirit prays but my mind is unfruitful."6 Is that meaningless prayer? Of course not! He who speaks to God in a tongue "utters mysteries in the Spirit." God, who searches our hearts, hears our cries, regardless of intelligible speech. But it must be in the Spirit. The apostle Paul knew that in prayer, especially, "we are not contending against flesh and blood, but against principalities, against the powers..." Since these evil powers will try to make prayer difficult, dreary, or impossible, we must "pray at all times *in the Spirit.*"7

This involves *silence*—being still—until we consciously know that God is God, and that he is with us at this moment. We must train ourselves to listen to him, to be led by his Spirit in prayer, to be sensitive to his will, for "if we ask anything according to his will he hears us."8

Our posture may help us to cultivate this inner silence. Although we may pray effectively while standing, kneeling, walking, or lying down, it is generally found that sitting upright in a chair, with both feet on the ground, arms relaxed on the thighs, is a good posture for releasing tension, which helps us to hear the still, small voice of the Spirit as he draws us gently into a conscious awareness of his presence. A few deep breaths and a deliberate relaxation of tension can help bring a profitable time of meditation and prayer.

Such stillness before God should lead us naturally to worship— the opening of the heart to the love of God, the coming of a child to his Father, the intimacy of communing. Passages of Scripture, particularly the Psalms, may encourage us to worship. So may hymns or Scripture songs. Beauty in creation may also stir us. And we should enjoy the freedom of confidence in prayer as true sons or daughters of our heavenly Father. "For you did not receive the spirit of slavery to fall back into fear, but you have received the spirit of sonship. When we cry 'Abba! Father!' it is the Spirit himself bearing witness with our spirit that we are children of God, and if children, then heirs, heirs of God and fellow heirs with Christ."[9] We have a new and living way into God's presence, and may draw near to him with the confidence of family members.

Because God longs for us to enjoy the glorious liberty of the children of God, we may express our worship in word, song, movement, dance, or language given by the Holy Spirit. "Bless the Lord, O my soul; and all that is within me, bless his holy name!"[10] The Scriptures are full of exhortations to use everything we have in praise to the Lord: "Let the sons of Zion rejoice in their King! Let them praise his name with dancing, making melody to him with timbrel and lyre!... Clap your hands, all peoples! Shout to God with loud songs of joy!... Sing praises to God, sing praises! Sing praises to our King, sing praises!... I will lift up my hands and call on thy name ... I will sing with the spirit and I will sing with the mind also..."[11]

Thanksgiving is another essential ingredient in prayer. Prayer becomes dull, if not meaningless, when we lose sight of the greatness of God, or forget his countless gifts. As soon as we take anyone for granted, our relationship with that person begins to crumble. Expressing appreciation for someone is an important part of building a relationship. "To say that God wants our praise is to say that he wants us to have the glorious joy of loving him and living in intimate communion with him ... Love grows and deepens only if it is expressed. Perhaps we have not grown in love and joy because we have failed to express our love and joy in praise. Love and praise call for each other."[12]

Interestingly, when Jesus burst into spontaneous thanksgiving to his Father, we read that he "was filled with joy by the Holy Spirit."[13] As we open our hearts to the Spirit, we shall begin to know God's joy, or his love and compassion, or even his grief. Prayer will simply be thinking God's thoughts with him, letting him use our bodies as a temple of his Spirit. When, in obedience to God, we push off into worship, thanksgiving, and prayer, whatever our feelings may be, we will often find the wind of the Spirit filling our sails, pressing us into the deeper waters of prayer.

## How We Should Pray

When it comes to prayer, there are no experts. We are all children learning from our heavenly Father. From Jesus' example and teaching, however, we may learn some characteristics of effective prayer.

1. *Humility.* There is only one way into the presence of God— through the blood of Jesus. We cannot even approach God's throne until we have confessed all known sin, and have found forgiveness and cleansing through the death of his Son. Even then, we need the help of the Holy Spirit, who gives us "access to the Father."[14] In other words, prayer is our humble response to God's initiative. In his great love, he gave us his Son, and sent his Spirit into our hearts. Prayer means saying Yes to God, submitting our lives to his will, bowing to his sovereignty, discovering and enjoying his Father-love.

We should not think of prayer as trying to twist God's arm, attempting to persuade a reluctant deity to do what he does not want to do. Apart from the futility of that, it betrays an utterly false image of God. He is far more willing to bless than we are to pray. He longs that we and others should know his inexhaustible love. But we can frustrate God's will for our lives by rebelling against him, and by insisting on our way, not his. When Jesus told us to pray "Thy will be done on earth as it is in heaven," he was not asking us to resign ourselves to some terrible fate! Such a thought is like that of the man in the parable of the talents who said to his lord, "Master, I knew you to be a hard man..."[15] Understanding that God is a gentle, tender, loving Father—strong, pure, holy, yes, but essentially loving—and seeing ourselves as his children, we can confidently submit to his perfect will for our lives.

We need simplicity when we pray. The disciples tried to protect Jesus from the annoyance of small children, but he rebuked them. "Let the children come to me, and do not hinder them; for to such belongs the kingdom of God. Truly, I say to you, whoever does not receive the kingdom of God like a child shall not enter it."[16] The kingdom of God is full of children and the child-like. In our thinking and living we are to become mature; but in our delight in the Father's love we should always be children.

*You must surrender yourself to me.*
*You must realize that you are neither big enough nor strong*
  *enough.*
*You must let yourself be guided like a child.*
*My little child.*
*Come, give me your hand, and do not fear.*
*If there is mud, I will carry you in my arms.*
*But you must be very, very little,*
*For the Father carries only little children.* [17]

There are many times when we shall have to admit, "I don't know." If we could understand all God's ways and workings, he would be no bigger than our minds and not worth believing in; he certainly would not be God. Sometimes we speak as though God were on trial, having to justify his existence to us, needing to explain his actions. When the psalmist was baffled by the age-old question of the prosperity of the wicked and the sufferings of the righteous, he tried to work it all out in his mind. It was "a wearisome task," he complained, *until* he went into "the sanctuary [or presence] of God." Then it was clear to him that he had become bitter towards God. He went on to say, humbly and wisely:

"When my soul was embittered, when I was pricked in heart, I was stupid and ignorant, I was like a beast toward thee. Nevertheless I am continually with thee; thou dost hold my right hand. Thou dost guide me with thy counsel, and afterward thou wilt receive me to glory. Whom have I in heaven but thee? And there is nothing upon earth that I desire besides thee..." [18]

When we do not understand, but still submit ourselves to the Father's will, we shall be profoundly aware of his love and know his peace and strength flooding into our lives again.

2. *Honesty.* We never have to pretend to God. Though he knows all about us already, he wants us to share every part of our lives with him, including our fears and failings, our moods and emotions, our thoughts and anxieties, even those things of which we are ashamed. Read the Psalms, and see the total honesty of the psalmist: "How long, O Lord? Wilt thou forget me for ever? How long wilt thou hide thy face from me? How long must I bear pain in my soul... ?" [19] He told God all his doubts and difficulties, his anger and despair, his confusion, pain and joy and kept nothing back. The mask was off. His prayer was real.

So it was with Jesus. We see no stoicism in the Garden of Gethsemane: "Father, if thou art willing, remove this cup from me..." Three times he prayed the same prayer, with his sweat falling like great drops of blood. He shrank from the appalling ordeal of the cross, even though he submitted himself perfectly to his Father's will. Or, look at the transparent honesty of the apostle Paul. In his letters he wrote specifically about his own weaknesses no less than twenty-two times. He admitted that at Corinth he was "nervous and shaking with fear." He sometimes despaired of life itself. His whole life had this refreshing touch of reality about it.

So don't be afraid of bringing your most secret thoughts and desires to God. As we are open with him, he will work gently in our lives to mold us into a closer likeness to Christ.

3. *Sympathy.* We may sometimes think that failure in prayer is due to "lack of faith." Often that may be true, but perhaps more often we fail through lack of sympathy or compassion. Jesus was "moved with compassion" when he saw the enormous needs of sinful, suffering men and women. Such compassion naturally led to prayer and practical help. "If we have God-given compassion and concern for others, our faith will increase as we pray. In fact, if we genuinely love people, we desire for them far more than it is within our power to give, and that will cause us to pray."[20]

Compassion means "suffering with" someone, feeling their pains and problems: "Remember those who are in prison, as though in prison with them."[21] Anne Townsend has written, "If I can imagine what it must be like to be the one for whom I am praying, then I find I can begin to intercede for that person. My imagination leads me on to want to be more deeply involved with him in his own life. This involvement leads to caring; caring to love; and love to intercession. I may never meet the one for whom I pray; but I may come to love him enough to offer him one of the most precious gifts one person can offer another; that of intercession, 'love on its knees.' "[22] Prayer is a totally unselfish expression of love; the individual who is blessed by God seldom knows that we are praying for him.

Compassionate praying will also be positive praying. It is never helpful to pray about all the problems in detail. If we do, at the end of our prayer we will be conscious only of the problems! Instead, we should focus our mind on the Lord, perhaps thinking of those aspects of his nature, those specific promises that he has given which are relevant to those problems: "Lord, thank you that you supply our needs... that your grace is always sufficient... that your steadfast love never ceases... that you are sovereign in all things..." Negative thoughts, often filled with fear, unbelief, anxiety, anger, or bitterness, may hinder God's working in our lives. We need to "take every thought captive to obey Christ" when we pray.[23] In Acts 4, when the disciples were threatened not to teach anymore about Christ, they came together for prayer. They said nothing about the considerable danger they were in, apart from "Lord, look upon their threats," but they rejoiced confidently in the Lord's sovereign control over everything.

Positive prayer, sensitively used, is also the prayer of the evangelist or healer. The recipient is encouraged to believe that God is doing something *now* in answer to the prayer of faith. Such prayer will also help us to believe, when we are praying secretly on our own. Even the psalmist in depression came through to the point where he could say, "Hope in God; for I shall again praise him, my help and my God."[24] Many of the prayers in the Psalms struggle through to this point of faith.

Compassionate praying will also be broad in its scope, not stopping with *our* circle of friends, our church activities or our evangelistic programs. We must be prayerfully concerned about social injustice and needs: unemployment, poverty, racial discrimination, the plight of the homeless and oppressed, the sick in mind or body, the brokenhearted, the lonely, the helpless and hopeless. It is not hard to see why the Clapham Sect, their deep spirituality coupled with compassionate concern for people, spent three hours each day in prayer. The church today has largely polarized different emphases; those engaged in social action often have little time for prayer; those committed to serious prayer are often detached from social needs. No wonder the church has largely lost its prophetic voice.

*4. Expectancy.* When you ask for something in prayer, start looking for the answer and expect God to work. When the early Christians gave themselves in prayer after Simon Peter's arrest, they could hardly believe it when Peter, freed, came to their door! They did not expect an answer to their prayers. Yet God "is able to do far more abundantly than all that we ask or think."[25]

The English word "believe" often has a weak connotation. We

believe that something *can* happen, but we may not be at all sure that it will. The word "believe" comes from two Saxon words: *be*, meaning "to be" or "to exist," and *liefan*, meaning "as if it were done." Thus, "to believe" means "to accept something as though it were already done, already true." Jesus once said, "Whatever you ask in prayer, believe that *you have received it*, and it will be yours."[26]

The Scriptures are full of illustrations of such expectant faith. When Mary was promised a son, she began to praise God that *it was now true:* "The Lord has done great things for me."[27] Jesus, about to raise Lazarus from the dead, "lifted up his eyes and said, 'Father, I thank thee that thou hast heard me...'"[28] Paul, describing the nature of saving faith, quoted the example of Abraham: "No distrust made him waver concerning the promise of God, but he grew strong in his faith... fully convinced that God was able to do what he had promised."[29]

Knowing and claiming the promises of God in the Scriptures can help us to pray with expectant faith. It is through these promises that we know the will of God, at least in general terms. And, "if we ask anything according to his will he hears us."[30]

5. *Seriousness.* There is possibly no area of our lives where we can be so careless and lazy as in the matter of prayer. Jesus rebuked the Pharisees for honoring God only with their lips, when their hearts were far from him.[33] Jesus also told his disciples that "they ought always to pray and not lose heart."[34] He underlined this principle with his stories of the importunate widow and the friend at midnight. God wants us to rely on him for everything, and in his wisdom he sometimes delays his answers to our prayers to see whether we want something for his praise and glory alone.

The first disciples knew the importance of persistence in prayer. After the ascension of Jesus into heaven, they all "with one accord devoted themselves to prayer."[35] Several times in Acts Luke uses this word "devoted" in connection with their prayer life; it means a refusal to give up or get discouraged, a determination to stick to it, knowing prayer is essential. When the early church in Jerusalem was expanding, the apostles appointed others to attend to the increasing pastoral and administrative demands, "but we will devote ourselves to prayer and to the ministry of the word."[36] As they did so, God's Spirit moved in power.

*6. Unity.* Jonathan Edwards used to say that every significant spiritual awakening in the church has been preceded by unusual, united, and persistent prayer. Neglect of prayer leads inevitably to a depressing sterility: the glory of the Lord departs. It is a painful lesson which the church has had to learn time and again. Because the flesh rebels against prayer, the devil will suggest endless reasons for not praying. Only the Spirit of God can help us to "keep alert with all perseverance."[37]

Partly for this reason, united prayer is strongly encouraged in the New Testament, as well as personal prayer. Jesus promised that he would be present whenever two or three of his disciples met for prayer.[38] The early church was always praying together. Similarly, in corporate prayer we encourage one another, stimulate faith, identify ourselves as members of the body of Christ, and use spiritual gifts to build each other up in him.

Corporate prayer needs good leadership by those who are sensitive to the Spirit. It may be helpful to start with a time of worship, consciously lifting our minds and hearts from ourselves to the Lord. We are to set our minds "on things that are above," to raise the level of corporate faith and expectancy. Short bursts of praise and prayer from as many as possible are far better than long "professional" prayers. We should encourage sensitivity both to the Spirit and to one another. "Pray through" one theme at a time, rather than jumping randomly from one topic to another. 1 Corinthians 14:26 is the New Testament model for such gatherings: everyone bringing a different gift to glorify Christ and to strengthen his body.

*7. Forgiveness.* To pray effectively, we must first know God's forgiveness by confessing known sin to him, repenting of it, and asking for his cleansing. Here we must distinguish between the Spirit's conviction and the Devil's nagging. The Devil is the accuser of the brethren.[39] The symptoms of his nagging will be a *general* sense of guilt, or a lack of peace, but no specific reason for this. When the Holy Spirit convicts, however, he will place his finger on some particular area of our life which is not pleasing to God. We must ask the Spirit to search our hearts, but not allow the Devil to rob us of God's peace.

We must also forgive one another. "Whenever you stand praying, forgive, if you have anything against anyone; so that your Father also who is in heaven may forgive you your trespasses."[40] Jesus repeatedly emphasized forgiveness. Nothing can more quickly damage our relationship with God and with one another than an unforgiving spirit. It hinders prayer; as soon as I retain sin in my heart, the Lord will not listen.[41] Because he wants us to enjoy unbroken fellowship with him, he withholds his answers until we have repented of all known sin and returned to him with our whole heart. Paul urged the Ephesian Christians not to let the sun go down on their anger; if they failed to forgive, they were cutting themselves off from the grace of God, forfeiting his protection, and thereby giving "opportunity to the devil."[42]

Jesus once promised: "If two of you agree on earth about anything they ask, it will be done for them by my Father in heaven."[43] The word "agree" means literally to be "in harmony with." It is much more than a casual mental assent concerning the object of prayer. Rather, it is a promise for those who are living in love and harmony with one another; and, significantly, it is set in the context of the sorting out of relationships, even if this means forgiving someone "seventy times seven." Only when we forgive others can God forgive us—and only when God forgives us can we pray at all.

### When We Should Pray

Once again the example of Jesus is our perfect pattern. Although his whole life was one continual life of prayer, certain occasions are instructive for all true disciples.

1. *Every morning.* If we take the first chapter of Mark's gospel as depicting a typical day in the ministry of Jesus, we see the force of verse 35: "And in the morning, a great while before day, he rose and went into a lonely place, and there he prayed." In a few people, metabolism makes this virtually impossible, but the most important time of prayer for most Christians is in the morning, before breakfast. Tuning in to God from the start enables us both to commit the entire day to God, and to turn to him more readily during the day. In any war, every day begins with a careful check on communications, so that throughout the day orders can be passed on immediately and calls for help can be instantly heard. Without this, any army would be in chaos. The same principle applies in the army of Jesus Christ.

I have personally never found it easy getting up in the morning to pray! Every day is a real battle, but because it is worth winning, I have taken practical steps to "pommel my body and subdue it"! I use two alarm clocks to wake me up, since one on its own may fail to wake me. In the early days after my conversion, I used to have one alarm by my bed, and another cheap but very noisy alarm outside my door, set to go off ten minutes after the first. Because the second alarm would wake the whole household (and make me thoroughly unpopular), I had some motivation to get out of bed as soon as the first alarm had sounded. This scheme never failed!

2. *Before making important decisions.* The future of the Christian church rested on Jesus' choice of those first disciples. Although he probably knew in advance that one would betray him, another would deny him, and all would often fail him, making the right choices was crucial. Therefore "he went out to the mountain to pray; and all night he continued in prayer to God. And when it was day, he called his disciples, and chose from them twelve, whom he named apostles."[45] Humanly speaking, they were an unlikely bunch; uneducated fishermen, patriotic freedom-fighters, a traitor (tax-collector), a traitor-to-be, ambitious, impulsive, pessimistic, fallible men. Yet these were to be the leaders of the Christian church when instructed in the faith and equipped by the power of the Spirit.

"If any of you lacks wisdom, let him ask God," wrote James.[46] "But let him ask in faith, with no doubting..." Major decisions will nearly always call for special times of prayer.

3. *When under pressure.* When "great multitudes gathered to hear [Jesus] and to be healed of their infirmities," we read that "he withdrew to the wilderness and prayed."[47] Most Christian work is draining. Beyond the usual physical and mental demands there rages a spiritual battle. When ministering to others, Jesus knew that power had gone out from him.[48] Because he needed a constant renewal of body, mind, and spirit, he would regularly escape from people, both to relax and to pray.

God once rebuked his people through the prophet Jeremiah with these words: "My people have committed two evils; they have forsaken me, the fountain of living waters, and hewed out cisterns for themselves, broken cisterns, that can hold no water."[49] The Christian worker or the Christian church could be described in the same terms; all the right words and actions may be there, but the vital life-giving water of the Holy Spirit has dried up. Only the Spirit gives life and we need his living presence continuously flowing through us if we are to meet the spiritual thirst in others. "Beware of the barrenness of a busy life," warned Bishop Taylor Smith, about feverish activism of our Western society.

4. *When concerned about others.* "Simon, Simon," said Jesus tenderly on one occasion. I have prayed for you that your faith may not fail; and when you have turned again, strengthen your brethren."[50] We so often criticize one another, and slander, attack, or judge. But if we turn our concern for other Christians into prayer, we will be far more effective as a church against the forces of darkness. A friend of mine said that the army of Christ must be the only army in the world where its soldiers constantly fight with each other. This is really doing the Devil's work for him. But when we turn criticism into prayer, we lift up the shield of faith on behalf of the one being attacked, and release the Holy Spirit's power to encourage or convict (as the need may be), and we keep the love of God flowing between us when the Devil is out to divide us.

5. *When tempted.* "Pray," said Jesus to his disciples when they faced severe testing, "that you may not enter into temptation."[51] Even though tired and sleepy, the three disciples in the Garden of Gethsemane could have mutually encouraged one another in prayer. Sadly, they were soon overtaken by fear. When Jesus was arrested, they struck out in panic, then fled for their lives. Out of fear, Peter denied Jesus, and later they all huddled behind locked doors "for fear of the Jews."

In contrast, Jesus withstood the Tempter's deceit in the wilderness, and later in the garden through fasting and prayer. We cannot resist temptation in our own strength. Many times I have had to say to God, "Lord, I cannot do this thing by myself. I've tried, and failed. Please be my strength and shield in the midst of temptation." We might prefer some automatic security system to protect us from the Evil One, but God wants us to abide in his love, where we are safe from the ravages of sin.

6. *When in pain.* "Father, forgive them," prayed Jesus as the fierce nails were driven through his hands and feet; "they know not what they do." Consciously turning our thoughts towards God, and praying *for other people*, can wonderfully relieve our own pain. Even when seriously ill, I have spent much of the night in active prayer. It was the only thing that kept me sane, keeping me profoundly aware of God's never-failing presence and love in the midst

of what seemed like a nightmare. I have also seen incredible spiritual beauty in the lives of those who, racked with constant pain, deliberately gave themselves to sacrificial, unselfish prayer. No one in his right mind will ask for seasons of pain, but God can use them to transform us into the likeness of Jesus, if we accept prayerfully his sovereign will for our lives.

7. *At the moment of death.* Death has been described as the old family servant who opens the door to welcome the children home. Sometimes death takes people by complete surprise, but if we know that we are being welcomed home, how good it will be to greet the one whom we are meeting face to face.

Ideally, of course, our whole life should become a life of prayer. Whether we wake, eat, walk, play, work, rest, chat or retire for the night, we should enjoy the Father's presence: rejoicing in him, praising him, thanking him, talking to him, listening to him, saying we're sorry, keeping silent. As we share our life with him, we allow him to share his life with us.

Intercessory prayer cards or calendars may be helpful for systematic prayer, but as servants, not masters. We must learn to be spontaneous in prayer as well. If I pray for people as I meet them in a street or in a home; or pray before answering the telephone or going to the front door, my attitude will be much more positive and sensitive. If all of us, as Christian disciples, could seriously pray—however briefly—for all whom we meet each day, think of the cumulative impact of the love of God on society!

### The Power of Praise

The Psalms are shot through with praise and adoration. Even in times of pain, depression, loneliness, or fear, the psalmist turned his mind to some aspect of God's faithfulness, mercy, or justice for which to worship him. "Great is the Lord and greatly to be praised," not just because we happen to feel great, but because he is eternally great, and therefore eternally to be praised. Moreover, whenever we honor God by giving him a sacrifice of praise, he always blesses us.

It was often in response to praise that God's people experienced his presence in powerful and unmistakable ways. "When the song was raised, with trumpets and cymbals and other musical instruments, in praise to the Lord... the glory of the Lord filled the house of God."[52] Of course, praise by itself will not automatically produce the required results. In 1 Chronicles 13, David was bringing back the ark of God to Jerusalem, but he and those with him had been careless about the instructions given for transporting it, and although "David and all Israel were making merry before God with all their might, with songs and lyres and harps and tambourines and cymbals and trumpets," the anger of God broke out on Uzzah when he touched the ark, and he died there. God has to show his people, often in dramatic and tragic ways, that he requires obedience; without that obedience, all our praise, however fervent, is vain. Nevertheless, I have known numerous occasions when God's presence has been manifest through the worship and praise of his people.

At an international Anglican conference for spiritual renewal, held at Canterbury in July 1978, 350 international leaders were present, including 30 bishops and a good number from the Third World. The final Communion service was profoundly moving. There was a magnificent spirit of praise. I discovered that the man on my right was an American tourist who was drawn into the cathedral by the sound of singing and praise. I asked him what he thought of the service. "I have never been anywhere that is so alive," he replied. I gently enquired if he really knew the One who makes us alive, Jesus Christ, but he was not at all sure about it, so we slipped in behind the choir, and as the praise started up again I had to shout the gospel to him. Suddenly he grabbed me by the wrist: "Can we pray?" he asked. I led him in a simple prayer of commitment to Christ, shouting it at him phrase by phrase, and he shouting it back. In that context of praise he became a true Christian, and a few minutes later received the tokens of God's forgiveness and acceptance in the bread and wine. God broke into that young man's life in a marvelous way; but it all began with the power of praise.

In the Bible we also see God's victory experienced in answer to praise. The classic example of this is in 2 Chronicles 20, when Jehoshaphat and the people of Israel were faced with seemingly invincible enemy forces. They gave themselves to humble prayer and fasting, and God directed them, through a word of prophecy, to stand still and see the victory of the Lord on their behalf. They worshiped God for this promise of his help, and they sent the singers ahead of the army to sing: "Give thanks to the Lord, for his steadfast love endures for ever." Then we read these significant words: "When they began to sing and praise, the Lord set an ambush against the enemy," and they won an astonishing victory. Paul commanded, "always and for everything" give thanks to God,[53] and "give thanks in all circumstances."[54] It is by praise that we declare our trust in the Lord who saves, lift up the shield of faith to quench every fiery dart of the Evil One, turn our negatives into positives, and allow the Lord to demonstrate his power.

Praise also releases the Spirit of God in our lives. After the ascension of Jesus, the disciples met together constantly for prayer, "continually blessing God."[55] It was in this context that the Spirit of God was poured out upon them at Pentecost; and when he filled their lives, they worshiped in languages given to them by the Holy Spirit "telling... the mighty works of God." Day by day they praised him, and with such a worshiping, sharing and loving fellowship, it is scarcely surprising that "the Lord added to their number day by day those who were being saved."[56] Moreover, when they met their first strong and dangerous opposition, they immediately resorted to prayer and praise. The result was that "they were all filled with the Holy Spirit and spoke the word of God with boldness."[57]

Paul later urged the Ephesian Christians to be continuously filled with the Spirit, "addressing one another in psalms and hymns and spiritual songs, singing and making melody to the Lord with all your heart..."[58] Praise often precedes a fresh move of the Spirit of God, and afterwards it is the first sure sign of the Spirit's renewed presence. In the words of Pope Paul VI, "The fresh breath of the Spirit has come to awaken latent energies within the Church, to stir up dormant charisms, and to infuse a sense of vitality and joy. It is this sense of vitality and joy which makes the Church youthful and relevant in every age, and prompts her to proclaim joyously her eternal message to each new epoch."[59]

Praise also contributes greatly to the unity of all true Christians. When we fly in an airplane, the walls and fences which seem big at ground level at once lose their significance; and when the Spirit of God lifts us through praise more consciously into the glory and beauty of God, the barriers at ground level become meaningless. When there were tensions within the church at Colosse, Paul urged them to "put on love" and, three times in one paragraph, to be thankful.[60] Here is one of the great secrets of maintaining the unity of the Spirit in the bond of peace. Praise helps to fix our minds upon the Lord, opens our ears to hear his word, and prepares the way for God to pour his love into our hearts. A truly praising church will be a loving church.

Praise is (or should be) a foretaste of heaven. There, "day and night they never cease to sing" praises to God. "And I heard every creature in heaven and on earth and under the earth and in the sea, and all therein, saying 'To him who sits upon the throne and to the Lamb be blessing and honor and glory and might for ever and ever!' "[61] Praise is the language of heaven, and therefore can bring us a breath of heaven here and now.

We may have to break through the barriers of moods and feelings before we enter the realm of Spirit-inspired praise. When praise is the authentic expression of love and obedience, there is nothing which so glorifies Jesus Christ, and thus nothing which will be so opposed by the Devil. To begin with, praise is seldom easy. The Bible significantly talks about a "sacrifice of praise." And Dr. Leon Morris has rightly commented that "worship that costs us nothing is worth precisely what it costs."

In his most helpful book, *Praise, a Way of Life*, Paul Hinnebusch gives some vivid illustrations of the power of praise. A Christian businessman described a business trip to Saudi Arabia: "I felt very depressed by the difficulty of our negotiations there, the silence of the hotel I was staying at, and the oppressiveness of the city, where every man's mind and heart seemed totally opposed to Jesus Christ and to those who profess him as Lord. I got on my knees and began praying quietly to the Lord in "private prayer," but was soon led to pray in tongues, in the Spirit. Soon I raised my arms and started singing in tongues and then switched to singing some of our prayer meeting songs. I stood up and praised the Lord in a loud voice, rejoicing in the name of Jesus, uttered aloud in that place. Praise and worship of the Lord and the joy of his Holy Spirit filled my heart and being, and within the space of a few minutes my depression was replaced by that exultant joy. This joy increased to higher and higher levels for about an hour and a half. Praise God! I have never been so upborne."[62]

Similar experiences of the intense reality and glory of God have frequently been experienced by Christians as they have praised their Creator and Redeemer. When Richard Wurmbrand was in communist prisons for fourteen years, three times in solitary confinement thirty feet below ground level, he learned to praise God as an act of sheer obedience, and discovered a beauty in Christ he had never known before.

Today there is a growing concern for the spiritual renewal of the church. Ever since the outpouring of the Spirit at Pentecost, God has responded when prayer has been the priority on the hearts of God's people. Charles Finney was right when he said that "every minister ought to know that if the prayer meetings are neglected, all his labours are in vain." Prayer and praise are the greatest spiritual weapons God has given us in our constant battle against the powers of darkness. Nothing—absolutely nothing—can be a substitute for that.

# CHAPTER SEVEN

# THE WORD
# OF GOD

THE WILDERNESS BY THE DEAD SEA is as desolate and hostile as anywhere on earth: blazing hot, craggy, arid, and dusty. Put a man there, alone, without food, while wrestling for six long weeks with life's most profound questions and you will make him vulnerable to any temptation. If the man is the Son of God, with supernatural powers at his disposal, you begin to see the force of the totally reasonable suggestion from the Devil: "If you are God's Son, order these stones to turn into bread." Why not? It would have satisfied an obvious personal need. In view of his physical weakness and hunger, Jesus' reply is startling: "The scripture says: 'Man cannot live on bread alone, but needs every word that God speaks.' "[1] More important than all our other needs and wants, than physical life itself, is God's word to man. Exactly what this word is, how it comes to us, how we understand it and respond to it, are questions that we shall try to examine in this chapter. In brief, however, the "word of God" refers to God's total revelation of himself to humanity.

One reason for the church's spiritual decline today is a serious neglect of God's word, a loss of impetus in the Christian gospel, and a failure to proclaim the Good News of Jesus Christ with authority. In the imagery of Amos there is a famine, not "of bread, but of hearing the words of the Lord."[2] God, however, seems to be creating within our society again a renewed spiritual hunger. "Human hearts are crying... 'Is there any word from the Lord?'... They don't want our views, opinions, advice, or arguments. Is there any word *from the Lord?*"[3]

Since this question is of supreme importance, we should be alert to hindrances which make it harder for us to hear or receive God's word.

## Hindrances to God's Word

*1. Materialism.* Jesus specifically warned us about "the cares of the world, and the delight in riches, and the desire for other things"[4] that would choke God's word in our lives. We are being bombarded by the false seduction of material things that steal our hearts away from Jesus, close our ears to his voice, and turn our feet out of his path. Much Christian religion in the affluent West is disturbingly worldly. Why do we not listen to the radical teaching of Jesus? Why do we not demonstrate a genuine alternative lifestyle, God's new society on earth? Why have we lost our prophetic voice? Why have we little concern for the poor and the oppressed? Why does the institutional church make it hard for people to believe in Jesus? Because we have the covetous spirit of our age, and ignore the truth that we cannot serve God and mammon.

The world's subtle pressures are so pervasive that we can resist them only if we are continuously being renewed in our minds through the Scriptures. We need every word that God speaks. When the Devil showed Jesus all the kingdoms of the world and their glory, he said, "All these I will give to you, if you will fall down and worship me."[5] It was only through the Scriptures that Jesus was able to resist him. How much more do we need to "hide God's word in our hearts."

*2. Activism.* In his excellent book, *Celebration of Discipline,* Richard J. Foster comments: "In contemporary society our Adversary majors in three things: noise, hurry and crowds. If he can keep us engaged in 'muchness' and 'manyness,' he will rest satisfied. Psychiatrist C. G. Jung once remarked, 'Hurry is not *of* the devil; it *is* the devil.' "[6] Sometimes, we try to shield ourselves from personal pain, frustration, or insecurity by busyness. Jesus once had to re-mind Martha that instead of "fretting and fussing about so many things," she should be like Mary who listened to him, absorbing every word that he was speaking.

In our constant rush we think that we have no time for God, for-getting that God himself is the giver of all our time. From activism, increasing numbers are turning to yoga and transcendental medita-tion, which claim to purify the body, improve the health, strengthen the mind, and intensify spiritual growth. Such practices, however, seek to unite the individual with an impersonal, "universal con-sciousness" very different from the living God as revealed to us by Jesus Christ. TM and yoga may be psychologically helpful, but they are spiritually confusing. Instead, the Christian disciple should take seriously the many instructions in the Scriptures to be quiet before God and to meditate upon his Word.

3. *Humanism.* Jesus once rebuked Simon Peter by saying, "Get behind me, Satan! You think as men think, not as God thinks."[6] This is the classic description of humanism: with ideas starting from man, not from God, everything is seen from man's point of view, not from God's and man's thoughts about God become more important than God's thoughts about man. The independent spirit of this secular age resists external authority and results in anarchy or lawlessness. I do what *I* want, not what God or anyone else wants. I accept what is meaningful to me, and reject the rest.

The doctrinal and moral implications of secular humanism are both obvious and devastating: we stop listening to God and reject the authority of Scripture; our beliefs and behavior are shaped by human reasons or social trends. Because we start from man, we are left with man. Paul rightly commented about all who suppress the known truth of God: "They became futile in their thinking and their senseless minds were darkened. Claiming to be wise, they became fools." As a result, "God gave them up" to the destructive way of life they had chosen for themselves.[8]

4. *Textualism.* In A. W. Tozer's phrase, this is "orthodoxy with-out the Holy Ghost." Speaking of fundamental churches that can be textually sound but spiritually hard and dry, Tozer went on to say: "Everywhere among conservatives we find persons who are Bible-taught but not Spirit-taught... Truth that is not experienced is no better than error, and may be fully as dangerous." Until the Holy

THE WORD OF GOD

Spirit illumines our dull minds and warms our cold hearts, we cannot receive God's revealed truth, no matter how accurately we know the right words and teach them to others.

"Man needs every word that God speaks," (*ekporeuomeno*), or that "is continually coming out of" the mouth of God. The living God is constantly speaking to us, and we, in turn, need to listen to him. He speaks in a wide variety of ways, which we will discuss later in the chapter. Our vital response is to train ourselves to ask the question, "What is God saying to me through this passage, this person, or this event in my life?" It is not enough to know the text. What is God specifically saying *to me*—perhaps through that text—at this particular moment? If we are to keep spiritually alive and alert, we need *every word* that God is continually speaking.

Richard Wurmbrand once pointed out that in communist prisons he found Christians who knew Bible verses such as "My grace is sufficient for you," but found little comfort in these verses. *It is God's grace that is sufficient for us, not the verse about it.* "You could have beautiful love letters and pictures from a girl and still not have the girl. The question here is having God himself."

5. *Literalism.* This is an extension of textualism, and an inevitable reaction to the secular humanism of today. In our zeal to avoid the skeptical cutting away of all that is distinctively Christian, we may fall into the simplistic trap of blind belief: "It must be true because the Bible says so." To some this will seem to be obscurantist dogmatism that renders reasoned debate impossible. It leads easily to a legalistic Christianity, which denies the glorious liberty that should be our inheritance in Christ.[9] At worst, it degenerates into bigotry, a conviction of our total correctness, which will not consider the possibility that we are mistaken. Literalism refuses to listen to what other people are saying, and, worse, to what God himself may be saying through those people.

This is the attitude of most of the cults, but also of sections of the true Christian church which are becoming cultic. A cult is "devotion paid to a particular person or thing by a body of professed adherents." A cult nearly always follows a particular person and a rigid set of rules and teachings. It is a closed system in that it allows no deviation, no alternative interpretation of a given text. The science of interpretation, known as hermeneutics, is an exacting one. We need always to ask ourselves, what was the historical, cultural,

linguistic, and religious context of this particular verse in Scripture?
What was the original intent of this passage? What was it really
saying; and, in the light of this, what was it *not* saying? We shall consider one or two examples later; but we must be wary of those who
hold rigorously to some of the *words* of Scripture, without becoming
truly *biblical* in their thinking. It is dangerously true that you can
prove almost anything from the Bible if you ignore the principles of
biblical exegesis. The literalist narrows his mind and life to the
"letter of the law," instead of enjoying the liberating effect of the
spirit of it. "The written code kills, but the Spirit gives life."[10]

6. *Intellectualism.* Jesus came to bring us life. We need every
word that God speaks in order that we might *live.* We may have to
think about and discuss the Word of God, but if we stop there, we
miss the whole point of it. "You search the scriptures, because you
think that in them you have eternal life; and it is they that bear witness to me; yet you refuse to come to me that you may have life."[11]
An intellectual grasp of the Bible does not in itself bring spiritual
life. "Understanding is a creative act, even a creative art, which involves the whole personality of the reader. If he is not open to the
subject matter, indeed if he is not open to God, a knowledge of certain rules is no substitute."[12]

In the West we have often embraced Greek concepts of truth and
knowledge to the exclusion of Hebrew concepts. The Greeks saw
truth in terms of propositions, abstract statements and words;
whereas in Hebrew thought, truth was seen in terms of actions and
relationships. When Jesus talked about "knowing God," he used the
word for knowing (*ginoskein*) sometimes used for the intimate relationship between husband and wife. If we claim to "know the truth,"
and our attitude towards others is critical and unloving, it is questionable how well we know the one who is the Truth, Jesus Christ.

A purely intellectual knowledge of the Scriptures may feed the
mind; but if it aggravates a divisive, contentious spirit it can hardly
be called "sound," a word which means healthy or life-giving. The
Christian preacher is called, not primarily to impart theological
information, but to preach God's Word, and that Word is "living and
active."[13] It is a dynamic expression of the life and power of the
living God. Repeatedly in Genesis 1 we find the refrain, "God said
... And it was so," and in Revelation we find various references to
"the sword of his mouth," referring to the powerful thrust of God's

Word. That is what it should be like. For the disciple of Jesus, the study of the Bible should never be just an academic exercise. "To say that the Bible is our authority means both that we let our theological thinking be tested by it and that we let our lives be moulded by it. It shapes our thoughts, emotions, attitudes, desires, and wills."[14] A life-transforming experience!

7. *Anti-intellectualism.* Eastern mysticism, so popular today, places a dangerous emphasis on experience and rejects logic and rational thought, as in the following statement: "Guru Maharaj Ji (The Divine Light) comes down and he pours down that Grace and Knowledge with it. That Grace is *satsang.* Then when that *satsang* hits the mind machine, the very first thing it does is disconnect it... What we have to fight today is mind."

Some charismatic groups have fallen into this danger. The endless repetition of simple choruses or the name of Jesus *can* become a *mantra* or incantation; we need to beware of an unhealthy interest in the sensational and the demonic; we must be cautious about depending solely on subjective prophecies and visions in matters of guidance, rather than understanding biblical principles and prayerfully applying them. John Stott warns us about "the misery and menace of mindless Christianity," and pleads for "a warm devotion set on fire by truth."[15]

Those early Christians had a rich experience of God—sometimes a profoundly mystical one. The apostle Paul, however, was diffident about such experiences, and urged his readers to "set the mind on the Spirit," to "live by the Spirit," to "walk by the Spirit," and to "test the spirits."[16] This does not mean expecting one mystical experience after another; rather it means living a Christ-like life each day that demonstrates the fruit of the Spirit.

## Hearing God's Word

If every word that God speaks is vital for us, how does God speak today? How can we both hear and understand his word rightly?

Christianity is essentially a revealed religion. It is not man searching in the dark for God. It is God revealing himself to man in a personal way that calls for a response. "In many and various ways God spoke of old to our fathers by the prophets; but in these last days he has spoken to us by his Son."[17] Jesus is God's supreme revelation of himself to man, understandable by everyone of every age and culture.

It is important to distinguish three main expressions of the Word of God.

1. *The personal Word.* The Word of God became a human being and lived among us. Above all, God is personal. If we have seen Jesus, we have seen the Father.[18] If we want to come to God, we must come to the Son. "He reflects the glory of God and bears the very stamp of his nature."[19] "He is the image of the invisible God" and "in him all the fulness of God was pleased to dwell."[20]

2. *The written Word,* as given to us in the Scriptures. Although God is by definition our ultimate authority, the Bible is our final court of appeal as to what God has said. Here is the God-given, objective test for our belief and behavior. Not all theologians would agree with this. Although every true theist would accept the Bible's supreme authority, there have been three main views about how we are to understand God's Word.

First, there is *God's Word as interpreted by tradition:* i.e., what the church says, God says. But what does the church say? While many traditions are good and stabilizing, many are purely human and superficial. Jesus clearly corrected the Pharisees, the religious traditionalists of his day, when he said: "You have a fine way of rejecting the commandment of God, in order to keep your tradition ... [You make] void the word of God through your tradition..."[21]

Second, there is *God's Word as interpreted by reason:* i.e., what reason can accept, God says. That is why many professing Christians reject things like the virgin birth of Christ, his miracles, his bodily resurrection and his personal return. The rationalists of Jesus' day, the Sadducees, could not accept the idea of resurrection, but Jesus reminded them that God had revealed himself as the God of Abraham, the God of Isaac, and the God of Jacob; and since God is the God of the living, not of the dead, Abraham, Isaac, and Jacob must be still living even though physically dead. "You know neither the scriptures nor the power of God."[22] Their arrogant rationalism had become a stumbling-block to knowing God.

Third, there is *God's Word as interpreted by the Scriptures:* i.e., what Scripture says, God says. Jesus certainly endorsed Scripture as the Word of God: he knew it, taught it, lived it, fulfilled it. There is no doubt that for him the Scriptures were the inspired Word of God; and since this was "Christ's *textbook,*" as Dr. J. I. Packer has put it, "Loyalty to Christ, our risen Saviour and enthroned Lord, calls for total submission to Scripture, and anyone, or any church declining to believe and do what is written there, or failing in practice to be faithful to it, is to that extent a rebel against Christ."[23]

The various New Testament writers also claimed that what they were writing had come to them from God. "If anyone does not recognize this, he is not recognized [i.e., by God]."[24] Some argue that the Scriptures are fallible, being written by sinful men. But if the Scriptures are *God-breathed* (*theopneustos*, 2 Tim. 3:16) as Paul claimed, God is well able to speak by his Spirit through sinful men, accurately and infallibly, just as the Holy Spirit gave birth to God's perfect Son through Mary. By the breath of his Spirit, God breathes through individuals' backgrounds, personalities, experiences and understandings as shaped by the culture of their day: God's inspired Word brought to us through human beings.

Moreover, the Bible's claim for its own authority is not invalidated by a "circular argument," as some have maintained. If such a claim had first to be authenticated by some external authority, that authority would have to be superior. "To prove an 'ultimate' authority by appealing to a higher authority would be a contradiction in terms."[25] The Bible's own claim for divine authority may be tested only by its own consistency, reliability, and by the personal experience of those who seek to live by it. The testimony of Jesus and the apostles was self-authenticating. We must accept the Scriptures as the inspired Word of God, *as originally given*, while not despising good biblical scholarship as we try to determine both the details of the original text and its cultural and historical context. Having questioned the text, we must then allow the text to question us. Our conscience must become captive to the Word of God.

3. *The spoken word*, given through preaching, teaching, witnessing, or prophesying. God often speaks to us through the silent eloquence of creation, through pricks of conscience or peace of mind, through life's varied events. But we may also hear God's word when the Scriptures are expounded, when a prophetic word is given, or when a Christian brother or sister talks with us, for God did not stop speaking to us when the Scriptures were completed. We are not to expect any further revelation of doctrine and the spoken word, to be authentic, must be in accordance with the written Word, and must glorify the personal Word.

## The Prophetic Word

Since the apostle Paul exhorts us "earnestly to desire the spiritual gifts, especially that you may prophesy," and since there has been a recent upsurge of prophetic gifts in many parts of the church, along with spurious gifts among multiple cults and sects, some teaching about prophecy is necessary.

Although the foundational gift of prophecy was given once-for-all through the apostles for the completion of the New Testament canon, the early church clearly experienced different levels of prophecy. In 1 Corinthians 14, Paul envisaged this gift as a natural and healthy expression of believers when they "come together." The vast majority of prophetic utterances, even in New Testament times, were not "foundational," but were a normal part of upbuilding the body of Christ, and were clearly distinguishable from teaching or preaching. While the written Word is God's truth for all people at all times, the prophetic word is a specific word, inspired by God, given to a specific person or group, at a specific moment for a specific purpose. The prophetic utterance is in the speaker's own words and thought-forms since God uses our human idiosyncrasies and experiences to convey his word. Nor should we be suspicious if the prophecy makes use of scriptural phrases, (more than half of *the Revelation* comes to us in that way). Nor should we dismiss a prophecy if the word seems simple, even "trivial." In the Old Testament we read this: "Then Haggai, the messenger of the Lord, spoke to the people with the Lord's message, 'I am with you, says the Lord.' "[26] That was all! Not another word came to God's people for a whole month. It was not the most sensational word they had ever heard; but it was the word of the Lord.

God may give prophetic gifts for many purposes: guidance for future needs, as when Agabus "foretold by the Spirit that there would be a great famine over all the world";[27] or directions for the church's ministry, as when the Spirit told the leaders at Antioch to set aside Barnabas and Saul for the church's first great missionary exploit.[28] But mostly prophecy is for "upbuilding and encouragement and consolation."[29]

Since prophecy is God speaking through man, it must be carefully weighed and tested before it is received as the word of God. Speaking of the Montanists in the second century, Michael Green stresses the dangers both of abuse and of the over-reaction to abuse: "When they claimed that they personally embodied the Holy Spirit, when they wrote off other Christians as carnal and proclaimed themselves alone as 'Spirit-filled,' when they refused to have their teaching tested by the Scriptures but regarded it as every bit as authoritative as the New Testament records, then the church had to take action. That action was to reject the Montanists emphatically, and at the same time, to quench the prophetic spirit in the church. How much better it would have been for the church at large if the Montanists had determined to submit to the authority of Scripture, and to resist the temptation to be exclusive and write off other Christians. How much better if the Catholics had stressed tests for the genuineness of prophecy rather than writing off the whole movement, good and bad together."[30] That is a lesson highly relevant for the church of today.

What are the tests for prophecy, or for any other spiritual gift that purports to bring the Word of God? These questions should be asked:

1. *Does it glorify Christ?* The prophecy may not mention Christ by name, but does the whole message honour and glorify him? This is always the Spirit's primary work (John 16:14; 1 Cor. 12:1-4).

2. *Does it edify the body of Christ?* Seven times in 1 Corinthians 14 Paul emphasizes this point when discussing spiritual gifts, especially tongues and prophecy.

3. *Is it in accordance with the Scriptures?* If we twist the Scriptures, we do so to our own destruction (2 Pet. 3:16).

4. *Is the prophecy given in the spirit of love?* This is the hallmark of the Spirit's presence, even in correction or rebuke.

5. *Is Jesus lord of the speaker's life?* A false prophet will be known by the fruits of his or her life, said Jesus (Matt. 7:15-20).

6. *Does the speaker submit to the church leaders?* Strong personalities with independent spirits caused splits and divisions in the New Testament church, and do so today. Paul warned the Ephesian elders about those "from among your own selves" who would draw away disciples after them, and so divide the church of God (Acts 20:29-30).

7. *Does the speaker allow others to judge the prophecy?* Such weighing should be the rule, not the exception (1 Cor. 14:29).

8. *Is the speaker in control of himself when speaking?* The speaker may be "taken over" by an evil spirit, but that is never the

mark of the Spirit of God (1 Cor. 12:2f, contrast the passive "moved" and the active "speaking"; see also 14:32).

9. *Is the prophecy fulfilled, if it speaks about some future event?* Most prophecy is forth-telling, not foretelling. A Christian prophesying will normally "tell forth" God's word as an encouragement or exhortation for the whole congregation. Only on rare occasions will prophecy predict some future event. When it does, the biblical test is in the prophecy: fulfillment, or lack of it (Deut. 18:22).

### Logos and Rhema

In recent years, a popular but questionable teaching has arisen which attempts to distinguish between *logos* and *rhema*. Different teachers may express it differently, but in general, *logos* is taken to refer to the total, eternal teaching of the objective word of God in the Scriptures, whereas *rhema* is the particular, personal word that God is now speaking to an individual, to a local fellowship, or to a church as a whole. The distinction that some make between these two words has subtle but far-reaching ramifications.

First, although the *logos* of God is eternally true and important, the claim is that it is the *rhema* of God that we especially need to hear and obey. The *rhema* of God is said to be God's personal word to us for this particular moment in time; it is the sword of the Spirit,[31] the word that acts. It is not mere information, but a dynamic event. It is the word that changes people's lives, gives the church its sense of direction, and wins spiritual battles. What we need, the argument goes, is not so much the general exposition of the Scriptures, as the prophetic word of the Lord for today. If we obey the *rhema* of God, we will see him powerfully at work among us.

Second, although there may be areas of agreement about the *logos* of God, Christian unity depends in practice, it is claimed, on our response to the *rhema* of God. If the Lord speaks his *rhema* to us (perhaps through prophetic utterance), what matters is that we should obey it, even if it means withdrawing from other Christians in the process. As one leader wrote to me: "Unity is not built on a relationship to my brother, but on a response to the word of God. Thus you may have as much unity as you have agreement on the *rhema* of Jesus Christ." If there is not this agreement "in terms of the *rhema* of the Spirit," it is virtually impossible, in practice, to maintain any working fellowship. On these grounds, separation from other Christians is necessary.

From biblical, theological, and philological perspectives, however, the distinction is impossible to maintain. According to *Kittel's
Theological Dictionary of the New Testament,* there seems to be no
basic difference in usage between *logos* and *rhema.* Since *logos*
occurs 331 times in the New Testament (in all the writings except
Philemon and Jude), and *rhema* occurs 67 times (32 by Luke and 12
by John), large areas of overlap are inevitable. *The New International Dictionary of the New Testament*[32] concedes that "whereas
*logos* can often designate the Christian proclamation as a whole in
the NT, *rhema* usually relates to individual words and utterances";
but it immediately illustrates these individual utterances (*rhema*)
like this: "Man has to render account for every unjust word (Matt.
12:36); Jesus answered Pilate without a single word (Matt. 27:14);
the heavenly ones speak unutterable words (2 Cor. 12:4)." In no
New Testament dictionary or Greek lexicon of any substance can
the claimed distinction between these two words be found.

William Barclay, in his study on *logos* and referring to Jesus as
the *logos* of God, wrote: "By calling Jesus the *logos,* John said two
things about Jesus. (a) Jesus *is* the creating power of God come to
me. He does not only *speak* the word of *knowledge;* he is the word
of *power.* He did not come so much to *say* things to us, as to *do*
things for us. (b) Jesus is the incarnate mind of God. We might well
translate John's words, 'The mind of God became a man.' A word is
always 'the expression of a thought' and Jesus is the perfect expression of God's thought for men."[33]

In J. J. von Allmen's *Vocabulary of the Bible,* the article on
"Word," referring specifically to *logos,* makes the same point: "The
Word does not point to a reality of which it is only the intellectual
expression. It is that reality itself. It is an event. It is not rationality,
but a deed... The preaching of the Word is not confined to utterance, however appropriate it may be for the faithful transmission of
biblical "thought." Revelation is above all a *deed,* and it is this deed
as a whole which is the Word. The Word of God is more than an
utterance of God. It is an act of God. For God acts by his Word and
he speaks by his action.[34]

The massive weight of evidence shows that there is no clear distinction to be made between *logos* and *rhema* in the Scriptures.
Thus the two far-reaching inferences mentioned above are based on
a false premise. First, God has already given us his written Word in

the Scriptures; and as we read it, preach it, or hear it, it may at any time by the power of the Spirit become God's living word for us today. Although prophecy is one of the gifts of the Spirit, it is wrong to exalt the prophetic word above the written Word. Since *logos* and *rhema* are virtually synonymous, what is required is not a false distinction between two Greek words, but plain obedience to what God's Word says.

Second, Christian unity is always based upon our relationship with Christ. Although our response to God's Word is always important, it does not determine the boundaries of our unity. A true Christian is a man or a woman "in Christ"; if you and I are in Christ, you are my brother or sister, and I am your brother, no matter what your response to a certain *logos* or *rhema* of God. If we separate from one another, we sin against Christ and his body, since we are all one in him. The only theological grounds on which the Bible permits us to divide concern the divinity of Christ, his death for our sins and his resurrection from the dead. If a person denies any or all of these principal doctrines, a break in fellowship is not only possible, it is inevitable, for our unity is entirely in Christ. However, if we separate on the grounds of differing responses to some other *rhema* of God we have no biblical justification whatsoever. The confused teaching by some about *logos* and *rhema* is a reminder that a little "knowledge" can be a dangerous thing.

### Understanding God's Word
Having seen the different forms of God's Word, the authority of the written Word and the tests for the spoken word, the next important question concerns interpretation. Jesus constantly rebuked his religious hearers for their wrong interpretation of the Scriptures. In the Sermon on the Mount he said repeatedly, "You have heard that it was said... But I say to you..." In all the examples, Jesus never once changed the word of God as given in the Scriptures; he simply corrected the false *interpretation* of that word, and brought it back to its original meaning and purpose. As disciples of Jesus we must learn rightly to handle the Word of truth.[35]

Clearly, much depends on the Spirit of truth, the Holy Spirit. By his operation the personal Word, Jesus, was conceived in his mother's womb. By his inspiration the written Word of the Scriptures came into being, and true prophetic words are spoken today. Thus the

Spirit who inspired the Word must also be the Spirit who interprets the Word. "No prophecy of scripture is a matter of one's own interpretation, because no prophecy ever came by the impulse of man, but men moved by the Holy Spirit spoke from God."[36] We need the illumination of the Spirit to discern God's truth. "No one comprehends the thoughts of God except the Spirit of God;" and he is given to us "that we might understand the gifts bestowed on us by God."[37] Constantly Paul prayed for the Christian churches that God would "give you the Spirit, who will make you wise and reveal God to you, so that you will know him. I ask that your minds may be opened to see his light..."[38] Or again, writing to the church at Colosse, Paul said, "We ask God to fill you with the knowledge of his will, with all the wisdom and understanding that his Spirit gives. Then you will be able to live as the Lord wants..."[39] Without the Spirit's direct help, we would all be spiritually blind.

But along with the understanding given by the Spirit, our minds need some basic principles of interpretation. Two questions need to be asked. First, *what did the text mean to the original hearer?* We need to step back from the text, not bringing to it our own preconceived ideas, nor reading into it our own pet doctrines, nor drawing from it what is meaningful to us in our situation now, *before* we understand its meaning to the original hearers in their situation, which may have been very different. Only then can we ask the second question: *What does the text mean for us today?*

In particular, we need to examine carefully the words, the context, the literary form and the cultural setting of the text.

*1. The words.* A good translation is not a transliteration; some interpretation or paraphrase of the original is always likely in any version used for study. *The New English Bible,* for example, translates 1 Corinthians 14:13: "... the man who falls into ecstatic utterance..." though the strict translation from the Greek is "the one who speaks in a tongue." To describe speaking in tongues as falling into ecstatic utterance is a wild and somewhat alarming guess as to the precise nature of the experience. It would certainly confirm some people's worst fears about "tongues"; but it is inaccurate as a translation and misleading as a paraphrase. The many millions of Christians who speak in tongues as a normal part of the daily devotional life certainly do not fall into ecstatic utterance, except possibly on the most rare occasions. Wherever possible we need to get back to the original text, and inquire carefully as to what the word meant to those first hearers.

Beware, too, of assuming that the same word means the same thing in different places. For example, Paul says that a man is not justified by works, while James says that he is! A contradiction? Not at all. Paul is talking about the means of justification, which is certainly *not* good works; James is talking about the fruit of justification, which certainly *is* good works, for "faith apart from works is dead."[40]

Extreme care must also be taken when it comes to an allegorical interpretation of any passage. I have heard many intriguing theories about the "gold, silver, precious stones, wood, hay, straw" in 1 Corinthians 3, and am more impressed by the ingenuity of the speakers than by the accuracy of the exposition!

2. *The context.* This must be looked at carefully in two ways. First, any verse or passage must be understood in the light of the whole section of Scripture surrounding it. Verses used to support a favorite doctrine, idea, or line of action, are often lifted right out of their contexts, and an examination of the whole section may reveal that the verse is saying something very different from what is claimed. For example, the ten or more verses *before and after* Paul's reference to "gold, silver, precious stones," etc. are all about the tragedy of divisions in a local church and the importance of unity. In that context, the materials that will survive the fire almost certainly refer to those which strengthen the temple of the Spirit by maintaining the unity of God's people.

Second, we must try to grasp the historical context of any passage. That is particularly striking when it comes to the message to the seven churches in Revelation 2 and 3. Some knowledge of the history, geography, and commerce of each city is virtually essential before the imagery can be understood. The historical setting of each of the epistles is also of considerable importance if wrong conclusions are not to be drawn.

3. *Literary form.* The Bible is a library of books: 66 of them, drawn from numerous sources, written by at least 40 different writers over a period of more than 1600 years. Because the books, and passages in each book, fall into different categories, it is important to determine what each passage is claiming and saying. "So history must be treated as history, poetry as poetry, hyperbole and metaphor as hyperbole and metaphor, generalization and approxi-

mation as what they are, and so forth. Differences between literary conventions in Bible times and in ours must also be observed: since, for instance, nonchronological narrative and imprecise citation were conventional and acceptable and violated no expectations in those days, we must not regard these things as faults when we find them in Bible writers... Scripture is inerrant, not in the sense of being absolutely precise by modern standards, but in the sense of making good its claims and achieving that measure of focused truth at which its authors aimed."[41]

*4. Culture.* This is the most complex consideration of all. We are not to be conformed to this world, and in the right sense the gospel stands in judgment on the culture of every generation. Far too often has the church, accepting the existing culture without discernment, failed in its prophetic role to the world. At the same time, the application of its gospel must vary with every cultural setting, or else we will fail to communicate the timeless truths of God to our own rapidly changing society. What are the biblical constants, and what are the practical variables of those God-given constants? What divine imperatives should be applied to every culture, and what are the New Testament examples of first-century cultural application of those imperatives, which may differ in other cultural settings? These are the crucial questions behind such issues as divorce, homosexuality, apartheid, the role of women, the use of creative arts in worship and evangelism, methods of communication, contraception, capital punishment, pacificism, lifestyle, and a host of other major issues.

As an example of cultural variation, Eugene Nida records an argument between Western missionaries and African church leaders as to whether Christian women should go naked to the waist as did their non-Christian contemporaries. The missionaries stressed the biblical requirements for modesty in dress; but the African elders replied that they would not allow their Christian women to look like prostitutes, who were the only ones in that culture who could afford the colorful extra clothing!"[42] What is modesty in one culture may be extravagance in another.

A similar issue, but one nearer to our Western culture, is Paul's teaching in 1 Corinthians 11 that a woman should cover her head when praying in public. Some argue that the Bible says that women must wear hats in church, whatever today's cultural norm might be.

But the question to ask is: *why* was Paul stressing the need for women to be so covered in the Corinthian church in that first century? Every respectable woman in those days had her head, and probably her whole body, veiled—as do many Eastern women today as a sign of being under the headship of her father or husband. Any woman in Corinth not so veiled was a "loose woman," a prostitute. Some of the Christian women, rejoicing in their new-found liberty in Christ, were discarding their veils, thus causing unnecessary offense for the gospel. The hostile, pagan world was all too ready to criticize Christians; in that setting, unveiled Christian women would be a scandal. Is hatlessness scandalous in most Western countries today? If not, we miss the biblical point if we require women to wear hats in church when the majority of their respectable contemporaries outside the church do not.

Questions about sexuality and morality are often of a different nature. Christians still have bodies; and we cannot say that the New Testament strictures against fornication, adultery and homosexuality were merely reflections of the strict moral principles of those days. Far from it! They went right *against* the climate into which the young church was born. Of the first fifteen Roman emperors, fourteen were practicing homosexuals. Divorce, too, was common. We read of one woman in that first century marrying her twenty-third husband, she being his twenty-first wife! Christian standards were no easier to keep then than now, especially in the Gentile churches, where most of the converts came from this background. So Paul writes to the Corinthians: "Do not be deceived; neither the immoral, nor idolaters, nor adulterers, nor homosexual perverts... will inherit the kingdom of God. And such were some of you. But you were washed, you were sanctified, you were justified in the name of the Lord Jesus Christ and in the Spirit of our God."[43]

Basic Christian doctrines are not affected by what is culturally acceptable. In New Testament days, the Sadducees strenuously denied the resurrection; the Jews were offended by the preaching of the cross, but the church did not cease to proclaim Christ crucified and risen again, "a stumbling block to Jews and folly to Gentiles."[44]

Asking careful questions about the cultural setting of New Testament teaching is not, therefore, a slippery slope down which any or every Christian truth might disappear. Most issues of doctrine and practice apply to every age and to every culture, but some were specific issues at that moment in history. I suspect that the apostles would be horrified if they knew that their detailed instructions for Christians in their world would become rules and regulations for Christians for all time. When the result robs us of some of the glorious liberty of God's children, impoverishes the life of the body of Christ, and hinders the communication of the gospel in relevant terms for today, basic questions about interpretation need to be pressed.

Let me summarize. In any study of the Scriptures we must remain dependent on the Holy Spirit of God who inspired the writers of the original text and will also illuminate our minds as we receive the Word of God. God wants us to use our minds to ask two basic questions. What did the text mean to the original hearers, bearing in mind the written words, their context, the literary form of the passage, and the cultural setting? And then, what does the text mean for us today, probably in a very different setting? It is at this point that we must let God speak to us, and allow our hearts to be examined and shaped by his Word. "You do not interpret the text, it interprets you." As we listen to God today, most of us hear only what we expect to hear. We come with our preconceived ideas and go away with these same ideas. Many of us need that divine rebuke which came to Simon Peter when he was chattering away on the Mount of Transfiguration: "And a voice came out of the cloud, saying, 'This is my Son, my Chosen; *listen to him!*' "[45]

## Lessons for Spiritual Life

From our discussion, let us learn three primary lessons:

1. **Listening to God's word.** God's people in Bible times expected to hear God's voice. "I wait for the Lord, my soul waits, and in his word I hope."[46] "Speak, Lord, for thy servant hears."[47] In the New Testament, God spoke to Philip, Saul, Ananias, Peter, Cornelius, the teachers and prophets at Antioch, indeed to anyone within the Christian community. Paul implied that any member of a local church might receive a revelation from God.[48] Today, the majority of us find it extremely hard to hear the voice of God because we have forgotten how to be still before him, and we give little time (if any) for Christian meditation.[49]

God's Word can bring us consciously into God's presence. Let it speak to us, drawing us to the Father and glorifying the Son. As we meditate on one of the names of God or an aspect of his character the Spirit will help us to "see God." Words, phrases, or even whole passages of Scripture are invaluable for this fresh encounter with God. For some, praying or praising in tongues may also be spiritually refreshing. The purpose is not to empty the mind of everything, but to detach the mind from wordly cares in order to focus it on Jesus and his Word. "This aspect is often neglected because in many circles it is assumed that the most important thing about the Bible is its 'teaching.' However, much of its poetry... its parables, its humor and irony, is lost when it is reduced... to 'teaching.' It confronts us not just with information, but with verdicts... The evangelical approach may be criticized for being too cerebral. The question: 'What can I learn from all this?' is not always the right one to ask. Some parts of Scripture serve not to speak about joy, but to give joy; some serve not to instruct us about reconciliation but to reconcile us. The Bible is not only to tell us about Christ, but also to bring Christ to us."[50] Start with five or ten minutes in silent meditation and slowly increase the length of time. You will begin to hear God speak to you through his written Word or by his Spirit in your heart. Soon you will enjoy an increasing sense of God's presence and hear him as he speaks to you each day.

Dietrich Bonhoeffer writes: "Silence is the simple stillness of the individual under the Word of God... But everybody knows that this is something that needs to be practised and learned, in these days when talkativeness prevails. Real silence, real stillness, really holding one's tongue comes only as the sober consequence of spiritual stillness... The silence of the Christian is listening silence, humble stillness... Silence before the Word leads to right hearing and thus also to right speaking of the Word of God at the right time..."[51]

2. **Studying God's Word.** "Do your best to present yourself to God as one approved, a workman who has no need to be ashamed, rightly handling the word of truth."[52] From the very beginning of our Christian discipleship, we need to study carefully the written Word of God, and to let the Word of Christ dwell in us richly.[53] When the Berean Jews heard the gospel, "they received the word with all eagerness, examining the scriptures daily to see if these things were so."[54] Today a growing number of Christians, though spiritually alive and enthusiastic, are alarmingly ignorant of other

than superficial scriptural truth. How then can we study the Word
of God to its best advantage?

*Equipment.* Biblical scholarship is a gift of the Spirit for the benefit of the whole body of Christ, and is not to be neglected nor despised. It is helpful to have a translation that is known for its accuracy of translation and also a paraphrase, for its stimulating freshness.
Use a good concordance to follow a word through its use in different
parts of Scripture. Many valuable handbooks and dictionaries are
available today, and a Bible geography can provide useful background information.

Commentaries can be immensely helpful as we try to grapple with
the meaning of the original text but they vary so much in style and
scholarship that it would be impossible to say more than "get good
advice" before you buy. This equipment should only *supplement*
your own study of the Bible and your understanding of words and
phrases. If I rely too heavily on a commentary, for example, I may
be so fascinated by the thoughts of another writer that I may not
hear what the Lord is saying to me. In other words, do your own
study first, with prayer and dependence on the Spirit of truth; then
draw on other resources.

*Methods.* Variety is the key-word. Any one method can be a useful servant, but none should become master. To begin with, use
some systematic Bible reading aid—the Scripture Union, for example, has excellent material for almost all ages and educational backgrounds: notes, cassettes, booklets. I have also found the following
methods stimulating:

*a) Rapid survey:* I often read four or more Bible chapters a day,
following either one of the Anglican Lectionaries, or an old plan of
Robert Murray McCheyne. This gives me a broad sweep of the
Scriptures.

*b) Verse by verse study:* This is a valuable method for studying an
epistle or a chapter in one of the Gospels. Read the whole epistle
several times, in order to get the writer's main thrust, then begin a
more detailed study. Here commentaries and concordances are
especially useful. Preachers who learn how to "unfold" a passage,
help their congregations to see the great riches God has for us in his
Word.

*c) Book study:* Read through a book, several times in different
translations. Jot down its main themes, then see how the writer

develops each theme. Use commentaries for passages that need clarification, and watch for key words that are worth special study on their own. Investigate the background to any book, or you will miss much of its significance.

*d) Topical study:* Study either a word ("forgiveness," for example); or a theme (you might study all the references to the healing ministry of Jesus). Note, here, the danger of concordance work. The same Greek word in the New Testament may have several different English translations; and an English word may cover several different Greek words. And the same word or phrase (in both Greek and English) will not always mean exactly the same thing in different passages with different purposes.

*e) Character study:* The Bible is refreshingly honest about its characters. The men and woman in the Scriptures are seen as they really were, warts and all. David was a man after God's own heart but also a murderer and adulterer. Simon Peter was the rock-like leader of the early church but impetuous, self-confident and weak. Study a minor character first ("minor" because of little information given), such as Epaphroditus, Ananias or Philip to get the feel of it.

Bible study is valuable both privately and corporately. Look at the personal benefit of private meditation on the Word of God in Psalm 119. Then notice how Jesus taught his disciples as a group, a practice continued in the early church.[55] Both approaches are important. Arriving from Cambridge University to work in a dockyard parish, my naive suggestion to the members of our youth fellowship to read their Bibles quietly in their bedrooms brought roars of laughter. One lad was one of 13 children living in a small council house; a "quiet time" for Bible reading and prayer was impossible for him. Some could hardly read at all, and reading a Bible of 1,300 pages, not to mention Scripture Union notes, was beyond them. I soon saw that corporate study was the only realistic way for them to read the Bible at all, and some skill was needed to make a group work well.

**3. Obeying God's Word.** God speaks to us, not primarily to impart information, but to guide our choices, to re-direct our lives, to change us continually into the likeness of Christ. "Do not deceive yourselves by just listening to his word; instead, put it into practice."[56] J. Aitken Taylor has expressed it well: "'One does not pray, 'God, help me resolve the seeming contradictions I have found in the Bible.' One rather prays, 'God, help me to receive thy word wholly, unquestioningly, obediently. Let me make it indeed and altogether *the* lamp unto my feet and the light unto my pathway."[57] We must let God's Word address us, challenge us, activate us.

*Let the Bible shape your life.* If the world is not to squeeze us into its mold, we must let God re-shape our minds from within.[58] God's values are totally different from the world's. If we are to stand against the secularizing pressures of advertising and media every day, we need to saturate our minds and hearts with the Word of God.

*Let the Bible strengthen you in temptation.* Learn from Jesus, who overcame the attacks of Satan in the wilderness with "the sword of the Spirit, which is the word of God." The three recorded Scripture verses that Jesus used in that temptation come from Deuteronomy 6 and 8. Jesus may have been meditating on those passages at the time, and the relevant verses came quickly to him when facing temptation.[59]

*Let the Bible guide you*—not as a "promise box," with its random verses but because you know this book so well that increasingly you have "the mind of Christ," and can apply God-given principles to particular problems.

*Let the Bible help others through you.* I once talked with a lawyer for about two hours about the Christian faith, in general terms. It was mostly my word against his—a stimulating conversation, but little more. Then I opened my Bible, and showed him six or seven verses. In twenty minutes the Spirit of God spoke powerfully to him, cutting through his intellectual defenses. I was a young Christian at the time, but I never forgot this lesson. The Bible, when handled rightly and in a spirit of prayer, has the power to change lives.

Use it also to encourage, comfort, rebuke, or instruct. God's Word feeds our faith and renews us in his love. It wields authority and power that our own human arguments will never have. "Who else can we go to?" Peter asked Jesus. "You have the words of eternal life." And he was right.

# CHAPTER EIGHT

# SPIRITUAL WARFARE

EVERY CHRISTIAN KNOWS that discipleship is a struggle. On a personal level, why are we so often reluctant to pray? Why is it so hard for us to love and forgive? Why do we often shrink from keeping our hearts wide open to God and to other Christians? Why do we not more readily speak to others about Christ? Why are we still proud, selfish, angry, jealous, covetous, easily defeated? On a social level, why are relationships falling apart at every level? Why is there such oppression, injustice, and confusion? On an international level, why does hatred, violence and war occur nonstop around the globe? Why is it easier to fly to the moon than to find peace in Northern Ireland or freedom in Iran?

The Bible gives us the double reason: First, in our rebellion against God, we have become captive to sin: "I do not understand my own actions," wrote Paul. "For I do not do what I want, but I do the very thing I hate."[1] Second, we are involved in a spiritual battle, in which Satan seeks constantly to frustrate God's will for our lives.

Many people today find it hard to believe in a personal devil, (though some see satanic forces in every direction). C. S. Lewis predicted this double danger: "There are two equal and opposite errors into which our race can fall about the devils. One is to disbelieve in their existence. The other is to believe, and to feel an excessive and unhealthy interest in them. They themselves are equally pleased by both errors and hail a materialist or a magician with the same delight."[2] Even Christians who believe in the Devil's existence may be blind to the reality of spiritual warfare or the nature of the enemy's tactics. "Much of the church's warfare today is fought by blindfolded soldiers who cannot see the forces ranged against them, who are buffetted by invisible opponents and respond by striking one another."[3] The reason for much of the bitterness, misunderstanding, and hostility within the Christian church is that we are under spiritual attack, we fail to see its nature and in our frustration we strike out at more visible targets.

### The Biblical Witness

Those who find the whole concept of Satan's activity difficult to take seriously, dismissing it as fanciful or medieval, should note the volume of biblical teaching on this subject. Besides numerous passages in the Old Testament, we note that as soon as Jesus began his public ministry he "was led up by the Spirit into the wilderness to be tempted by the devil."[4] Later, when Jesus began to focus on his coming suffering and death, the supreme purpose of his earthly ministry, the battle against Satan is again explicitly mentioned. When Peter resisted the teaching that Jesus "must suffer many things... and be killed," Jesus rebuked him: "Away with you, Satan; you are a stumbling-block to me. You think as men think, not as God thinks."[5] Satan constantly tries to blind our minds to the purpose of God, and tempts us to see man as central. And when Jesus was facing the ordeal of the cross, he had another tremendous spiritual battle in the garden of Gethsemane—a battle won by prayer and obedience to his Father's will.

Jesus also talked about "the Evil One" snatching away the seed of God's Word,[6] and warned that the enemy who sowed weeds in the field was the Devil;[7] he told Jewish leaders that they were of their "father the devil,"[8] and prayed for his disciples to be kept from the Evil One.[9] Much of his healing ministry involved the casting out of evil spirits and demons. There was no doubt about the power and personality of the devil in the life, teaching, and ministry of Jesus.

The apostles, too, gave careful instruction about this spiritual battle. For example, Paul warned his readers that "even Satan disguises himself as an angel of light."[10] He stressed that he had forgiven those who had wronged him "to keep Satan from gaining the advantage over us; for we are not ignorant of his designs."[11] Elsewhere he urged Christians to "give no opportunity to the devil."[12] He wrote about "the snare of the devil"[13] and "the doctrines of demons."[14] He exhorted the Ephesian church to "put on the whole armor of God, that you may be able to stand against the wiles of the devil. For we are not contending against flesh and blood, but against the principalities, against the powers, against the world rulers of this present darkness, against the spiritual hosts of wickedness in the heavenly places."[15] He encouraged the Colossians by saying that, through the cross of Christ, God had "disarmed the principalities and powers... triumphing over them in him."[16] James said, "Resist the devil and he will flee from you."[17] And Peter warned, "Be sober, be watchful. Your adversary the devil prowls around like a roaring lion, seeking some one to devour. Resist him, firm in your faith."[18]

### The Historical Evidence

Throughout church history, Christian leaders have taken the spiritual conflict seriously and taught others how to experience victory. Ignatius Loyola (1491-1556) wrote a manual on spiritual warfare and conquest, (still used widely at Jesuit retreats), and included "Rules for the Discernment of Spirits," showing the contrast between Holy Spirit conviction of sin and the satanic counterfeit of condemnation leading to despair as well as the contrast between the Spirit's illumination and the Devil's false "enlightenment" which leads to further sin and spiritual darkness.

The Reformers largely accepted Loyola's directions as biblical; and although they rejected much of the medieval superstition that had erupted, they took seriously the spiritual conflict. Martin Luther (1483-1546) knew long and painful attacks by the Evil One, such as depression. Later, numerous works on spiritual warfare were written, including *Christian Armour* by William Gurnall (1616-1679). The full title of this book is this: "The Christian in Complete Armour, or, A Treatise on The Saints' War with the Devil: wherein a Discovery is made of the Policy, Power, Wickedness, and Stratagems made use of by that Enemy of God and His People. A

Magazine Opened, from whence the Christian is furnished with Spiritual Arms for the Battle, assisted in buckling on his Armour, and taught the use of his Weapons; together with The Happy Issue of the Whole War." My copy of 1837 has 818 pages of detailed exposition of Ephesians 6:10-20.

John Bunyan (1628-1688), well-known for *Pilgrim's Progress, The Holy War,* and *Grace Abounding to the Chief of Sinners,* sees the powers of darkness as lions chained on a short tether on either side of the road to the Celestial City. These lions will maul travellers who wander from the path, but cannot touch those who center their walk in God's will. With vivid imagery and biblical accuracy he shows that the forces of evil are held in check by the victory of Christ, and can do nothing which ultimately destroys God's kingdom and glory.

John Wesley (1703-1791) and George Whitefield (1714-1770) were under no doubts about the reality of spiritual struggle, as their writings and sermons indicate. Whitefield's *Journals* often refer to this battle in the heavenly places: "Satan endeavoured to interrupt us... Satan is disturbed... By and by, I expect Satan and his emissaries will rage horribly. I endeavoured to forewarn my hearers of it. Lord, prepare us against a day of spiritual battle!"

Jonathan Edwards (1703-1758) was especially alert to the counterattacks of Satan during times of spiritual revival. He saw Satan's main strategies as persecution, accusation, and infiltration. If possible, Satan sets Christian against Christian, leader against leader, to divide and conquer. Edwards also observed how the Devil, if unable to prevent a revival, pushed those involved to unhealthy extremes: "If we look back into the history of the church of God in past ages, we may observe that it has been a common device of the Devil to overset a revival of religion, when he finds he can keep men quiet and secure no longer, then to drive 'em to excesses and extravagances. He holds them back as long as he can, but when he can do it no longer, then he'll push 'em on, run 'em upon their heads."[19]

In this century, with the confusing counterfeit work of Satan during the great 1904-05 revival, Evan Roberts and Jessie Penn-Lewis wrote *War on the Saints.* And in more recent years, with the growing interest in the occult, many serious Christian books have been written from a clear biblical and pastoral perspective.[20] Because of the perplexities surrounding this subject, and the sensationalism of the "lunatic fringe," some church leaders today are skeptical about the reality of satanic conflict with God—it lacks intellectual respectability—but serious teaching about this warfare can be traced through the centuries since the days of the early church.

## Discerning the Spirits

"The ability to distinguish between the spirits" is one of the spiritual gifts given by God for the benefit of the whole body of Christ. Undoubtedly this played a significant part in the ministry of Jesus and the apostles. Jesus instantly recognized what he was dealing with, when confronted by those who were tormented or possessed by evil spirits: "You dumb and deaf spirit, I command you, come out of him, and never enter him again."[21] The effect was immediate; in this case a boy whose affliction had defied the attempted help of the disciples was made whole. Jesus never treated ordinary physical diseases like this, but he knew at once when faced with his enemy. Peter, too, was able to unmask Simon Magus who had joined Philip's converts; Paul set free the girl with the spirit of divination. In each case they accurately discerned the nature of the conflict.

"A good deal of the church's history becomes somewhat more intelligible if biblical principles for the discernment of principles are employed. They must be applied with *exquisite caution* (italics mine). But some rather tumultuous periods of renewal, counterinfiltration, and counterattack can only be sensibly interpreted with their use. Otherwise the scene is as confusing as a football game in which half the players are invisible."[22] In his First Letter, John tells us to "test the spirits to see whether they are of God,"[23] an important test in an age when cults and sects are proliferating; but this should be done with "exquisite caution," lest a genuine work of God be regarded as spurious, heretical, or even demonic. Some have written off the whole charismatic movement, good and bad together; they would have been wiser to exercise the caution of Gamaliel, for "if it is of God... you might even be found opposing God!"[24]

Satan is described as the "god of this world" who blinds people's minds to the truth of Jesus Christ.[25] He is "the deceiver of the whole world,"[26] using a host of evil spirits to persuade men to believe lies about God, to reject God's Word, and to indulge in the works of the flesh which bring further spiritual darkness and misery. The New Testament mentions the existence of the spirits of error, lust, and fear; unclean spirits, seducing spirits, deaf spirits, dumb spirits, lying spirits which deceive men by false guidance and false prophecy; familiar spirits working through occult practices; and a host of others. These demonic agents work within the institutions of the church and even in certain academic theological studies. The denial of some church leaders and scholars of the deity of Christ, his resurrection from the dead, and his expected return, is one example of Satan's blinding influence.

He is also called "the prince of the power of the air," who opposes the rule of Christ and controls evil movements and unjust political systems. He seems to be behind the massive, illicit use of drugs, the pornographic industry, the dehumanizing bondage to materialism, and the obscene violence which increasingly threatens our world. Paul warned Timothy that "in these last days there will come times of stress. For men will be lovers of self, lovers of money, proud, arrogant, abusive, disobedient to their parents, ungrateful, unholy, inhuman, implacable, slanderers, profligates, fierce haters of good, treacherous, reckless, swollen with conceit, lovers of pleasure rather than lovers of God, holding the form of religion but denying the power of it."[27] Although the root of all sin is to be found in the heart of fallen man, the extent of corruption and evil is sometimes great enough to warrant the adjectives "satanic" or "demonic."

Times of spiritual renewal, while refreshing the church, are also occasions for Satan's activity. Richard Lovelace comments: "Periods of renewal are times of vigorous activity both among agents of God and agents of darkness. Behind the scenes of earthly history in awakening areas we can dimly discern the massing and movement of invisible troops of darkness and of light. While this may seem fanciful to anyone in the twentieth century, it is simply realistic according to the biblical world picture, in which the angels of God are portrayed as locked in combat with the occupying powers of darkness at critical junctures in the unfolding of world history."[28]

### Direct Attack

There are a number of well-tried tactics of the Evil One that we need to understand. First, Satan seeks to destroy God's work by the direct attack of persecution, or by various assaults on the bodies, minds, and spirits of God's people, especially those involved in

Christian work. When Peter told his readers to watch out for the Devil as a "roaring lion," he went on to say, "Resist him, firm in your faith, knowing that the same experience of suffering is required of your brotherhood throughout the world." He had previously been talking about the "fiery ordeal" which would come upon them, telling them to "rejoice in so far as you share Christ's sufferings."[29]

Every active work of God has been contested in this way, from the vicious persecutions against the early church under the Roman emperors to the tortures and imprisonments of Christians during this century, especially in communist and Islamic countries. It is estimated that there have been more martyrdoms for Christ during the twentieth century than during the rest of church history. Such attacks are usually accompanied by false accusations based on gross misunderstandings of Christian faith and work. Right-wing dictatorships and totalitarian governments of every political hue have accused Christians of subversive influence, of revolutionary intrigue, and of law-breaking. Trumped-up charges followed by the mockery of justice have led to wanton aggression against Christians, often diabolical in its intensity.

It is notoriously difficult discerning the root causes of physical or mental afflictions, but the timing, significance, and ferocity of some indicate the work of the "roaring lion." Sudden illness, accident or death, may be examples of his activity. Many Christians have, for example, battled depression. Charles Spurgeon, the great Baptist preacher, knew "by most painful experience what deep depression of spirit means," especially on Monday mornings after the intensity of preaching the day before.[30] Writing of Luther's similar conflicts, Spurgeon said, "his great spirit was often in the seventh heaven of exultation, and as frequently on the borders of despair... He sobbed himself into his last sleep like a great wearied child." Luther himself, however, could view this practically; his remedy for depression was: "Don't argue with the devil. Better to banish the whole subject... Seek company or discuss some irrelevant matter, e.g., what is happening in Venice... Dine, dance, joke and sing... Shun solitude... Manual labour is a relief; harness the horses and spread manure on the fields." We shall often have to discern the interplay of four different sources of affliction: physical factors (sickness, fatigue, malnutrition, hormonal or chemical imbalance); psychological factors (personality types); fallen human nature; and demonic attack. The Devil may of course take advantage of any area of weakness, but where there is some disorder, various responses may be appropriate concurrently.

### Spiritual Accusation

Second, Satan aims to disrupt God's work by the indirect attack of accusation. He is the "accuser of the brethren," who seeks to overwhelm us with a flood of lies.[31] Opposition to the work of God's Spirit may come from within the church as well as from without. Within the church, spiritual hunger or renewal may be politely ignored altogether, especially by the leaders of the church. Or renewal may be caricatured in exaggerated proportions (reinforced by the aberrations and excesses that inevitably exist) and then vigorously opposed. Criticisms of one group of Christians by another often reveal misunderstandings of the truth of the situation. The accusations of good, honest Christian leaders would have often left me almost speechless, but for the fact that I have probably made similar accusations myself, unwittingly. Such extraordinary twisting of the truth can only be the "accuser of the brethren" at work.

Then, Satan often capitalizes on the genuine faults and failings of Christians, both to divide the church and to cause the name of God to be "blasphemed among the Gentiles."[32] Paul was concerned that Christians guard their behavior, that the name and the Word of God not be discredited.[33] The popular image of the church in secular Western society is of a pathetic and useless relic. *Some* elements of the church's existence may lead to such an image—it is not wholly false. But it is such a distortion of the real picture that it is effectively a lie that is, sadly, believed by much of the population. Such is the Devil's skill. He is the "slanderer" as well as the "accuser."

The work of the accuser also causes mental distress for countless Christians. With frightening accuracy and frequency he reminds us of our sins and weaknesses, and we fall into self-condemnation and despair. Blasphemous or evil thoughts may assail the mind, even during worship or prayer, and many believers consequently feel appalled by their sinful disposition. We need to understand clearly that these are no more than the "flaming darts of the evil one."[34] However, unless we learn how to lift up the shield of faith by claiming Christ's victory, we may become bound by obsessive guilt and continuing depression.

## Spiritual Exploitation

Third, Satan is out to damage God's work by exploiting the carnality of Christians to dilute the Spirit's activity.

God is a God of truth; but Satan can use a powerful personality in the church to turn the truth of God's Word into narrow, hard-line bigotry. A Christian can become so sure that he is right and others wrong that he lashes out with biting criticisms at fellow-believers.

God is a God of love; but Satan can use the frailty of human flesh to turn a genuine experience of God's love into emotional entanglement, or even into an adulterous or homosexual act. The immense pressure on Christian marriages today is natural in the context of the general breakdown of family life in society, but some of it seems devilish as it targets outstanding Christian workers and leaders.

God is a God of peace; but Satan can play on our weaknesses so that we become peace-lovers rather than peace-makers. We avoid conflict; we fail to resolve tensions in relationships; we allow sin to continue unchallenged within the fellowship; we agree with all points of view in a muddy ecumenism instead of clear unity in Christ. Christ the Bridegroom looks for moral and doctrinal purity in his bride, the church. In his Word he tells us to "speak the truth in love" so that we can grow up in every way into him. He knows that we are not perfect: we will all make mistakes, and we do not yet see things clearly. But only as we sort out our relationships with honesty, love, and forgiveness, will the God of true peace be with us.

## Spiritual Counterfeit

Fourth, Satan seeks to discredit genuine movements of the Spirit of God through counterfeit movements, which deceive many. As the "angel of light" he seduces deeply religious people with "deceitful spirits and doctrines of demons,"[35] bringing them into the bondage of legalism or license. He deludes weak Christians by those who are disguised as "servants of righteousness"[36] and by counterfeit miracles—"pretended signs and wonders."[37] He may draw them into a false religion which has all the outward form, but none of the life and power, of the Spirit of God.[38] In the experiential mood of today, alongside genuine charismatic experiences, a host of occult practices and Eastern mysticism have mushroomed. Sects that promise spiritual fulfillment and reality have grown like a cancer, encouraged by the spiritual ill-health of much of the orthodox church.

This has been the pattern of church history since New Testament times. The apostles and church fathers saw gnostic heresies and mystery religions as expressions of deceiving spirits. They were alert to the "spirit of antichrist" and the "spirit of error." They warned other Christians about false prophets "secretly bringing in destructive heresies,"[39] naming those who opposed the truth, "men of corrupt mind and counterfeit faith."[40] When we see the same confusing influences in church and society today, we cannot simply dismiss these apostolic warnings as first-century superstition. More humbly we ought to acknowledge our own limited vision of the spiritual realm, accept the teachings of Scripture as God's Word, and warn Christians about the danger of counterfeits today.

### Spiritual Temptation

Fifth, Satan tries continually to defeat God's people with temptation. He is called "the tempter." Generally his actions encourage inconsistencies in Christian witness. We are tempted to lose our temper, to be lazy, to covet what is not ours, to feed our pride, and to nurse grievances. Such temptations are aimed at our specific weaknesses.

What may be harder to detect, but is in the long run much more powerful and effective, is Satan's temptation to a sub-Christian lifestyle of worldly materialism, social distinctions, middle-class morality, Western affluence—covered with a thin veneer of spirituality. The unbeliever sees through this disguise. He demands to see a genuine alternative lifestyle which gives credibility to Christian witness. If he sees nothing substantial to distinguish the believer from the unbeliever, why should he join this "religious club" having little to say about real life and only a few religious activities? The temptation to avoid the challenge of true discipleship is both subtle and considerable. It is devastatingly effective, and it keeps the Christian powerless as an ambassador for Christ.

As Christians we are clearly called to live in the world and yet not be conformed to its values. When the world is mentioned, some Christians think at once of drink, drugs, sex or gambling. All of these may be poor substitutes for Christ in our hearts. But John tells us that "the whole world is in the power of the evil one,"[41] including its education, politics, philosophy, economics, industry, entertainment, television, radio, and press. These things are not necessarily wrong in themselves; but they are part of the system that is controlled by Satan. Everything that is not directly under the lordship of Christ belongs to the kingdom of this world and is in opposition to the kingdom of God.

Jesus once said, "As it was in the days of Noah, so it will be in the days of the Son of man. They ate, they drank, they married, they were given in marriage..."[42] Notice that Jesus did not say that they lusted, they fornicated, they gambled, they murdered. No! These evils may well have been true, but Jesus refers instead to the ordinary, natural things in life which they went on doing "until the day when Noah entered the ark, and the flood came and destroyed them all." Why did God's judgment fall? *Because that was their whole world, their entire life.* They were preoccupied with everything but God. God was not at the center of their lives as he always ought to be.

The problem for a Christian, therefore, is not how to avoid eating, drinking, marrying and giving in marriage but how to avoid the *power behind* these things, since the whole world is controlled by the Evil One. Even harmless, everyday things belong to the world which is in the control of Satan. How, then, can we be free from the strong pull of the world? How can we overcome the natural desires, ambitions, and attractions which so easily draw us away from the love of God? The answer is that in Christ and through his cross we have already been crucified to the world, and the world has been crucified to us.[43] We no longer belong to that old realm. We have been transferred into the realm where Jesus reigns.

This truth will be real to us only as we keep our hearts open to the love of God, and trust his Spirit within us to control our lives and to change us continuously into the likeness of Jesus. "Because he cleaves to me in love, I will deliver him..."[44] We cannot love God and the world at the same time. Only as the love of God is poured into our hearts each day by the Holy Spirit are we able to experience freedom from the pull of the world. This is no once-for-all spiritual battle. Though we belong in that realm of grace where Jesus reigns, each day we still need to submit every part of our lives to his sovereign rule, to be renewed in his love, to be filled with his Holy Spirit, and thus increasingly experience the "glorious liberty of the children of God."[45]

## Demon Possession

Sixth, Satan may mock God's work by taking possession of something that was created by God for his glory, usually a human being. Satan, as the "murderer" and "destroyer,"[46] desires to destroy God's work, and the destruction of the human personality by indwelling evil spirits is a frightening reality. We see it happen often in the Gospels. The man with the unclean demon was thrown down by the demon before he left him at the command of Jesus.[47] The "Legion" demons caused their victim to break the chains with which he had been bound, then drove him into the desert; when Jesus finally cast them out of the man, they destroyed a whole herd of swine.[48] The boy with the unclean spirit was tormented and convulsed by it; it "tore" at him, "shattered" him, and would "hardly leave him" until rebuked by Jesus.[49] Indeed Jesus warned that if an unclean spirit went out of a man, he would be "seeking rest"; later, if he found a man's life swept but empty, he would bring "seven other spirits more evil than himself" to dwell there, "and the last state of that man becomes worse than the first."[50]

I have personally witnessed the destructive power of demonic forces in the lives of several individuals. I have seen mocking, lying or tormenting spirits take hold of the personality of a human being created in God's image, causing him to say and do evil and violent things beyond his power. I have heard demonic voices speak through people. I have witnessed the wretched existence of those who are manipulated by the powers of darkness—usually through personal involvement in occult practices, although there are other means. I have prayed through hours of terrible conflict until those who are possessed by satanic forces begin to turn to Jesus for deliverance. Though I have been frightened by the reality of such evil, I have experienced the greater power of Jesus Christ. From what I have personally known over the last ten to fifteen years, I could not possibly doubt the existence of the Devil, even if I had intellectual difficulties with some of the concepts involved.

Normally, however, the destructive character of Satan is expressed in less bizarre, though still dangerous, forms. Satan works through human institutions that humiliate the individual, through social and political systems that oppress the poor and weak, through human avarice that exploits the defenseless for "filthy lucre," and through sinful lust that abuses young people as expendable objects of sex. "The involvement of the forces of darkness in stirring up and shaping these works of destruction against God's creation does not eliminate human responsibility and guilt. It simply explains the fearfully logical strategy often apparent in evil and the blindness and virulent energy present in human beings involved in such genocidal actions as the murder of six million Jews under Hitler."[51] If we fail to see the spiritual conflict, we shall be tempted to respond in bitterness and hatred towards *people*. However, Satan's human tools for evil in this world are not our enemies, nor are we to regard them as such. That is why Jesus told us to love our enemies and to pray for those who persecute us. All men, good or evil, are to be loved by Christians who follow God's example and love the sinner, though hating the sin. We see clearly that we are not contending against flesh and blood. Our real warfare is against the spiritual principalities and powers that control the lives of men and the system in which we live. In view of the scale, subtlety, and intensity of the spiritual conflict, there is great need for God's gift of spiritual discernment. As we pray for this specifically, God will increasingly give it to us. Paul prayed that the Colossians would be filled with the knowledge of God's will, and "with all the wisdom and understanding that his Spirit gives."[52]

## God's Freedom Fighters

Because the New Testament writers assumed that most readers were already familiar with spiritual warfare, only occasional exhortations are given to encourage the churches in it. Today we can make no such assumption, so a brief summary of some of the main principles of spiritual victory and freedom may be helpful.

1. *Know your enemy.* Speaking of Satan, Paul said, "We are not ignorant of his designs."[53] We should be well acquainted with the character and strategy of the Evil One, neither dwelling on it too much nor ignoring his active and destructive work: "Watch and pray that you may not enter into temptation," said Jesus to his sleepy disciples;[54] and in the Lord's Prayer we say, "Deliver us from evil" or from the Evil One.

2. *Keep yourself in the love of God.* Jude, writing about worldly people devoid of the Spirit who in the last days would scoff and divide the church, went on to assure his readers that God "is able to keep you from falling"; on their part they were to build themselves up in their faith, pray in the Holy Spirit, and keep themselves in the love of God.[55] It is sometimes said that the Christian who sins is a

fool because, if he abides in Christ, he need not sin. In the same way, although we must recognize Satan's power, we are not to be frightened of it. If we walk in the light with Christ, we have nothing to fear from the powers of darkness. Paul knew that "neither death, nor life, nor angels, nor principalities, nor things present, nor things to come, nor powers..." absolutely nothing, could separate a Christian from the love of God in Jesus Christ. Therefore if we keep ourselves in that love, we are perfectly and eternally safe. The Evil One will not touch us.[56]

3. *Be strong in Christ.* Paul instructed the Ephesian church: "Be strong in the Lord, and in the strength of his might."[57] Christ is "far above all rule and authority and power and dominion, and above every name that is named... all things [are] under his feet"[58] and "he who is in you is greater than he who is in the world."[59] In particular, our victory over Satan is to be seen in the cross of Christ, for it was there that God "disarmed the principalities and powers,"[60] and it is "by the blood of the Lamb" that we are able to conquer the accuser of the brethren.[61]

The power of the cross can dramatically release people from satanic bondage. Reading verses and passages about the cross are powerful weapons in spiritual warfare, especially in the most severe expressions of it. Generally speaking, a prayerful and confident trust in God's power over Satan through the cross of Christ is all that is required. We should exercise caution about "deliverance ministries" and indiscriminate exorcisms. Not every malaise can be ascribed to satanic oppression or possession and to do so may create serious disorder. The less sensational principles described in this section will be effective in the vast majority of cases. Christ has won the victory for us. We are to stand firm in it, proclaim it and rejoice in it. That is the way to resist Satan.

4. *Be filled with the Spirit.* Paul, having warned the Ephesians about "the unfruitful works of darkness" and the days "that are evil," urged them to continue to be filled with the Spirit.[62] All the gifts of the Spirit were needed to equip them for effective warfare. He told Timothy to be inspired by the "prophetic utterances which pointed to you," so that "you may wage the good warfare."[63] Repeatedly, and perhaps painfully, God will remind us of our own utter weakness without him. Pride, seen in self-confidence and self-reliance, so easily dominates our thinking. Like Simon Peter, we think we can

do it ourselves: others may fail, but we shall stand firm. We are shocked by the sin of another Christian, but blind to our own weakness. We need to come to that point, in every area of our lives, where we *have* to depend on the Holy Spirit. Unless we are daily cleansed from our sin by the blood of Jesus, and daily filled with the Spirit as we yield to him, we shall never overcome the Evil One.

5. *Be active in Christian witness and service.* In the same context of being filled with the Spirit, Paul urged his readers to "make the most of the time" and to wake out of sleep. Jude, too, exhorts Christians to convince those who doubt and to snatch others out of the fire. In other words, in view of the cosmic struggle in which we are engaged, there is not a moment to lose. Every day we need to know what the will of the Lord is, *and do it*. Isaac Watts was right when he said that "Satan finds some mischief still for idle hands to do," which must be balanced with Carl Jung's comment, noted earlier, that "Hurry... is the Devil." In the Gospels we see Jesus maintaining this balance—working to the point of exhaustion, yet calm and at peace in his spirit, busy but not rushed, alert but not tense. He perfectly accomplished the work that God had given him to do, and Satan had no foothold in his life.

6. *Be quick to put right your wrong relationships.* Every church is a fellowship of sinners. Inevitably we shall hurt others and feel hurt ourselves. Jesus knew the need for an emphasis on forgiveness, seventy times seven, if need be. Paul knew that we would at times be angry, justly or unjustly. But unless we deal immediately—before the sun goes down—with our anger, and with the problem that prompted it, we will give "opportunity to the devil."[64] If we go to bed angry, we may be sleepless; and find ourselves both depressed and irritable in the morning. If there is any break in fellowship between two Christians, the Devil will be quick to exploit it.

We also need to keep our lives constantly open to one another in love and thus help each other in the spiritual battle. If I don't know what is happening in your life, and you don't know what is happening in my life, how can we help when either of us is in trouble? However, if we are genuinely sharing our lives, when you are down I may be able to lift you up, and when I am down you may do the same for me. "Two are better than one... For if they fall, one will lift up his fellow; but woe to him who is alone when he falls and has not another to lift him up... And though a man might prevail against one who is alone, two will withstand him. A threefold cord is not easily broken."[65] Paul's instructions about the battle were written to a church, not just to individual Christians, and they could stand together, pray together, lift each other up only as they were genuinely united in love.

7. *Put on the whole armour of God.*[66] God gives us all the protection that we need. But we must make sure that we are walking with the Lord, that our lives are right ("righteous") with God and with one another, that we make peace wherever we go, that we lift up that shield of faith together to quench all the flaming darts of the Evil One, that we protect our minds from fears that easily assail, and that we use God's Word to good effect in the power of the Spirit. Remember, it was by the repeated sword thrusts of God's Word that Jesus overcame his adversary in the wilderness.

8. *Be constant in prayer.* "Pray at all times in the Spirit, with all prayer and supplication. To that end keep alert with all perseverance, making supplication for all the saints."[67] If, through prayerlessness, we lose our close contact with God, we can never stand firm in the battle. We need daily his "marching orders." We must come to him, wait upon him, renew our strength in him, listen to him, trust in him, and then go out into the world to face the enemy. If Jesus knew the constant need of this for his own ministry, how much more should we acknowledge our weakness by humble, persistent prayer?

9. *Use the festal shout.* "Blessed are the people who know the festal shout," sang the psalmist.[68] Through the centuries, God's people were often encouraged to shout praises to God, particularly in battle. Joshua told the people: "Shout; for the Lord has given you the city... So the people shouted, and the trumpets were blown. As soon as the people heard the sound of the trumpet, the people raised a great shout, and the wall fell down flat... and they took the city."[69] When Jehoshaphat faced a powerful enemy, he called God's people to prayer and fasting. The Lord spoke to them through prophecy, promising them victory in the battle. They fell down to worship, and the singers stood up to praise the Lord "in a very loud voice." As they went into battle, the singers went ahead of the soldiers, singing praises to God. And the Lord gave the victory.[70] "Shout to God with loud songs of joy!" sang the psalmist. "God has gone up with a shout."[71] In Acts 4 when the believers were faced

with a powerful conflict against the rulers who had murdered their Master, they raised their voices together to God and said, "Sovereign Lord..." and they praised him with a loud voice that he was in control of everything, and asked merely for boldness to speak his Word. No wonder they were filled afresh with the Holy Spirit; and no wonder the powers of darkness were driven back!

In Festivals of Praise around the world, I have encouraged many thousands of Christians to give the festal shout, "The Lord reigns!" As large congregations have joined together in "loud shouts of joy," many have told me afterwards what an encouragement this simple act had been. We need to strengthen each other's hands in the Lord. When people all over the world are stirring up each other with shouts of hatred, shouts of violence, shouts supporting this political candidate or that football team, surely we ought to follow this biblical principle and shout praise to God. After all, "if God is for us, who is against us?"[72] Let us proclaim together that Jesus Christ is the Lord who reigns.

# CHAPTER NINE

# EVANGELISM

CHRIST'S CALL TO DISCIPLESHIP is not primarily for the benefit of the disciple. His own apostles were slow to realize this, always wondering what they were going to get out of it, and who would be the greatest among them. Jesus challenged that idea: "Even the Son of man came not to be served but to serve, and to give his life a ransom for many."[1] And Jesus laid down his life for one reason: because he had compassion for people in need. "When he saw the crowds he had compassion for them, because they were harrassed and helpless, like sheep without a shepherd."[2]

So, how did he reach the people? He chose twelve potential leaders, gave them instructions, and sent them out to preach and heal, saying "The kingdom of heaven is at hand."[3] A little later, seventy others were sent out for much the same purpose, "to go into every town and place where he himself was about to come."[4] He told them it would not be easy; some would reject them, others persecute them; they would be involved in a great spiritual battle. In fact, the seventy came back bubbling over with joy; the mission had been for them a wonderful learning experience. As disciples, they

were called and sent out; and in going out they grew in their discipleship. Later, Jesus made it clear that every disciple is called both
to be his witness and to be committed to the task of evangelism. "As
the Father has sent me, even so I send you... You shall be my witnesses... to the end of the earth."[5] If Christ's first call to us is
*Come*, his second is *Go*—"Go your way... Go and preach the
gospel... Go and make disciples..."[6]

## Jesus' Plan of Action

Naturally they were not launched into powerful and effective evangelism overnight. Jesus had to help them to lose their fears, to overcome their inertia, to see the urgency of the harvest, and to watch
and pray. He had to teach them about the kingdom of God. He had
to strip them of pride and self-confidence, and to show them, sometimes in humbling and painful ways, that they could do nothing on
their own; only by prayer and fasting could they expect to see the
power of God at work. At times he had to test the reality of their
love, challenge their commitment, and prepare them for spiritual
battle. Often he warned them of hard times ahead, but promised
them also the power of his Holy Spirit, by whose inward help they
would be able to do the works that he had done, and even greater
ones.

When we look at the early church, frail with its human fears and
failings but alive in the Spirit, we see everyone gossiping about the
gospel. Who first carried the good news of Christ to the great Gentile city of Antioch, and up and down the Phoenician seaboard? It
was not the professionals. It was the "little people," the nameless
laity—the *idiotes*, as they were later called—who went everywhere
preaching Christ. No opposition could stop them. It was the whole
church, active in witness and bold in evangelism, that dramatically
changed the world of that day.

In the church today we need to think seriously how we can encourage the same spirit of evangelism that made such an impact on
the first few centuries of the church's history, and is so effective
today in southwest Asia, much of Africa and Latin America. How can
we overcome the natural reticence, partly cultural, that makes most
Western Christians like the great Canadian rivers in winter, frozen
at the mouth? How can our congregations be released from the
natural fear of men and resistance to change? How can good news

spontaneously flow from our church services and fellowships out
into the streets, homes and places of work—where people are?

### Breaking the Ghetto Mentality

Following a mission to Oxford University, Bishop Stephen Neill
wrote, "We are still faced with the problem of the real outsider. In
this mission, as in so many others, most of those attending were
good Christians, or part-Christians, or "spoiled-Christians." How do
we make contact with the real outsider, and to what kind of message
is it likely that he will give an ear?... Most of our so-called evangelism takes place within or on the fringes of the church; we do not
seem yet to have found the way to break out of the Christian ghetto
into the world."[7] There is a valid place for Christian missions and
festivals, when Christians unite together for evangelism or joyful
celebration. Spiritual renewal always precedes effective evangelism.
For the last few years I have been involved in festivals in different
parts of the world, when the gospel is proclaimed in the context of
music and praise, dance, drama, color, and joy. Such events have a
triple aim: evangelism, renewal, and reconciliation between Christians—three inseparable strands of Christian mission[8]—but we
must admit that only a few real outsiders find Christ in this way. The
vital necessity is *personal witness leading to effective discipleship.*
There are other ways of reaching the outsider, but nothing can re-
place this personal approach.

In view of this, the church needs to give training and support to
Christians at home and at work. It is the daily, unspectacular witness of Christians who are alive in Christ, that will most likely break
into areas that the church is not otherwise touching at all. "Men of
business, trade, industry come and worship with us, and we tell
them to be good husbands and appoint them our treasurers. We do
almost nothing to equip them for their daily work, which is where
God's kingdom has to come effectively today... We need to develop among all God's people, not merely the professionals, the sense
of vocation as to where we live and work. What seems to be lacking
in a divine strategy now is a mobile task force at God's disposal."[9]

In many Western countries—in Europe, for example—the
church is in a missionary situation. Most people know little or
nothing about the Christian faith, and regard the church as irrelevant. The church needs deeply committed Christian trade unionists,

teachers, politicians, social workers, craftsmen, artists, so that the church can be what Christ called it to be, the salt of the earth and the light of the world. The Christian dramatist, Murray Watts, put it forcefully like this: "We look at the TV today and say, 'How terrible! The violence, the immorality, the pornography—the meat has gone bad!' Of course, it's gone bad, because the salt never got there in the first place." Instead, others have got there before the Christians. Secular, revolutionary, and cultic groups have infiltrated strategic sections of society with philosophies that cannot begin to match the gospel of Christ. They have been successful for one reason only: they mobilize trained and dedicated disciples who are willing to sacrifice everything to achieve their goal. If we Christians pray that God's kingdom may come, we must be willing to be the answer to our own prayers, with all the imaginative boldness of the early disciples.

### The Witness, an Evangelist?
It is important to stress here that not every Christian is called to be an evangelist. All are witnesses to Christ, all must be committed to the church's task of evangelism, but only some are evangelists.[10] It is Peter Wagner's belief that only about ten percent of those in any church have this particular gift.[11] This means that while those ten percent should be trained and encouraged in this gift, the other ninety percent (with other needed gifts) must resist a nagging sense of guilt that they are not evangelizing as the others are. But that does not relieve us of the responsibility to be witnesses.

### The Marks of a Witness
1. *A witness must have a first-hand experience of Christ.* Hearsay is not acceptable in a court of law, nor in the court of this world's opinion. People will listen only to what we have personally seen and heard.

2. *A witness must be able to express himself verbally.* We may witness effectively through our lives, our work, our relationships, our attitudes, our suffering and even our death, yet we must still "be ready at all times to answer anyone who asks you to explain the hope you have in you."[12] We must do so "with gentleness and respect," and with the integrity of our lives demonstrating the truth of our words.

3. *A witness will have confidence in the power of God.* He relies on the power of the message of Christ and him crucified, and the power of the Holy Spirit. He knows that God can break through any defenses, and change any heart. This confidence will not be brash, but humble and sensitive, marked by much prayer. He knows that without God he can do nothing, but that with God all things are possible.

4. *A witness will have compassion for the spiritually lost.* He will care for them as individuals who matter deeply to God: made in his image, redeemed by his Son, and to be indwelt by his Spirit.

## The Marks of an Evangelist
An evangelist will of course have, at least potentially, the qualities required for effective Christian witness; some of these may be more fully developed than in the life of someone who is a witness but not an evangelist. As well as these, he or she should have the potential for three other abilities:

1. *An evangelist will have a certain clarity* in explaining the gospel to others. He must be sure about his message, and able to communicate it with simplicity and relevance.

2. *An evangelist will be able to make an appeal to the will.* After laying the groundwork of gospel facts, he can call people to lay down their arms of rebellion, to turn to Christ in repentance and faith, and to accept him as Lord and Savior.

3. *An evangelist will have a God-given faith* that, if the Holy Spirit is truly at work in this situation, there can be a definite response to Christ here and now.

Repeatedly we have stressed the need to perceive the "potential" in people. As we encourage one another to pray and work for this potential it will be developed in our lives. Also, others may discern God's gifts to us more easily than we can ourselves; this may protect us from selfish ambition that could spoil those gifts, which are to be used for the glory of God and for the benefit of his people.

## The Motivation of Evangelism
Today, there are more training courses in evangelism than ever before; but even with all the knowledge of what to say and how to say it, the question still faces us, How can Christians be motivated to do it?

It is worth taking a look at one of the New Testament disciples, Philip the evangelist. We know little of his background. He is first mentioned in Acts 6 when he and six others were appointed to a practical administrative task in the church. His subsequent impact as an evangelist, however, was considerable. What caused Philip and many others like him in the early church, to preach Christ so readily?

*1. He was full of the Spirit.* This is the one outstanding fact we know about the seven, including Philip, who were appointed in Acts 6 to help in the pastoral care of the church at Jerusalem: they were full of faith, wisdom, and the Holy Spirit. And the Spirit who filled them is the Spirit who comes to bear witness to Christ. "The urge to witness is inborn in the church, it is given with her nature, with her very being. She cannot *not* witness... Pentecost made the church a witnessing church, because at Pentecost the witnessing Spirit identified himself with the church and made the Great Commission the law of her life... So spontaneous was the response of the church to the Spirit-effected law, that the need of consciously obeying the command of Christ was not felt... It formed no part of her motivation."[13] As the love of Christ was continuously poured by the Spirit into the hearts of those first disciples, it naturally overflowed to others.

Paul once wrote that "our gospel came to you not only in word, but also in power and in the Holy Spirit and with full conviction."[14] The Greek word for "full conviction," *plerephoria*, suggests a cup so full to the brim that it overflows. When people "bump into" us, the Spirit filling our hearts "to the brim" will spontaneously touch their lives with the presence of Christ. If our hearts are not full of the Spirit, we may be reluctant to bear witness. Since we have no witness to bear, we are as limp as half-filled balloons. And if, from a sense of duty, we do speak about Christ, our words will seem empty, devoid of the reality of Jesus.

An agnostic professor of philosophy at Princeton University became a true Christian, after carefully studying the lives of some of the great saints of God down the centuries. What really gripped him was the spiritual radiance of their lives! Often they suffered intensely—many of them far more than most other human beings, yet through all their pain their spirits shone with a luster that defied extinction. Convinced that some supernatural Being was the source of their extraordinary joy, the philosopher found Christ.

A friend of mine once said that the most important thing about us is not just what we say, nor what we do; it is "our unconscious influence, impregnated with the fragrance of Jesus." Jesus wants us to *be* his witnesses. He wants us to be with him, to spend time with him, to be in constant communion with him. St. Ignatius of Antioch once said, "It is better to keep silence and to be, then to talk and not to be."

The following is simple poetry, but it states a great truth:

*Not merely in the words you say*
*Not only in your deeds confessed,*
*But in the most unconscious way*
*Is Christ expressed.*
*Is it a calm and peaceful smile?*
*A holy light upon your brow?*
*No, more! I felt his presence while*
*You laughed just now.*
*For me 'twas not the truth you taught,*
*To you so clear, to me so dim,*
*But when you came to me you brought*
*A sense of him.*
*And from your eyes he beckons me,*
*And from your heart his love is shed,*
*Till I lose sight of you, and see*
*The Christ instead.*[15]

2. *He had seen God at work.* We cannot say precisely what Philip had seen, but since he was well-known in the rapidly growing church in Jerusalem, he may have been present when the pentecostal Spirit was poured out on those first disciples. Overwhelmed with the love of God and with the presence of the risen Christ, perhaps he worshiped God in a language given by the Holy Spirit. He may have seen the apostles' "many wonders and signs" and joined in prayer to the sovereign Lord for boldness to speak for him in the face of mounting opposition, or been present when the room shook with power as all those present were filled with the Spirit. Undoubtedly he experienced the loving care and generosity of that newborn church, and knew of God's dramatic judgment falling on Ananias and Sapphira when they both lied to the Holy Spirit. Certainly he witnessed the church's astonishing growth from 120 on the

Day of Pentecost to many thousands who had "filled Jerusalem" with their teaching.

There is nothing so inspiring as seeing God at work. When men and women are won for Christ, when lives are changed (sometimes dramatically so), when Christians give spontaneously to God's work, when some are healed of sickness and others delivered from demonic powers, when there is a sense of God's presence in the praise of his people, when there is an almost tangible experience of the love of God within the body of Christ, how can we fail to "speak of what we have seen and heard"?[17] Spiritual renewal is vital to evangelism. If the life of a church is at a low level, it is a battle to believe and hard to witness with any ring of truth. But when there is a demonstration of the love and power of God in the lives of his people, it is natural to explain spontaneously what it is all about.

3. *He was spurred on by suffering.* Shortly after Philip's appointment in the church, Stephen, another of the seven, was arrested and brought to trial. Courageously, Stephen pointed out from Israel's history that whenever God did something new among them, his work was opposed and rejected. "You stiff-necked people," concluded Stephen, "uncircumcised in heart and ears, you always resist the Holy Spirit. As your fathers did, so do you." Stephen was martyred for his boldness, but his suffering gave courage to the church. From the resulting persecution, the church was scattered throughout Judea and Samaria; and "those who were scattered went about preaching the word."[18] Perhaps the truth of Stephen's message and the radiance with which he said it spurred Philip to go to the "untouchables" in Samaria.

Paul later wrote that through his own suffering and imprisonment "most of the brethren have been made confident in the Lord . . . and are much more bold to speak the word of God without fear."[19] "The blood of martyrs is the seed of the church," and in every age the persecution of Christians has nearly always led to the spread of the gospel. Bonhoeffer used to say that "the church is a community of those who are persecuted and martyred for the gospel's sake," and he himself was one of the millions who have laid down their lives for Christ.

Michael Green writes of three Ugandans, accused of political crimes against General Amin, who were converted in prison. "They grew in the power and love of the Holy Spirit. Then they were led out to die by public executioner. They urged Bishop Festo Kivengere, who was allowed there to encourage them, to go and tell the gospel to the executioners, while they bore witness joyfully to Christ before the crowd, and continued praising the God who had forgiven and would soon be receiving them right up till the moment when the shots rang out from the amazed firing squad. That story went round the country like wildfire."[20]

The church in the West is far too comfortable. It costs little to be a Christian. The church is too flabby to warrant persecution and it is on the retreat anyway. But when the church begins to be God's new society, an effective counterculture force that challenges the sterile spirit of the age, growing in influence, it will certainly be persecuted. When selfish human ambition is threatened by the light and love of Jesus Christ seen in the church, it will strike back. If the church is willing to be renewed by the Holy Spirit, and when persecution follows as a direct result, Christians will either summon courage to witness boldly for Christ, or they will drop out of the race altogether. The time of purifying for the church will be a time of powerful evangelism.

The Church of England's report on evangelism observes: "When Jesus said to his disciples 'I will make you fishers of men' the picture that he and they had in mind was that they would 'launch out into the deep' of the particularly treacherous lake of Galilee, dragging or casting a net over the side of the boat and then trying to bring the net ashore. It was a dangerous occupation in a dangerous milieu, but their livelihood depended on it. It was their full-time occupation. The commonest modern image of a fisherman in England (with apologies to deep sea trawlermen) is of a man safely sitting alone under an umbrella on a river bank with a baited rod and line occasionally landing a small fish out of the river and into his bucket. He runs no risk and catches very little worth catching. His is a weekend pastime not a daily occupation. His living does not depend on it."[21] As long as we play at evangelism, with no risk to ourselves and no price to pay, we shall make little impact on our society. When we see evangelism, not as a gentle Sunday sport, but as the serious, costly business of everyday life, we may have to ride out many storms but there will be a fishing harvest for God's glory. In some parts of the world Christians are being urged by church leaders *not* to evangelize because, it is said, religious and political situations are too sensitive. How would Stephen or Philip have reacted to that?

## The Message of Evangelism

There was nothing vague, defensive, or apologetic about Philip's message. He "went down to a city of Samaria, and proclaimed to them the Christ"; "he preached good news about the kingdom of God and the name of Jesus Christ"; "he told him the good news of Jesus" (Acts 8:5, 12, 35). God's message entrusted to us is Jesus Christ. It centers, not on a proposition nor on a philosophy, but firmly on a Person.

*The central theme.* Evangelism is "the presentation of the claims of Christ in the power of the Spirit to a world in need by a church in love."[22] The claims of Christ are on the basis of his unique person, his death for our sins, his resurrection from the dead, and his return to judge the living and the dead. The message of the letter to the Hebrews is simply this: *There is no one like Jesus!* He is described as God's last word, the Creator of the world, reflecting God's nature and glory and upholding the universe by the word of his power. He has once for all offered himself as a sacrifice for sins, so that we now have confidence to come into God's presence, by his blood. There is no one like him.[23]

Without Jesus, therefore, we have missed the main purpose of our existence. Facing the Jewish leaders who had recently secured the death of Jesus, Peter affirmed, "There is salvation in no one else, for there is no other name under heaven given among men by which we must be saved."[24] Paul wrote that one day "We must all appear before the judgment seat of Christ."[25] Christ himself taught clearly and repeatedly about the judgment to come. In his great love for us he not only told us about our greatest need, but died to bear our sins and so meet that need. It is now urgent that we turn from our sins, trust him as Lord and Savior, and receive his Spirit into our hearts. How shall we escape God's righteous judgment if we neglect such a great salvation?[26]

*The gospel essence.* How, too, shall we help others to escape if we are diffident about this gospel, ashamed of it, apologetic about it? How shall we convey the urgency of it all if we rewrite the gospel in sophisticated philosophical terms or dilute its content until it is not worth anyone's life response? How will others believe in Jesus if he is not central in our message and the consuming passion of our lives? How will they believe that "there is no one like Jesus" if they see us quarrelling, unwilling to work together, preoccupied with things that are trivial in comparison with Christ? How will lost men and women be convinced of their need of God if we are not burdened for them, if we are apathetic about evangelism, and if we are not willing to pay the price of reaching them for Christ?

God has entrusted us with the ministry of reconciliation, calling people to be reconciled to God through Jesus Christ, "God making his appeal through us."[27] But Christ himself proclaimed the kingdom of God and it is God's declared purpose to "unite all things in him";[28] God intends the whole world to be reconciled through Christ. Thus evangelism which is solely concerned with personal salvation is not New Testament evangelism.

I talked about this with Dr. William Glasser at Fuller Theological Seminary, and he asked me a rhetorical question, "What is the gospel for South Africa? That Christ died for your sins?" When I led evangelistic missions in South African universities I could not expect a hearing unless I spoke to some of the burning issues facing those students. What does God say about *apartheid?* What does it mean for a Christian to "be subject to the governing authorities" (Rom. 13)? Certainly I preached about God's answer to man's sin through the death and resurrection of his Son. But the evangelist will take seriously the questions his hearers are asking; only then will he be relevant.

*An incomplete gospel?* Professor David J. Bosch from South Africa put it in this way: "If we communicate only that part of the gospel which corresponds to people's 'felt needs' and 'personal problems' (Are you lonely? Do you feel that you have failed? Do you need a friend? Then come to Jesus!') while remaining silent on their relationship to their fellow-men, on racism, exploitation and blatant injustice, we do not proclaim the gospel. This is the quintessence of what Bonhoeffer called 'cheap grace' " and again: "Christianity which does not begin with the individual, does not begin; but Christianity which ends with the individual, ends."[29] God is infinitely concerned with the salvation of the individual; but his purpose is for the healing of creation and the proclamation of his kingdom.

Philip's preaching of the kingdom of God was therefore accompanied by many signs of the kingdom: "And the multitudes . . . gave heed to what was said by Philip, when they heard him *and saw the signs which he did.* For unclean spirits came out of many who were possessed, crying with a loud voice; and many who were paralyzed or lame were healed. So there was much joy in that city."[30] Much of our society today is marked by depression, frustration, and despair. More than ever we need to proclaim and demonstrate the good news of the kingdom of God. When people see his power to change people's hearts, to restore broken relationships, to lift oppression, to bring justice, to heal emotional hurts and physical diseases, then they will begin to take notice.

How should we communicate with joyful enthusiasm the most glorious good news in the world? Drama and mime, music and dance, have a real part in the telling of this news to a world that is increasingly *word-resistant.* "Today we need overdrawn images, parables, stories, fantasies if you like. Secular Western man is too sad, too dull, suffering from personality malnutrition. It is time to stand up and tell our story with enthusiasm."[31] With a team gifted in music, dance and drama I have witnessed the joyful surprise of many "outsiders" at the vitality and relevance of the Christian gospel. In prisons, on the streets, in schools and universities, I have seen this fresh form of communication cutting through the apathy and antagonism of many towards the church.

One leading terrorist wrote to me from a prison in Northern Ireland after a service in that prison: "I had been considering for some time becoming a Christian, but after seeing your team I no longer had any doubts, and have now been saved by the blood of Christ." His letter revealed two interesting facts. First, in spite of a life sold out to violence he was spiritually hungry. Second, it was the communication of the whole team, not my words, that really got through to him. Why should the Devil monopolize effective communication?

It is worth noting that Philip's evangelistic ministry was not perfect. He lacked spiritual discernment in the case of Simon, the occult magician: "After being baptized (presumably by Philip) Simon continued with Philip." But Peter unmasked this counterfeit conversion: "Your heart is not right with God. Repent therefore... For I see that you are in the gall of bitterness and in the bond of iniquity." We all need a plurality of gifts within the body of Christ. Philip also required the ministry of Peter and John before the believers in Samaria received the Holy Spirit. It has been argued that before the Samaritans, with their corrupted Judaism, could be received into the body of Christ, apostolic witness and confirmation were needed. It is also possible that Philip's evangelistic message had neglected direct reference to the Holy Spirit, as with Apollos in Acts 18. Today, when there is no reference to the Holy Spirit at the point of conversion, confusion may later arise. Peter's instructions on the Day of Pentecost were clear: "Repent, and be baptized every one of you in the name of Jesus Christ for forgiveness of sins; and you shall receive the gift of the Holy Spirit."[32]

## The Method of Evangelism
The most striking feature of Philip's evangelism was his obedience to the Spirit of God. Obediently he crossed the Jewish-Samaritan divide, and the power of the Spirit was with him. Obediently he then left that fruitful ministry and travelled to the desert road between Jerusalem and Gaza, not knowing why he was going there. Obediently he confronted a particular traveller, because the Spirit told him to. Later he obediently left that man and "preached the gospel to all the towns till he came to Caesarea." As we focus attention on Philip's personal evangelism with the Ethiopian eunuch, we see that he went to the right man at the right time with the right words and the right ministry.

The right man. The Ethiopian queen's treasurer was clearly a man in whom the Spirit had been working long before Philip came along. A searcher after God, he had been to Jerusalem to worship. Frequently I pray this prayer of Bishop Taylor Smith: "Lord give me eyes to see, and grace to seize, every opportunity for Thee." Believing that God's Spirit is at work throughout the world, let us observe what the Spirit is doing in people's lives, and then, boldly and sensitively, take the opportunities God sends. Ethiopian tradition holds that this statesman became not only the country's first convert, but its first evangelist. He was certainly the right man.

The right time. When Philip ran to the Ethiopian's chariot, he heard the man reading aloud from the Scriptures; not just anywhere in the Scriptures, but from Isaiah 53! What perfect timing! There is a time to speak, and a time to keep silence. In my evangelistic experience, there are certain moments in a person's life when God seems to be especially near and easily found. We are to "seek the Lord while he may be found, [and] call upon him while he is near."[33] Although there is urgency with the gospel, we should expect God to guide us to people just when his Spirit is drawing them to himself, whether they realize this or not. The moment when Jesus met the Samaritan woman at the well is another example of this.

**The right words.** Philip asked a question which immediately related to what the man was doing: "Do you understand what you are reading?" It drew a positive response, and an invitation to Philip to join him in the chariot to talk further. Several interesting points follow from this.

*Our words should be relevant to the person concerned.* Philip's opening words were not only relevant, but courteous and led easily to further conversation. A great friend of mine, an Anglican clergyman, won his janitor for Christ a little time ago. He said, "Bill, I want to introduce you to the greatest janitor in the world. He will stoke your furnace any time of day or night!" Bill was fascinated by this, and it was immediately relevant. He soon understood that Jesus had come to put new life and warmth into his heart. When Jesus approached the woman at the well who had come to draw water, he spoke to her of living water which would quench her eternal thirst.

*Pray also for what could be called a "prophetic witness."* A woman longed to speak to her neighbor about Christ, but she seemed to find no opportunity. So she prayed one morning, "Lord, what *can* I say to my neighbor that will show her that you love her?" This Christian woman was not used to hearing direct answers to such prayers, so she was startled when she had a strong impression, almost as though the Lord had spoken to her aloud, that she was to go to her neighbor and tell her not to be afraid. Obediently she went and started out nervously, "I think God wants to say something to you this morning. I think he is saying to you, 'Don't be afraid.' " Her neighbor at once burst into tears. She had heard only that morning that her daughter needed an operation, and her mother-heart was full of fear. That God could care about her enough to send a message to her personally broke through all her defenses.

*In evangelism, we must know our Bibles.* Philip recognized at once the passage that the Ethiopian was reading, and from that passage he shared with him the good news of Jesus. In particular, we need to know from the Scriptures both the way by which anyone can find God, and also brief answers to common questions. In my book *Is Anyone There?*[34] I have glanced at some of the questions or comments that I hear repeatedly:

What about the suffering in the world?
The church is so dead and irrelevant.
What about the truth in other religions?
There are too many things I don't understand.
I've tried it before, but it didn't work.
I am afraid of getting involved.
How does God guide me?
I could never keep it up.
Can't I keep it to myself?
I'm doing O.K.; I don't feel any need of God.
Isn't being moral or going to church good enough?
I can't accept the Bible.

We are not expected to have a complete answer to all these questions; with many of them, such as suffering, that would be impossible. Anyway, if we could know all about God and his ways of working, he would be no bigger than our finite minds, and not worth believing in. But it is helpful to have some thoughtful and biblical responses to these questions to prevent them from becoming excuses, or barriers, to belief.

*Often those who don't believe don't want to believe.* It is a matter of the will:

*Convince a man against his will,*
*He's of the same opinion still.*

Also, if a person's faith rests in a clever argument, he will always be vulnerable to an even cleverer argument. Paul was concerned to preach "Jesus Christ and him crucified" in the Spirit's power so that the faith of those who responded "might not rest in the wisdom of men but in the power of God."[35] When the Samaritan woman raised a "theological" question as to where God should be worshipped, in Jerusalem or in Samaria (Jesus was touching very personal areas in her life which called for repentance), Jesus did not fully answer her but brought her back to the spiritual issues: "God is Spirit, and only by the power of his Spirit can people worship him as he really is."[36] It is good, then, to be acquainted with the common problems that are raised, have some positive remarks to say about each one, but also seek to turn the conversation back to a more personal and helpful direction.

## Leading a Person to Christ
If I am lost and I ask someone the way, I want them to say to me,

"Turn left, turn right, turn left, up the hill, and there you are!" They could describe it in much more accurate terms, but those simple directions are all I need to hear at that moment. If someone is lost spiritually and he asks us the way, he too wants simple directions. We could describe it in complicated and theological terms, but something clear and simple is all that he needs to hear at that moment. What simple directions are there to Christ? This is one of my favorite explanations, perhaps because it was through it that I found Christ personally at the age of 21:

Think of the way of salvation as four steps, A B C D. Each of these four steps I state, explain, illustrate and apply. This is how I might word it to someone.

*Something to Admit.* First, admit your need of God, especially that you have sinned and therefore need his forgiveness. Sin means going your way, not God's; doing what you want, not what God wants. In the Bible Paul says, "There is no distinction, since all have sinned and fall short of the glory of God" (Rom. 3:22-23). As far as a good life is concerned, you could be on the top of Mount Everest; and in comparison with you, I could be at the bottom of the valley. But there is really "no distinction," since neither of us can touch the stars. We both come miles short of God's perfect standards shown to us in the Bible, and in the life and teaching of Jesus Christ. Our sins have separated us from God, and we need his forgiveness.

*Something to Believe.* Believe that Christ died for you. Suppose that this hand (holding out my left hand) represents you, and this object (putting a book on my hand) represents your sin—a barrier between you and God. That is why God seems unreal and distant. This other hand (holding up my right hand) represents Jesus—perfect and sin-free as he was. Isaiah 53:6, speaking of the coming sufferings of Jesus on the cross, says: "All we, like sheep, have gone astray; we have turned every one to his own way; and the Lord has laid on him (transfer the book from my left hand onto my right) the iniquity (or guilt) of us all." Now, where is your sin? It was taken by Jesus when he died on the cross. Simon Peter, who at one time could not understand why Jesus had to die, later put it like this: "Christ died for our sins once for all. He, the just, suffered for the unjust, *to bring us to God*" (1 Pet. 3:18).

*Something to Consider.* Jesus must come first in your life. Jesus once said, "If any man would come after me, let him deny himself and take up his cross and follow me" (Mark 8:34). You must say *No to sin*, being willing with God's help to turn away from all that you know is wrong in your life. You must say *No to self*, being willing for Jesus to be Lord over every part of your life: home, work, time, money, ambitions, relationships, everything. You must say *No to secrecy*, being willing to be known as a Christian, even if some may mock and oppose you, opening your life to the one person who loves you and cares about you more than anyone else in the world, and who wants only the best for your life. (I may refer to Mark 8:35-38 to help a person think through his "profit/loss" ledger).

*Something to Do.* Give your life to Jesus, and, as you do that, he will give his life to you, by his Spirit coming to live within you. Think of the marriage analogy. When my wife and I were married some years ago, the clergyman who married us said,

"David, will you have this woman?" "I will."

"Anne, will you have this man?" "I will." At that moment a new relationship was established. In the same sort of way:

"Savior, will you have this sinner?" Always he says, "I will."

"Sinner, will you have this Savior?" The moment you say "I will," and really mean it, a new relationship will be established. Other points follow from this analogy.

When I said "I will" at my wedding, I had to promise to "forsake all others," or put Anne first. When you say "I will" to Jesus, you must be willing to put him first.

When I said "I will" at my wedding, I didn't need feelings at all; it was an act of my will. With Jesus, the relationship does not depend on feelings, but on commitment and trust.

When I said "I will" at my wedding, it was only the beginning of a new relationship. We had to work hard at it, and it hasn't always been easy. When you say "I will" to Jesus, it is only the beginning of a new relationship, and there may be moments of doubt, disobedience, rebellion, and so on. But working through the difficulties matures and develops any relationship.

Putting the directions like this on paper may seem stiff and stereotyped. Every person is different, and every conversation will flow differently. We must make sure that each step is understood before proceeding to the next, and this may involve asking a few questions and adding more explanations and illustrations. The key to it all is prayer, sensitivity to the Spirit, and genuine love for the individual concerned. J. I. Packer once expressed our dependence on the Spirit of God in evangelism in this way: "However clear and cogent we may be in presenting the gospel, we have no hope of convincing or converting anyone. Can you or I by our earnest talking break the power of Satan over a man's life? No. Can you or I give life to the spiritually dead? No. Can we hope to convince sinners of the truth of the gospel by patient explanation? No. Can we hope to move men to obey the gospel by any words of entreaty that we may utter? No. Our approach to evangelism is not realistic till we have faced this shattering fact, and let it make its proper impact on us."[37] It is only through our prayer, as we humbly acknowledge our helplessness and seek for the illumination of the Spirit, that the scales may fall from a person's eyes to enable him to see the light of the gospel of the glory of Christ.[38]

Once a person appears to understand the steps to Christ, offer some practical action. "If you like," I often suggest, "I will lead you in a simple personal prayer, which you can echo phrase by phrase in your own heart, either silently or aloud; or I can give you some literature to help you understand more fully the step you are taking." I may encourage a prayer of commitment to Christ right then, for I have often seen the parable of the sower enacted—after the seed has been sown, the devil is quick to snatch it away before it has time to take root in the heart's soil. If the subject is willing to pray, I sometimes go quickly through the prayer beforehand to see if he is happy to echo it for himself. Then I pray slowly, a few words at a time, something like this:

Lord Jesus Christ,
I know that I am a sinner,
and I need your forgiveness.
Thank you for dying on the cross for me,
to take away my sin.
I am willing to turn from all that is wrong in my life.
I am willing for you to be first in my life.
And now I come to you; it is my choice.
I say "I will."
I give my life to you, my Lord and my Savior.
Please give your life to me by your Spirit,
and come to live with me forever.
Thank you, Lord Jesus. Amen.

The person may follow me in prayer, aloud or silently, and then I will pray another short prayer of encouragement, thanking Jesus for hearing our prayer, and asking that this person might be filled with the Spirit, discover God's purpose for his life, grow in his relationship with Jesus (with the help of other Christians), and share the love and truth of Jesus with others in this needy world.

After that I may point out one more promise of Jesus to help him stand firm against any doubts which may later come to him; and then plan a time in a day or two when we can talk together again. Nearly always I give some suitable literature before we part, so that he has something to read that will help him to grasp the basic steps that he has taken.[39] The young Christian will then need careful follow-up, either through personal sessions or through a church "beginners' group," which studies subjects such as: assurance, growth, prayer, the Bible, foundational truths of the faith (God, Christ, the Holy Spirit, the cross and resurrection, the church, spiritual gifts, etc.); also we need to look at witness, guidance, giving, and a lot of other issues as they arise.[40]

Remember that winning a person for Christ is only the beginning. With the love of God and the sensitivity of his Spirit, we are to encourage and serve that person until he or she becomes a true disciple of Christ. When we see that person winning someone else for Christ, or at least taking responsibility in the body of Christ, we can rejoice that in the Lord our labor is not in vain. William Barclay once said, "There is no joy in all the world like the joy of bringing one soul to Christ." That is the privilege and responsibility of every disciple.

# CHAPTER TEN

# DISCIPLESHIP AND SIMPLE LIFESTYLE

TWO SHARPLY CONTRASTING ILLUSTRATIONS will demonstrate the present-day scandal of economic inequality within the world-wide family of God.

*Time* magazine[1] carried a revealing article about American evangelists and their weekly television shows. Searching questions could be asked of some of them concerning the content of their gospel and the style of their presentation. For all my personal misgivings, I hope I have the generous spirit of the apostle Paul who wrote, "Christ is proclaimed; and in that I rejoice."[2] I am sure that some, at least, come to know God's love, peace and healing through these programs. What disturbs me much more is the lifestyle of these and other well-known preachers. One evangelist, according to the article, received annual gifts from listeners of $51 million, a fiftieth of which he keeps as personal income. He already owns a luxurious home, a fleet of cars, and numerous other material advantages. The *Time* journalist was understandably critical.

One month after reading that article I attended the International Consultation on Simple Lifestyle, held in England under the joint chairmanship of Ronald Sider and John Stott. On the opening evening an evangelist from Columbia spoke through an interpreter. He told us of an exhausting day's preaching in one village, and of returning, tired and very hungry, to the pastor's house where he was staying. The pastor, his wife and five children were there, but the table was set with only one plate—for the visiting evangelist—with one egg and one small potato on it. "Is that all?" he thought to himself. "But I'm so hungry!" Nevertheless he bowed his head to give thanks to God for the food before him, then asked if the others had already eaten. Hastily the pastor's wife replied that she would fix something later. Since it was already 10:30 in the evening, the evangelist made further inquiries. He discovered that they had no money and no food in the house but this one egg and one small potato. He asked the wife to put seven other plates on the table and divided his already tiny meal into eight minuscule portions, invited them all to sit down with him, bowed his head and again gave thanks.

Is this kind of staggering difference in lifestyle between members of his family what God intended? How far does the lifestyle of the Western church, in particular, help or hinder the task of mission and evangelism in the world? For many of us, on both personal and corporate levels, there is an urgent need for a totally new image, a radical discipleship modelled on the simplicity of Jesus, if we are to demonstrate with credibility the values of the kingdom of God and thus speak with authority about the God who so loved the world.

The Christian dramatist, Murray Watts, once told me of a man born deaf, from a middle-class Christian home, who was brought to a living faith in Christ on a train in India. He found himself in the same carriage as a beggar who was materially destitute, but overflowing with thanksgiving and praise to God. This amazing sight broke through to the deaf man and allowed the love of God, which had always surrounded him, to flow into his heart.

This true incident is a parable: The world is increasingly deaf to a church that has sold out to materialism. Only as the world is confronted with a church wholly dependent on God, that accepts material poverty for the sake of the countless poor whom God is trying to reach, will any impact be made. Affluence and spiritual complacency are often partners, and material bankruptcy may accompany spiritual wealth. When others see that we have "nothing but God," and therefore have everything to praise and thank him for, the reality of his presence among us will move those who have doubted his existence.

Today there is no shortage of pious words, affirmations of faith, discussions about hunger, or expressions of spirituality. But the world is still waiting for the demonstration, in hard, costly and practical terms, of what we glibly proclaim with our lips. Let it not be that "I was hungry, and you formed a committee to investigate my hunger... I was homeless, and you filed a report on my plight... I was sick, and you held a seminar on the underprivileged... You have investigated my plight. And yet I am still hungry, homeless, and sick."

"The life of Jesus and his disciples," writes John Taylor, "was not only eucharistic but also defiant. He knew it was not enough to say these things; the world is waiting for concrete examples and realizations. So in our day it is not enough to point out the contrast between our idolatry of growth and the Bible's theology of enough; we have to opt out of the drift and help one another to live in cheerful protest against it..."[3]

Thus Jesus not only taught and challenged his disciples on the issues of money and possessions but shared his whole life with them. Unless their obedience was demonstrably true, he knew that he would be building a castle in the air instead of a church on the rock, against which the gates of hell could not prevail. How then can the vital ingredients of effective discipleship be proved and developed?

## Obedience and Material Possessions

From the very beginning Jesus taught his followers the necessity of total obedience to him as Lord of their lives. The kingdom of God involved his rule over every area of their lives, whether or not they understood and agreed. In Luke 5, when Jesus, the carpenter's son from Nazareth, told Simon, the experienced Galilean fisherman, to cast his nets into the sea in broad daylight, we can understand the professional protest: "Master, we toiled all night and took nothing!" Yet such was the commanding presence of Jesus in his boat that Simon added, "But at your word I will let down the nets." The catch was staggering. One minute's obedience to Christ is worth infinitely more than striving, even to the point of exhaustion, in the wisdom and energy of the flesh.

We need to learn obedience especially when it comes to material possessions. Juan Carlos Ortiz remarked about the way we tend to select Bible verses which are comforting but ignore those that we find disturbing. We happily respond to the reassuring words of Jesus: "Fear not, little flock, for it is your Father's good pleasure to give you the kingdom"; but all too easily ignore the next verse, "Sell your possessions and give alms."[4] Yet this sacrificial act of obedience may well be a vital part of the way in which God will give us the kingdom. When we fail to take the challenge of Jesus seriously, we may wonder why the kingdom of God fails to come in the power that Jesus promised. It is because we have embraced the independent spirit of the world which says "Yes, but . . ." However hard we try to rationalize it, saying "Yes, but . . ." to Jesus is essentially disobedience. That is why there is not a greater demonstration of the power of the Spirit: God's Spirit is given only to those who obey him.[5]

*The choice.* In Matthew 6:19-24 Jesus highlights the issue in a series of sharp contrasts. We must make our choice between two treasures (earthly or heavenly), two conditions (light or darkness), and two masters (God or mammon). In other words, we have to face up to the searching question, Who or what comes first in our lives? Nowhere is this question more clearly answered than in our attitude to possessions.

It is important to stress that Jesus is not forbidding the ownership of private property. Even when the sharing among Christians was at its most generous, Peter assured Ananias about the sale of his land, "While it remained unsold did it not remain your own? And after it was sold, was it not at your disposal?"[6] That several of the disciples had possessions of their own is implied by the statement that they went on continuously (Greek imperfect tense) selling what they had to provide for those who had not.[7] Further, Jesus is not against some wise provision for the future. As Paul later wrote: "If any one does not provide for his relatives and especially for his own family, he has disowned the faith and is worse than an unbeliever."[8] Nor is Jesus encouraging us to ignore or despise the numerous good gifts of God's creation. Matter is not intrinsically evil as the gnostics wrongly taught. "Everything created by God is good, and nothing is to be rejected if it is received with thanksgiving."[9] Paul knew "how to be abased, and how to abound," and he found the Lord's peace in facing either plenty or hunger, either abundance or want.[10]

What Jesus spoke strongly against was hoarding up treasures *"for yourselves."* This is not only foolish (all earthly treasures will sooner or later decay or disappear); it is selfish in the light of the vast needs of a world of men, women, and children—a straight denial of the love of God; worst of all, it is idolatrous, "for where your treasure is, there will your heart be also."[11]

"Worldly possessions tend to turn the hearts of the disciples away from Jesus. What are we really devoted to? That is the question. Are our hearts set on earthly goods? Do we try to combine devotion to them with loyalty to Christ? Or are we devoted exclusively to him? Where our treasure is, there is our trust, our security, our consolation and our God. Hoarding is idolatry... Everything which hinders us from loving God above all things... is our treasure, and the place where our heart is... If our hearts are entirely given to God, it is clear that we *cannot* serve two masters; it is simply impossible... Our hearts have room only for one all-embracing devotion, and we can only cleave to one Lord...[12]

"The eye is the lamp of the body"[13] said Jesus. In other words, without the clear vision of the eye my whole body has to walk and move in darkness. It cannot see what it is doing or where it is going. It is only as my "eye" is set wholly on the light of Christ that my whole life can have clear direction. But if my eye looks to another master—it cannot have two—my whole life will be left in deep darkness. "The love of money is the root of all evil";[14] every day reveals the inescapable and ugly truth of that statement. When Jesus told the lovable, talented, promising, seeking, rich young ruler, "Sell all that you have and distribute to the poor, and you will have treasure in heaven,"[15] the man went away sad. But Jesus allowed no compromise, for no one can serve two masters.

There are details in this well-known incident that are instructive. First, as Ron Sider comments, "When Jesus asked the rich young man to sell his goods and give to the poor, he did not say, 'Become destitute and friendless.' Rather he said 'Come follow me.' In other words, he invited him to join a community of sharing and love, where his security would not be based on individual property holdings, but on openness to the Spirit and on the loving care of new-found brothers and sisters."[16] Second, what Jesus looks for first and foremost is not poverty but obedience. Obedience may lead to poverty, if that is what Jesus requires of us; but choosing poverty in itself could be choosing my own way of life, or some religious ideal, which is not the command of Jesus. Third, having made that point, many of us are so skilled at spotting the loopholes and saying "Yes, but..." that Ron Sider rightly observes that "what 99 percent of all Western Christians need to hear 99 percent of the time is: 'Give to everyone who begs from you,' and 'sell your possessions.' "[17] Fourth, we must never minimize the seductive danger of riches.[18] Covetousness is perhaps the most serious sin in the West today, and no covetous person will inherit the kingdom of God. Always we are brought back to this basic issue: Who or what comes first in my life? Only when the lordship of Christ is clearly recognized—and our attitude to possessions will test this as nothing else can—can we truly be his disciples. While we must be wary of attitudes like pharisaism or legalism about lifestyle, we must recognize that God requires of us a true biblical radicalism which refuses to be conformed to this world.

### Faith

This is crucial if we are to see God's power at work. "He who *believes in me* will also do the works that I do," as Jesus promised his disciples in John 14:12.

When Jesus warns us against anxiety in Matthew 6:25-34, he is asking us another crucial and penetrating question: On whom or what are you really depending? What is the clear object of your faith? Again, the logic is compelling, for we have to face up to this alternative: *either* we are trusting our heavenly Father for everything; *or* we are ultimately trusting in some form of worldly security. Material possessions often *create* anxiety. We worry about having enough money to buy what we want; then, when we get it, we worry about keeping it safe or in good condition. We worry about its sufficiency for the future. We worry about changing currency values, about economic instability, inflation, and recessions. Jesus warned us about the spiritual damage done by such anxiety: the seed of God's Word can easily become "choked by the cares and riches and pleasures of life."[19] But if we trust our heavenly Father, we shall live a day at a time: "Don't worry at all then about tomorrow. Tomorrow can take care of itself! One day's trouble is enough for one day."[20]

If this all sounds naive and irresponsible, we must realize that Jesus is calling us out of the kingdom of this world into a different kingdom known for the loving care and generous sharing of the people of God. In fact, it is especially in this quality of shared life that we experience the reality of God's love, which casts out our fear and encourages deeper faith in him.

This was the lifestyle that Jesus adopted for himself, instructing his disciples to do the same. The power and effectiveness of their ministry depended on their willingness to trust God for everything. Remember Jesus' commission to the twelve: "Preach as you go, saying, 'The kingdom of heaven is at hand.' Heal the sick, raise the dead, cleanse lepers, cast out demons. You received without paying, give without pay. Take no gold, nor silver, nor copper in your belts, no bag for your journey, nor two tunics, nor sandals, nor a staff..."[21] Most of us will readily understand that their faith was sometimes unable to rise to such levels. How could the 5,000 be fed? What about when they were hungry themselves? Jesus gently rebuked them, "O men of little faith!"[22] However much we might sympathize with them, their little faith over these material matters meant little faith in spiritual ministry. When the disciples later asked why they could not cast out a demon from a boy, Jesus replied, "Because of your little faith."[23] That is why he constantly tested and stretched their faith over the ordinary, everyday matters of lifestyle; only as their faith developed *there* would they be able to believe for the even more vital work of the kingdom of God.

The same testing was given when the seventy were sent out: "Carry no purse, no bag, no sandals... Wherever you enter a town and they receive you, eat what is set before you; heal the sick in it and say to them, 'The kingdom of God has come near to you'..." Off they went, inexperienced, untaught, but with simple faith; and "they returned with joy, saying, 'Lord, even the demons are subject to us in your name!'" Jesus too rejoiced, "I thank thee, Father... that thou hast hidden these things from the wise and understanding and revealed them to babes"—that is, to those who exercised an unwavering faith in the reality and faithfulness of their heavenly Father.[24]

Most of us would like to find some happy compromise. Of course we want to seek first the kingdom of God; but earthly treasures continue to attract us, cause us anxiety, and erode our faith. Wanting the best of both worlds, we lose the transforming power of the kingdom of God. We must stress again that Jesus is not forbidding personal property; but when we start craving any of these things we may well "wander away from the faith" and pierce our hearts "with many pangs."[25]

"It is want of faith that makes us opt for earthly rather than heavenly treasure. If we really believed in celestial treasures, who among us would be so stupid as to buy gold? We just do not believe. Heaven is a dream, a religious fantasy which we affirm because we are orthodox. If people believed in heaven, they would spend their time preparing for permanent residence there. But nobody does. We just like the assurance that something nice awaits us when the real life is over... We must be suspicious of any faith about personal justification that is not substantiated by faith in God's power over material things in our everyday life. Faith about pie in the sky when I die cannot be demonstrated. Faith that God can supply my need today *can* be demonstrated."[26]

That was precisely the challenge for the rich young ruler. Having told him to sell what he had and to give to the poor, Jesus promised him that he would have "treasure in heaven." "Come," said Jesus, "follow me." But at that critical point, the young man, with all his good living and a religious enthusiasm, did not have enough *true* faith in Jesus to obey him. Jesus admitted to his startled disciples that it is not easy for a rich man to enter the kingdom of heaven. But, he promised that "every one who has left houses or brothers or sisters or father or mother or children or lands, for my name's sake, will receive a hundredfold, and inherit eternal life."[27] In some measure the disciples were experiencing the greater riches that God had promised; they discovered a depth of relationships in common life that they had never known before. They lived together, worked together, prayed together, learned together. They had given up everything and, as a result, had gained all that mattered.

## Integrity
Because of the constant danger of false prophets, whose work was (and is today) marked by deceit and corruption, Paul and other early church leaders repeatedly stressed their own integrity in all their evangelistic, teaching, and pastoral work: "We are not, like so many, peddlers of God's word; but as men of sincerity, as commissioned by

God in the sight of God we speak in Christ... We have renounced disgraceful, underhanded ways; we refuse to practice cunning or to tamper with God's word, but by the open statement of the truth we would commend ourselves to every man's conscience in the sight of God... We put no obstacle in any one's way, so that no fault may be found with our ministry, but as servants of God we commend ourselves in every way... Open your hearts to us: we have wronged no one, we have corrupted no one, we have taken advantage of no one..."[28] Without a hint of hypocrisy or pride, Paul could say, disarmingly, "You yourselves know how I lived among you all the time from the first day that I set foot in Asia, serving the Lord with all humility... You know what kind of men we proved to be among you for your sake... You remember our labour and toil, brethren."[29]

The integrity of the messenger is vital to the authority and converting power of the message. Jesus could throw out a challenge to his critics, "Which of you convicts me of sin?"[30] Although Jesus came from a reasonably secure family business, his family was far from wealthy. Willingly becoming poor for us that we through his poverty might become rich, Jesus saw that a marked simplicity of lifestyle was a vital part of the credibility of his whole ministry. He set the example for his disciples; they shared a common purse; they gave regularly to the poor;[31] they denied themselves many of the material possessions and comforts that they had been used to. And later they taught others to live in the same way: "If we have food and clothing, with these we shall be content. But those who desire to be rich fall into temptation, into a snare, into many senseless and hurtful desires that plunge men into ruin and destruction..."[32] "Keep your life free from the love of money, and be content with what you have."[33]

One of the marks of the false prophet was that his heart was "trained in greed";[34] he would flatter people "to gain advantage."[35] By contrast, a prospective leader in the church must be "no lover of money" and "not greedy for gain."[36]

"The poverty of Christ's messengers is the proof of their freedom ... As they go forth to be the plenipotentiaries of his word, Jesus enjoins strict poverty upon them... They are not to go about like beggars and call attention to themselves, nor are they to burden other people like parasites. They are to go forth in the battledress of poverty, taking as little with them as a traveller who knows he will get board and lodging with friends at the end of the day. This shall be an expression of their faith, not in men, but in their heavenly father who sent them and will care for them. *It is this that will make their gospel credible*"[37] (italics mine).

In the commercial and advertising world of today most of us understandably suspect exaggerated sales talk or a promotional push. How genuine is it? What is the catch? Is it all that it seems to be? If the salesman benefits personally from what he is trying to sell, we are doubly cautious, and it is imperative that, as Christ's messengers offering the free gift of God, we make no personal or financial profit from the work God has called us to do.

Just today, some literature from quite a well-known evangelist came in my mail. After an impassioned statement about the needs of "this hour," there was a strong appeal to "yield yourself to the Holy Spirit and ask for His guidance in your special thanksgiving gift— for his goodness to you!" And, in case I had missed the point, there was a postage-paid envelope for my reply, together with a slip for me to complete, entitled *MY GIFT TO REVERSE THE TREND!* I was encouraged to sign this slip, which says, "Dear Brother (name of evangelist), I am thankful to God for His goodness, His love in choosing me, in challenging me to rise up and become one of His Partners in prophecy for the Healing of the Nations... I have felt led of the Holy Spirit to send $___ as my November gift to overtake the Heathen..." At the end of the form I was reminded that "this is God's hour!" No doubt many vulnerable Christians will respond financially to the challenge. Several widows in my own church have given generously to similar appeals. No doubt this evangelist will continue to enjoy "success." Since he seems to preach Christ, it may be that God will bless his efforts in one way or another. But the whole approach smacks of the world and lacks the credibility of the Master.

When I am interviewed by secular media people concerning my work as an evangelist, one inevitable question is, "What do you get out of it?" They are asking not about job satisfaction, but about financial reward. To be able to speak truthfully in answer to this question is a vital part of my integrity when it comes to anything else I may want to say. Covetousness is one of the commonest and most blatant of sins, so it is vital that the church should guard herself against the strong and subtle pressures of this temptation.

These snares may seem even more attractice to those with an independent ministry not firmly rooted in the discipline of a local church. Certainly, within a local congregation, there should be explicit, regular biblical teaching about the Christian responsibility to give generously to the Lord's work. However, the main aim of this teaching is both that God may be glorified through the joyful offering of our possessions, and that Christians may be blessed through such giving. With fund-raising techniques, on the other hand, the main aim is obviously to fill the empty coffers! Instead of a concern with the worship of God and the freedom of God's people, the focus shifts to the economic prosperity of some religious project, and at this point the integrity of those involved comes under question.

### Identification

Just as obedience, faith, and integrity were perfectly exemplified in the life and ministry of Jesus, so the model of identification is found in its purest form in his incarnation. The Word of God became a human being and dwelt among us. Listen to Martin Luther's simple words about Jesus: "He ate, drank, slept, waked; was weary, sorrowful, rejoicing; he wept and he laughed; he knew hunger and thirst and sweat; he talked, he toiled, he prayed ... so there was no difference between him and other men, save only this that he was God and had no sin."

Although the primary theological debate today rages over the divinity of Jesus, many less academic, orthodox Christians find difficulty in coming to terms with his genuine humanity. Possibly because we tend to think of him as intrinsically different, separate from ordinary men, the church, as a whole, has often retreated to its own religious ghetto, and failed to be God's agent in the healing of the whole creation. We have wrongly divided the sacred and the secular. In keeping ourselves "unstained from the world," we may have kept ourselves from the world altogether, thus failing in our God-given ministry of reconciliation. Paul rejected such religious detachment. "I have made myself a slave to all, that I might win the more ... I have become all things to all men, that I might by all means save some. I do it all for the sake of the gospel, that I may share in its blessings."[38] Here the vital incarnational principle is applied in effective evangelism and compassionate service.

Throughout the Scriptures God is clearly seen to be on the side of the poor. Although he is no respecter of persons, and is rich to all who call upon him, he is also a God of justice. Therefore, since by greed or neglect, the rich oppress the poor and inevitably add to their weight of suffering, God must be on the side of the poor. Moreover, he identifies with them: when we are kind to the poor, we lend to the Lord.[39] When we offer practical help to those who are hungry, thirsty, lonely, naked, sick, or in prison, we are doing it to Jesus.[40] Jesus was loved and welcomed by ordinary and often poor people because he consciously identified himself with them. He had come "to preach good news to the poor," and he could do so because he himself had "nowhere to lay his head." On the cross he was literally stripped of everything. No one could be more destitute than a naked man fastened to a cross. Yet the apostle Paul repeatedly refers to "the power of the cross"—materially nothing, spiritually everything.

The early church continued the same pattern. Peter and John had neither silver nor gold to offer to the crippled beggar at the Gate Beautiful, but because they had the power of the Spirit of Christ they could say: "In the name of Jesus Christ of Nazareth, walk."[41] When we see the extraordinary quality of sharing and the generosity of giving in the young church, it is not surprising that God was able to work through them with "many wonders and signs." Because God found them faithful in handling lesser material riches, he was able to trust them with much greater spiritual riches. Their willingness to live by the principle of "enough," so that any abundance might be passed on was proof of the grace of God among them.

The church of the West today, however, appeals largely to the affluent middle-class. Our church buildings, our styles of dress, language, and music, can all become highly selective factors that determine which sections of the community we reach for Jesus Christ. It is not that we should aim for damp and draughty buildings instead (some of us have these anyway!); but as soon as we become materially ambitious for our buildings we stand in great danger of shutting the door of the gospel on some who desperately need the Savior. It is sobering to remember that the fastest period of growth in the entire ministry of the church was almost certainly during the first three centuries, when there were no church buildings and few material assets.

On a recent visit to the United States, I went to several churches of different traditions that were all, in their way, immensely impressive. I was immediately struck by their diversified facilities, the efficiency of their organizations, the quality of their printed service sheets for every Sunday, the colorful information and welcome cards at every seat, the precise timing of each service, the musical quality of organist and choir, together with the bright colors of their robes, and, not least, the size of the congregations. My general impression was that of quality performance backed up with obvious business efficiency. Our little efforts in England looked shabby and amatuerish by comparison, and I felt that we had much to learn. After all, administration is one of the gifts of the Spirit. At the same time, in such lavish environments I had to struggle to sense God's presence and hear his voice. There was little freedom in worship, and I wondered how many genuine conversions took place among those outside the social and cultural ethos of those churches. I feared that the genuinely "un-churched" members of society would have felt uncomfortable and conspicuous in the distinctive middle-class conformity of those congregations.

In contrast I went to Calvary Chapel in Placentia, California, a church without buildings of its own, which used a huge school gymnasium for its Sunday services. Every week an enthusiastic team rolled out carpets, set up 2000 chairs, erected a stage, and organized an effective sound system. The contrast between the more conventional churches and this one was staggering. With an almost total absence of structure and organization, the services were relaxed, the worship sensitive and intimate, and within the gentle control of the main pastor there were opportunities for many to bring spiritual gifts to edify the whole body of Christ. The congregation had grown from nothing to 2000 in four years, and the vast majority of these were genuine conversions, many among those who had become disillusioned by the conventional formality of the more established churches. There was no mistaking the manifest presence of the living God in that gymnasium. His love, joy, life, and generosity were tangibly expressed there through conversions, healings, deliverance and blessings every week. Anyone searching for spiritual reality would have found every activity meaningful. In terms of material facilities they had very little; in terms of spiritual power, *God was there.* Here was the incarnate body of Christ. In that setting, the ordinary sinners heard the gospel gladly.

## Love

This is the supreme quality of all, without which all our eloquent preaching would be a noisy gong or a clanging cymbal. The love of Christ controlled and compelled that persecuted early church. "So being affectionately desirous of you, we were ready to share with you not only the gospel of God but also our own selves, because you had become very dear to us."[42] Their infectious love drew people to them, and to the Lord, like a magnet; the poor and the outcast, the sick and the lame, Jew and Gentile, slave and free, male and female, even a few who were rich and influential—they all came, except for those whose hearts were jealous or hard towards God. As those Christians loved one another, others were sure that they were the disciples of Jesus and that God was abiding in their midst.

Christian love, however, is always marked by sacrificial giving: "God so loved the world that he gave his only Son." In the same way the evidence and demonstration of love must be much more than mere words, as the early Christians' lives showed so eloquently: "All who believed were together, and had all things in common; and they sold their possessions and goods and distributed them to all, as any had need . . . And the Lord added to their number day by day those who were being saved."[43] "Now the company of those who believed were of one heart and soul, and no one said that any of the things which he possessed was his own, but they had everything in common. And with great power the apostles gave their testimony to the resurrection of the Lord Jesus, and great grace was upon them all. There was not a needy person among them, for as many as were possessors of lands or houses sold them, and brought the proceeds of what was sold and laid it at the apostles' feet; and distribution was made to each as any had need."[44] It is interesting that the remark about the power of their evangelism is sandwiched between the comments about their shared life. In other words, it was in the context of this loving, sacrificial care of one another that the good news of Jesus Christ made such an impact.

In Acts 6 we see the pattern repeated again. The needs of some Greek widows were not being met, but when the apostles set aside seven men "full of faith and of the Holy Spirit," to attend to their material needs, "the word of God increased; and the number of disciples multiplied greatly in Jerusalem . . ."

There was no compulsion to sell property or to give money, nor was there any bias against private ownership. It is clear that many Christians kept some of their possessions and lands, even though a number of them went on selling what they had as the needs continued. But this new community in Christ longed to express God's love towards their brothers and sisters as obvious needs arose. "If any one has the world's goods and sees his brother in need, yet closes his heart against him, how does God's love abide in him?"[45] When widespread famine was prophesied, the newly-formed Gentile church at Antioch responded at once in love towards their Jewish brethren in Judea by sending such money as they could "every one according to his ability."[46]

When attempting to teach the biblical values about lifestyle in Western churches, I have usually encountered strong and determined opposition, except perhaps from students. Most Christians will readily agree with teaching about faith, love, hope, service, mission. But the area of money, possessions, and a simple lifestyle, is a very sensitive spot indeed. The reason may be that our security is materially-based (however much we may consciously deny this) or that the God of mammon exercises a much more powerful influence in our lives than we will admit, or that most of us instinctively know that we cannot withstand the pressures of the world and live by biblical standards on our own. Very few Western churches know anything of the degree of the sharing of lives and possessions that was the norm in New Testament times and is best exemplified today in Third World churches or where there is active persecution. For countless Christians in the West "discipleship" means little more than going to church regularly, giving a proportion of one's income and getting involved in a limited number of church activities.

Consequently, the lifestyle of most Western Christians and churches can give no prophetic challenge to the affluent society all around. In fact it is scarcely distinguishable from it. We have, quite unconsciously, adopted the values and standards of the world; and as the standard of living has risen considerably over the last thirty years, so we Christians, along with our neighbors, spend that much more on our cars and carpets, TV sets and washing-machines, furniture and stereo equipment, until we regard most of these things as necessities. Where is there any serious attempt to live on "enough," to be "content with food and clothing," and to give the rest away for every good work? Where is there that commitment to one another in love, so that we really share our possessions, reduce our standard of living—despite inflation—and express the love of Christ in costly, tangible, sacrificial terms?

Ron Sider has expressed it like this: "In the New Testament we see Jesus calling together a new community of people who began to live a whole new lifestyle. The early church was a new society. It was one new body where all relationships were being transformed . . . If anything is clear in the New Testament it is that they were sharing financially in a massive way . . . Extremes of wealth and poverty are simply not what God wills among his people . . . Now, if the one world-wide body of believers today would dare to implement that vision so that something like economic equality existed within the universal body of Christ . . . it would probably be the single most powerful evangelistic step we could take. When the church in Jerusalem shared dramatically they found the work of God increased. The evangelistic impact of the first Christians' financial sharing was just astounding. Unfortunately, the radical character of New Testament *koinonia* is largely missing from the contemporary Western church."[47]

I, myself am only just beginning to learn the first lesson in all this. But I do know that some personal steps towards a simpler lifestyle have been encouraged partly through living in an extended household for eight years, where together we seriously commit ourselves to this end, and so are free "to stir up one another to love and good works." Although our progress has been slow and small, we have begun to discover in a new way the riches of Christ and the depths of Christian fellowship and have found at least a degree of liberation from some of the snares of this world. We are far from being, with Paul, "as poor, yet making many rich; as having nothing, and yet possessing everything,"[48] but I think we know a little bit more of what the apostle meant. In this way we have been able to release both money and manpower for the kingdom of God.

## Money Talks

I was asked by a leading Anglican bishop recently if I thought it right to try to reproduce a New Testament church in this highly complex, technological twentieth century. My reply was that I believed the New Testament principles to be timeless, but that the outworkings of them must always be relevant to this particular generation. We are not to follow the exact pattern of the early church slavishly. At the same time, when the evangelistic impact of the Western churches is mostly very weak, when the needs of this present day are increasing all the time, and when the crisis of the church today is primarily in its lack of spiritual power and life and love, it is imperative that we examine closely those basic principles that made the church so effective 2000 years ago and today, especially in the Third World.

If the life and love of Jesus are to be clearly manifest—and without this all our gospel words will be empty—the church must learn again what it means to be the body of Christ on earth. It needs to demonstrate God's new society, marked by love and seen in the costly, practical sharing of lives and possessions together. Money talks, not least in this covetous generation. When others see that our faith really means something, in practical and material ways, then the good news of Jesus Christ will be seen to be more than religious words.

James K. Baxter once wrote: "The first Christians did not start to share their goods in a free and full manner till after the bomb of the Spirit exploded in their souls at Pentecost. Before then, they would be morally incapable of this free and joyful sharing. The acquisitive habit is one of the deepest rooted habits of the human race. To say, 'this is yours, not mine' and to carry the words into effect, is as much a miracle of God as raising of the dead."[49] It is by such miracles of God's grace that others may catch a glimpse of the realities that we proclaim so glibly with our lips. But without such tangible evidence of the love of God among us, we shall have to accept E. M. Forster's rebuke when he referred to "poor, talkative, little Christianity."

"Little children, let us not love in word or speech but in deed and in truth."[50]

*The substance of this chapter was given as a keynote address at the International Conference on Simple Life-style, held in England, March 1980.*

# CHAPTER ELEVEN

# THE COST OF DISCIPLESHIP

JESUS NEVER PROMISED his followers an easy life. It is true he came to meet the deepest needs of every one of us and only in him can we find forgiveness for the past, a new life for the present, and a glorious hope for the future.

Yet Jesus came to build a body, the church. Far from being a comfortable club existing entirely for the benefits of its members, the church is to be God's agent for the healing of the whole of creation, existing mainly for the benefits of its nonmembers. Thus church membership necessarily involves discipleship, and that means accepting the full demands that Jesus clearly made. Jesus was, in fact, so honest about the cost of discipleship that many of the enthusiastic crowds who flocked after him "turned back and no longer went with him." There were only 120 of them waiting for the promise of the Holy Spirit in that upper room; and, although more than 500 saw the risen Christ, those 120 presumably represented most of those who were willing to accept his call. In sheer numbers his three years of ministry had not been exceptionally fruitful, and it is not hard to see why. Although he healed the sick and relieved the oppressed without any conditions attached, he spelled out the cost of discipleship in clear and forthright terms to all those whom he called and to those who wanted to join his number.

When one man eagerly responded, "I will follow you wherever you go," Jesus replied, "Foxes have holes, and the birds of the air have nests; but the Son of man has nowhere to lay his head."[1] Jesus was warning this would-be disciple where the obedience of faith would lead. In worldly terms it means a life of uncertainty and insecurity; but in spiritual terms it means a life of continuous certainty in things not seen,[2] and of total security in the love of God. Jesus calls people to put their whole trust in God, and not in the uncertain riches of this world. Faith is the essence of all true discipleship, for without faith it is impossible to please God. To test the reality of his faith the disciple must therefore expect to find himself frequently in situations where he has to trust in God. Like their Master, those first disciples often did not know where their next meal was coming from, or where they would sleep for the night. In following the call of Jesus, they had left their homes and their jobs, their money and their possessions, and were trusting wholly in him. Although he never failed them and promised them that their Father in heaven would meet all their needs, their faith often faltered when it came to the test. "O you of little faith! Why did you doubt? Have you no faith?" were Jesus' humbling rebukes. Constantly he encouraged his disciples, taught them, guided and strengthened them; but until they learned, sometimes the hard way, to trust him and obey him, Jesus knew that all his training would be in vain.

## The Path of Obedience
From the earliest days of Christ's ministry "the people were astounded at his teaching; unlike their own teachers he taught with a note of authority."[3] Sometimes they asked each other in amazement, "Who then is this, that even wind and sea obey him?"[4] What many did not appreciate was that "all authority in heaven and on earth" *had been given* to him.[5] Jesus was not just a wonder-worker with unusual authority; he was the Lord of glory, with all authority. At his name every knee must bow and every tongue confess that he is Lord. There can be no half measures with him. If we want to be his disciples, we must accept his supreme authority as Lord over every part of our life, without exception. If we are not willing for

him to be our Lord, he cannot be our Savior. With Jesus it is all, or nothing. To be in the kingdom of God is to accept Jesus as King; and if he is King, his word has final authority and must be obeyed.

The first disciples understood this clearly. In Acts 4, when Peter and John were "charged not to speak or teach at all in the name of Jesus," they replied, "Whether it is right in the sight of God to listen to you rather than to God, you must judge; for we cannot but speak of what we have seen and heard." Later, they prayed again for boldness to speak the Word of God. Again, in Acts 5, after further serious threats, Peter and the apostles answered, "We must obey God rather than men. The God of our fathers raised Jesus whom you killed by hanging him on a tree..." No wonder their opponents "were enraged and wanted to kill them"; no wonder that the Word of God spread like wildfire through that ancient world! Those first Christians learned obedience, no matter the cost in terms of personal sacrifice. For many, it meant literally giving up their lives for the gospel of Christ. God was powerfully working through them; he gives his Spirit to those who obey him.[6]

In the words of J. B. Phillips: "Perhaps because of their very simplicity, perhaps because of the readiness to believe, to obey, to give, to suffer, and if need be to die, the Spirit of God found what he must always be seeking—a fellowship of men and women so united in faith and love that he can work in them and through them with the minimum of... hindrance."[7]

This call of Jesus to his disciples was also a call of love. Their obedience to his Word meant trusting in his love. It is because Jesus loves us and has laid down his life for us that he looks for a total response of love on our part, a love whose reality is tested by obedience. Do we really want to be his disciples? Do we genuinely want God's perfect will for our lives? Are we honestly willing to trust ourselves to one who demands all, but who loves us more than anyone could ever love us and who longs only for our highest good? The test must be unquestioning obedience to his Word. If we reject his Word, we question his wisdom and doubt his love, and we cannot be his disciples.

This truth is behind some of the words of Jesus which may seem to us, as they seemed to the crowds in his day, "a hard saying." "If any one comes to me and does not hate his own father and mother and wife and children and brothers and sisters, yes, and even his own life, he cannot be my disciple."[8] This was an idiomatic way of saying that our love for Jesus must be so unhesitatingly first that by comparison our love for those who are nearest and dearest to us is like hatred. The lordship of Jesus means that no one can have equal claims with him to our loyalty and allegiance. There can be no condition or compromise. "Whoever does not bear his own cross and come after me, cannot be my disciple... Whoever of you does not renounce all that he has cannot be my disciple."[9]

With such a call to a life of total and uncompromising obedience, we should not be surprised if we are strongly tempted to qualify Christ's call, to modify its stringent demands by taking a more "reasonable" line in the light of modern culture, which, we tell ourselves, is so different from that of the first century. With our intellectual and theological approach we may try to hold a "more balanced" view or reinterpret the teaching of Jesus in order to avoid its direct and disturbing challenge. It is important, we say, not to take things too literally. We must not become legalistic. We must not ignore the vital principles of hermeneutics. Jesus may have *said*, "Do not lay up for yourselves treasures on earth"; but what he *meant* was, "Enjoy the beautiful things in this world, but do not allow them to hold a central place in your hearts." Jesus may have *said*, "Love your enemies"; but what he *meant* was, "Do not take active revenge against someone who has wronged you." When Jesus *said*, "Seek first the kingdom of God," what he really *meant* was, "Although there will be many other things you must seek in order to exist and have a normal life, make sure that you do not leave God's kingdom out of your life altogether." In these ways we evade the clear call of Jesus to absolute obedience; in this our whole attitude to him is wrong. We do not believe that he loves us and plans only for what is best for us. And our unbelief and disobedience disqualify us as his disciples.

## The Necessity of Faith
We have already seen that Jesus' aim in testing our obedience is to bring us to the point of genuine faith in him. Everything ultimately depends on God's grace—his undeserved love as he takes the initiative in reaching out to us when we are helpless—but although God's gifts are given "by grace," they are received through faith. Faith is the open hand by which we take what God's grace offers us. We are

justified by faith. We enter God's presence by faith. We receive the Spirit by faith. Christ dwells in our hearts by faith. Those upon whom the Spirit fell at Pentecost and on other occasions were sometimes described as "full of faith and of the Holy Spirit"; it was "by faith in his name" that God was able to work with unusual power among them. We see Philip, later termed the evangelist, acting by faith on the unusual promptings of the Spirit of God in Acts 8, which brought new life to the Samaritans and to the Ethiopian eunuch. See the faith of Ananias as he went nervously to the feared Saul of Tarsus, arch-enemy of the Christian church; note the faith of Jewish Simon Peter (reluctant as it was) as he walked into the house of Cornelius, the Gentile. The whole story of the early church is a continuous demonstration of faith in the risen Christ. Their evangelistic enterprise makes a magnificent *volume* 2 to the epic stories of the heroes of faith summarized in Hebrews, chapter 11.

In all these examples, however, we see that the faith which is able to receive God's grace will be proved by obedience to God's Word. Without obedience there is no faith. "By faith Abraham *obeyed* when he was called to go out to a place which he was to receive as an inheritance; and he went out..."[10] Paul gives as a reason for his apostleship the need to bring about "the obedience of faith." To quote Bonhoeffer: "Only he who believes is obedient, and only he who is obedient believes... When people complain that they find it hard to believe, it is a sign of deliberate or unconscious disobedience... Only the devil has an answer for our moral difficulties, and he says, 'Keep on posing problems (of faith) and you will escape the necessity of obedience.' "[11]

John suggests in his Gospel that the opposite of believing in Jesus is disobeying him: "He who *believes* in the Son has eternal life; he who *does not obey* the Son shall not see life, but the wrath of God abides on him."[12] Paul also makes it clear that, while we are saved through believing in Jesus, God's righteous judgement will one day come "upon those who do not know God and upon those who *do not obey* the gospel of our Lord Jesus."[13] Just as faith and obedience are paired, so unbelief and disobedience are two sides of the same coin. It is no good calling Jesus "Lord" unless we do what he says.

Calvin once said, "While it is faith alone that justifies, the faith that justifies is never alone." Always it is accompanied by good works, since faith without works is dead. And the basis of the good works that James commends in his epistle is obedience to the Word of God: "Be doers of the word, and not hearers only, deceiving yourselves."[14]

"The issue at point is crucial—the one that matters most. We do need more "decisions" in evangelism, more effective church management and organization, more money to run churches, and sometimes we may even need better buildings and facilities. But woe be to us as Christians if we do not see that the greatest need of the hour is to help Christians clearly understand and obey the teachings of Christ... Praying a prayer to invite Christ into one's heart, having an emotional experience, testifying for Christ, sharing the 'plan of salvation,' entering into the fullness of the Holy Spirit, teaching the Bible, and many other Christian acts are valid and good. But they mean nothing, *absolutely nothing*... if Jesus is not obeyed in our private lives."[15]

The disciple of Jesus is the follower of Jesus. He has committed himself to go the way that Jesus goes. He has pledged himself to absolute obedience. When he fails to obey he must repent and ask for Christ's forgiveness at once, for sin breaks the discipleship and spoils the relationship. Without obedience there is no faith; and without faith there is no discipleship.

### The Way of the Cross

Jesus repeatedly taught his disciples that there was only one way that he could go: "the Son of man must suffer many things, and be rejected by the elders..."[16] Notice the clear distinction between suffering and rejection. If Jesus had only suffered he might have drawn immense sympathy from all his Jewish contemporaries. His passion would have been marked with great dignity and honor. But the agony and irony of it all was that, although he loved and welcomed all men, he himself was "despised and rejected by men." Humanly speaking his passion was shameful: "as one from whom men hide their faces he was despised, and we esteemed him not."[17] He bore the excruciating pain of the cross. He was mocked by the soldiers, tortured by the scourging, thorns and nails, jeered at by the crowd, sworn at by one of the thieves, forsaken by almost all his friends. There was no dignity about the cross. Klausner, the Jewish historian, wrote that "crucifixion is the most terrible and cruel death which man has ever devised for taking vengence on his fellow men."

Cicero called it "the most cruel and the most horrible torture."

Yet this was how Jesus had to go; and he saw any attempt to dissuade him from it as the work of the Devil, even if the suggestion came from one of his closest disciples. Christ would not have been Christ without the cross. That was the lesson that Peter had to learn immediately after his great confession. It was upon this rock that Christ was going to build his church. But the church could never have been the church without the cross. The cross has always been offensive to man. Even religious man finds it a "stumbling-block," partly because it cuts out all human pride, and partly because it is a reminder that if we are to follow Jesus it must be by way of the cross. "A servant is not greater than his master. If they persecuted me [Jesus], they will persecute you."[18] The disciples soon experienced the truth of this. "All who desire to live a godly life in Christ Jesus will be persecuted," wrote Paul.[19] A disciple is a disciple only if he shares Christ's life, including his pain, his suffering, his rejection, even his crucifixion. "Do you not know that all of us who have been baptized into Christ Jesus were baptized into his death? We have been united with him in a death like his. We know that our old self was crucified with him... We have died with Christ... I have been crucified with Christ... Those who belong to Christ have crucified the flesh with its passions and desires..."[20]

What does the way of the cross mean for us today? Most of us will probably not face crucifixion or any other form of martyrdom. A young man once asked an older Christian, "What does it mean to be crucified with Christ?" The older man thought for a moment, and then replied: "To be crucified with Christ means three things. First, the man who is crucified is facing only one direction; he is not looking back. Second, the man who is crucified has said goodbye to the world; he is not going back. Third, the man who is crucified has no further plans of his own. He is totally in God's hands. Whatever the situation, he says, 'Yes, Lord!' "

### Death and Discipleship

What, then, has to die—or, as the New Testament expresses it, what has already died—when we become true disciples of Jesus Christ?

*1. Our old self has died.* Paul expounds this great truth in Romans 6. In the first three chapters of Romans, Paul declares the

universal fact of sin: all alike have sinned and are under God's judgment. Then Paul asks, how can God be both just and the justifier of
the sinner at once? How can a sinner be forgiven and accepted by a
holy God? It is by God's grace, received through faith in Christ and
his death on the cross. In Romans 4 Paul expands on the nature of
true faith—faith that saves. Then, in chapter 5, he compares and
contrasts Adam and Christ. Referring to Figure 11-1, we see that by
virtue of Adam's disobedience we are all naturally in the kingdom

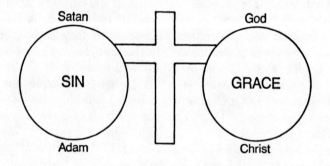

*Figure 11-1*

of Satan where sin reigns (left-hand circle). By virtue of Christ's
obedience unto death we can enter the kingdom of God, where
grace reigns, passing from death into life. We are dead to that old
life. By accepting the cross of Christ as our entry-way from the kingdom of Satan into the kingdom of God, we identify ourselves with
the crucified one; we have died with him to the old world of self and
sin. This should no longer have any part in us. "You must consider
yourselves dead to sin and alive to God in Christ Jesus. Let not sin
therefore reign in your mortal bodies, to make you obey their
passions."[21]

Emil Brunner once put it powerfully: "In the cross of Christ God
says to man, 'that is where you ought to be. Jesus my Son hangs
there in your stead. His tragedy is the tragedy of your life. You are
the rebel who should be hanged on the gallows. But lo, I suffer
instead of you and because of you, because I love you in spite of
what you are. My love for you is so great that I meet you there...
on the cross. I cannot meet you anywhere else. You must meet me

there by identifying yourself with the one on the cross. It is by this identification that I, God, can meet you in him, saying to you as I say to him, 'My beloved son.'"

Such identification, however, while allowing us to "be called children of God," also guarantees our suffering for Christ's sake. Some imagine that, since Jesus has died for us once for all to bear away our sin, we shall not be called to a life of suffering today. Certainly we shall never suffer to atone for our sins, since Jesus *finished* that work of atonement on the cross; "There is no longer any offering for sin."[22] But the cross, far from being an escape from sufferings, is the promise of sufferings for all those who are Christ's disciples. Paul once said, "I rejoice in my sufferings for your sake, and in my flesh I complete what is lacking in Christ's afflictions for the sake of his body, that is, the church."[23] There was nothing lacking in Christ's death when it came to taking away the sin of the world. But the way of Christ is the way of the cross, and today he still suffers in his body, the church.

Although in Christ we are now in the kingdom of God where grace reigns—and in that sense we are freed from the authority of sin and Satan over our lives—the spiritual battle will continue until Christ comes to vanquish all his enemies. We are free in Christ, yes, *free to fight!* The writer to the Hebrews exhorted his readers not to give up this constant battle against the forces of evil: "Consider him who endured from sinners such hostility against himself, so that you may not grow weary or fainthearted. In your struggle against sin you have not yet resisted to the point of shedding your blood."[24]

That is Paul's argument in Romans 6 and elsewhere in his letters. He expounds what Christians are in Christ, and then urges them to lead a life worthy of their calling. *We must become what we are.* The old self has died to sin through the cross of Christ. We must live in the light of our new life in him, refusing to allow that old realm of sin to dominate us. In one sense, the Christian who sins is a fool! Of course we all do sin, either through ignorance, through weakness or through our own deliberate fault. We still listen to the voice of the Tempter. We are still attracted by the deceptive pleasures of this world. Yet Sin is foolish, it spoils our relationship with Christ (and with others), it destroys our peace of mind, it enslaves us, paralyzes us in the service of Christ, and negates the joy of our salvation. God, in infinite patience and mercy, longs to restore us, and will do so as soon as we repent. But we often have to learn the hard way that God's Word is right. We are free to ignore it if we want to, but we are not free to ignore the consequences of ignorance.

Maintaining our freedom and fruitfulness in Christ is never easy. That is why we need the mind of Christ, who humbled himself and became obedient unto death, even death on a cross.[25] We should note carefully the example of Christ's sufferings, and follow in his steps.[26] We should not be surprised at the "fiery ordeal... but rejoice in so far as you share Christ's sufferings, that you may also rejoice and be glad when his glory is revealed."[27]

At the heart of any self-denial or self-emptying is not a determination somehow to do away with our old self-life; all that has already been crucified with Christ. Rather it is a determination to do the will of God and to stand fast in the freedom that Christ has already given us through his own sufferings. We may lose that freedom by falling into either of two opposite errors, legalism or license; but neither is inevitable.[28] We can win through the struggle; but it will be a struggle, and no disciple of Jesus can avoid suffering, in one form or another.

2. *The pull of the world must die.* This is why the rich young ruler had to give up all his selfish ambitions, sell all his worldly possessions, give to the poor; and *then* follow Jesus. Without this death to the world, with its values and standards, we remain in bondage to it and cannot be Christ's disciples. "Do not love the world or the things in the world. If any one loves the world, love for the Father is not in him. For all that is in the world, the lust of the flesh, and the lust of the eyes and the pride of life, is not of the Father but is of the world."[29] We need to relinquish all worldly attachments, which so subtly and powerfully draw our hearts away from Christ. Jesus wants us not to be "out of the world," but to be kept from the Evil One, as we move into the world to redeem it for him. We are free to do this only if we are free from the world's pull on our own life.

God calls us to make a complete break from our former relationship with the world. In Christ we become new people altogether—"the past is finished and gone, everything has become fresh and new."[30] In this new realm, therefore, our relationship with everyone and everything must be "in Christ" if it is to be good and right in God's sight. In the first century, the gnostics (who have their successors today) taught a false duality of spirit and matter; that God is interested only in the development of our spirits, and therefore we can either indulge our flesh or deny it altogether. The gnostics thus became known either for their gross permissiveness, especially in terms of sexual morality, or else for their extreme asceticism, "Do not handle, do not taste, do not touch." Paul rightly commented: "These have indeed an appearance of wisdom in promoting rigor of devotion and self-abasement and severity to the body, but they are of no value in checking the indulgence of the flesh."[31] Elsewhere he called this "doctrines of demons," and wrote positively that "everything created by God is good, and nothing is to be rejected if it is received with thanksgiving."[32] In other words, many things are basically good, since they were created by God. But we live in a fallen world, under the control of the Evil One, and we can enjoy the good things God has given us in his world only when they are redeemed by Christ and brought under his lordship, and received and enjoyed with thanksgiving.

Abraham is the classic example of this. God called him to leave his country and his father's house. He did not know where he was going, but he did know with whom he was going. Later he was challenged to sacrifice his only son, the son of God's promise. Because he was willing to let go his most precious possession, confident that God was able even to raise the dead, he could enter into God's promised blessings by faith. Bonhoeffer made this comment: "Abraham comes down from the mountain with Isaac just as he went up, but the whole situation has changed." In New Testament terms, Abraham had brought his precious relationship with Isaac under Christ's lordship. It was now "in Christ." "Christ had stepped between father and son. Abraham had left all and followed Christ, and as he follows him he is allowed to go back and live in the world as he had done before. Outwardly the picture is unchanged, but the old is passed away, and behold all things are new. Everything has had to pass through Christ."[33] Every part of our life must go through the same basic process to be redeemed for Christ, and received with thanksgiving.

Learning to be *in* the world but not *of* the world may cause us suffering. "Obedience to the gospel in a world where Satan is still active means living with tension. This is part of the meaning of the Incarnation. The Incarnation makes sense only through faith in God. If it is faithful, the church's career will largely parallel that of Jesus

Christ. We, as Christians... are constantly forced back to total dependence on the incarnate Christ. We should be alarmed when we are at home in the world or have total 'peace of mind.' Christian life in a non-Christian world is tension, stress, and at times even agony. A whole system of social techniques aims to adjust the individual to the world and eliminate tensions. But being a Jesus-follower means accepting the scandal of Jesus' statements that he came not to bring harmony but discord; not peace but a sword (Matt. 10:34-36). For only thus may true peace finally come."[34] When the whole of creation is groaning, waiting to be set free from its bondage to decay, we Christians must "groan inwardly as we wait for adoption as sons, the redemption of our bodies." But at this moment in time, we must wait in patience.[35]

### The Pain of Relationships

No man is an island. Our lives are woven together, so that who we are and what we do always influences other people. The New Testament knows nothing of the solitary Christian. Christ calls us into fellowship both with him and with all his other disciples. Although he wants us to keep our God-given individuality (God loves variety), he insists that we lose our independence, since this is the root of all sin. We are to submit to his authority, and we are to submit to one another out of reverence for him. As members of the body of Christ "joined and knit together," we manifest the life of Christ on this earth today. When we are deeply united with one another in love the world will begin to believe and accept the truth about Jesus Christ. But it is here that problems arise.

The German philosopher Schopenhauer once said that people are like a pack of porcupines on a freezing winter night. The subzero temperature forces them together for warmth. But as soon as they come close together, they jab and hurt one another. So they separate, only to attempt, repeatedly, to huddle together again. Our natural but sinful independence is largely a defense against the risk of close relationships.

Many churches know little of the deep Christian fellowship which the New Testament considered normative. Many congregations consist of isolated individuals who may select a small circle of like-minded friends with whom to share, if at all. But that is totally foreign to the biblical picture of fellowship. We are called, as disciples of Christ, to share our lives, and, if need be, our possessions. We are to open our hearts, to take off our masks, to become real and honest. And when, as fellowships of Spirit-empowered Christians, we try to do this we discover two things. First, that deep and loving relationships as brothers and sisters in Christ can prove enriching and fulfilling. Second, we will also find pain, since sin makes us sharp and, huddling together for warmth, we hurt and jab one another. The temptation then is to separate, to pull back to a safe and comfortable distance, to erect little barriers, and to protect ourselves from the vulnerability of close relationships. In so doing, we shall destroy, or weaken, the love and unity that Christ commanded, prayed for, died for, and sent his Spirit to accomplish. Had Jesus pulled back from his disciples when they hurt him, the Christian church would never have been born.

*Burden-bearing.* Jesus, our sin-bearer, calls those of us who profess to follow him to be burden-bearers: "Bear one another's burdens, and so fulfil the law of Christ."[36] In the context this means bearing not only another's anxieties but also his sins. In the previous verse Paul wrote: "Brethren, if a man is overtaken in any trespass, you who are spiritual should restore him in a spirit of gentleness... Bear one another's burdens..." I can do this by forgiving the sin that he has committed, which may be a grievous sin against me. In this way I release my brother from his sin and guilt, and at the same time I am released from my own prison of unforgiveness. The essence of forgiveness is release. Forgiveness is never easy. It cost Jesus his life; and it may mean for me the crucifixion of pride, bitterness, resentment, or revenge. I may have good reasons to justify my unforgiveness. They may be logical and humanly understandable. But there is nothing that so grieves God's Spirit as lack of forgiveness. It destroys the health of his body. It hinders his work. The "root of bitterness" causes trouble, and by it many may become damaged. Reasons and excuses mean nothing at the foot of the cross, where I begin to see how much God has forgiven me in Christ and am compelled by his love to forgive my brother, even if he has sinned against me seventy-times-seven. I may not have the grace to do it. But if I have the wilingness, as a disciple of Christ, then God's grace will always be sufficient for me in this vital area of forgiveness.

*The Christian's rights.* We sometimes think of the cost of discipleship in terms of giving up all our sin. Certainly it will include that; but it will also include much more. Jesus had no sin, but *he gave up his rights,* and made himself weak and vulnerable towards others. Because it cost him his life, he could minister life to others. If we, too, are to be obedient to God, remaining in unbroken fellowship with him and with one another, we must lay aside not only our sin, but also our rights, making ourselves vulnerable and weak towards others. We may get hurt in the process. But this is how the life of Jesus and God's glory will be seen in the church.

Phil Bradshaw expressed it this way: "Christ had no defences. In his life and death he absorbed the sin of the whole world without giving sin back in return. 'When he was reviled, he did not revile in return...' (1 Pet. 2:23). If we want to pursue this road (i.e. of maintaining that quality of fellowship among us that Jesus had with his Father) we do not even need to look to the world in order to know the cost. Our own Christian brother will heap on us his sin—his anger, judgment, frustration, accusation, demands, fears. The challenge to us is not to return our own sin... If we want unity in the biblical sense, scriptural teaching is that it will cost us our lives in givenness to the Lord and to each other. That kind of fellowship is produced by gentleness, and the price of gentleness is brokenness of spirit. What produces brokenness is laying aside our rights... So, unity does cost a lot. But... the reward is something that has the power to heal and restore and bring people to the knowledge of the truth. It is something that will make the corporate life we share amongst ourselves the glory of God on the earth."[37]

Jesus had one supreme concern during his earthly ministry: to glorify his Father.[38] His terms of discipleship may seem severe because his plan, both for his church and his world, is so far-reaching that he cannot afford to have half-hearted disciples. Christ once said to the lukewarm Laodicean Christians, "I will spew you out of my mouth."[39] God's glory will be seen in those who are prepared to accept the path of obedience, the way of the cross and the pain of relationships. That is how Jesus lived, setting his face like a flint, doing always what pleased his Father. As we follow Jesus this way we can bring his salvation to the world.

# CHAPTER TWELVE

# *ABOUNDING IN HOPE*

F. R. MALTBY SAID THAT JESUS promised his disciples three things: they would be absurdly happy, completely fearless, and in constant trouble—a fair characterization of the New Testament church! Almost everywhere in the biblical witness of God's dealings with his people we find this paradoxical theme:

*Joy and woe are woven fine,*
*A clothing for the soul divine.* —William Blake

### The Tapestry of Life

We find this contrast vividly expressed in the earthly life of Jesus. At his birth, the display of heavenly glory, the burst of angelic praise, was followed by the appalling massacre of the infants. At his baptism, heaven was opened, the Spirit came down, and God himself confirmed that this was his beloved Son; yet immediately afterwards we see Jesus wrestling with his adversary in the wilderness for six exhausting weeks. The dazzling glimpse of his deity on the Mount of Transfiguration preceded the casting out of evil spirits and the rebuke of the disciples for their powerlessness and lack of faith.

When the Seventy returned from their mission excited by their experience of God's power, "Jesus was filled with rapturous joy by the Holy Spirit";[1] yet soon after he was accused of being demonically inspired. The joyful enthusiasm of crowds waving palm branches and shouting "Hosanna!" contrasted sharply with Jesus' sorrow over Jerusalem's spiritual blindness and coming judgment. The tender intimacy of the Last Supper was the prelude to betrayal, arrest, denial, and despair: Peter wept bitterly and Judas hanged himself. Although Jesus healed the sick, raised the dead, and fed the needy, the Jerusalem mob thirsted for his blood, "Crucify him! Crucify him!" Although he saved others, he would not save himself. Although he promised that he would never forsake those who trusted in him, in his extremity on the cross he cried out, "My God, my God, why have you forsaken me?"

The same pattern is also true in the New Testament church. The mighty wind of the Spirit at Pentecost, the thousands of conversions, the dramatic healings and "wonders and signs" were followed by imprisonments and beatings, and God's swift judgment on Ananias and Sapphira for lying to the Holy Spirit. The extraordinary multiplication of the church in Acts 6 preceded the martyrdom of Stephen in Acts 7 and the wave of persecution against the church in Acts 8. Bishop Cuthbert Bardsley once said, "We hear marvelous stories of what happens when there is an outpouring of the Holy Spirit—conversions, speaking in tongues, miracles, large congregations. But it also brings fears, frustrations and pain."[2]

Peter warned the Christian refugees scattered throughout Asia Minor, "Beloved, do not be surprised at the fiery ordeal which comes upon you to prove you, as though something strange were happening to you. But rejoice in so far as you share Christ's sufferings, that you may also rejoice and be glad when his glory is revealed. If you are reproached for the name of Christ, you are blessed, because the spirit of glory and of God rests upon you."[3] Note the juxtaposition of contrasts: beloved, fiery ordeal, rejoice, sufferings, glory, reproached, blessed. This pattern for God's people was also reflected in the Psalms. "When the Lord restored the fortunes of Zion, we were like those who dream. Then our mouth was filled with laughter, and our tongue with shouts of joy." Then the sigh and cry for further refreshment is heard: "Restore our fortunes, O Lord... May those who sow in tears reap with shouts of joy."

Tears, however, are mixed with hope that he who weeps now "shall come home with shouts of joy, bringing his sheaves with him."[4] Our lives are cyclic, like the seasons of the year. We cannot always have harvest. We need the cold, hard winter to develop spiritual muscles; we need rain. Yet in those bleaker days we also need the hope of spring and summer: "If winter comes, can spring be far behind?"[5]

Much of the church today has suffered through a long and barren winter, with bare branches, fruitless orchards, rocky soil and no hint of harvest. Spiritual deadness, however, coupled with the gathering gloom of today's hostile world, has led to spiritual hunger, an expectation that God is about to do something new in his church. Cardinal Suenens expressed it like this: "The church has never known a more critical moment in her history. From a human point of view, there is no help on the horizon. We do not see from where salvation can come, unless from *him;* there is no salvation except in his name. At this moment, we see in the sky of the church manifestations of the Holy Spirit's action which seem to be like those known to the early church. It is as though the Acts of the Apostles and the letters of St. Paul were coming to life again, as if God were once more breaking into our history."[6] God is certainly doing a new thing by his Spirit in the church. We see spring's tender green shoots pushing through the hard soil; the dark clouds are broken by shafts of sunlight. "The Spirit of God can breathe through what is predicted at a human level, with a sunshine of surprises."[7]

But before harvest we must expect suffering: "Unless a grain of wheat falls into the earth and dies, it remains alone; but if it dies, it bears much fruit."[8] What does this mean? It means dying to our respectability, to our rights and privileges, to our prejudices, to our ambitions, to our comforts, to our independence and self-sufficiency, to our self-preservation. Unless we die to ourselves there will be no fruit, no harvest, and no hope for this world.

Our ideas about spiritual life and power are very different from the example shown by Jesus. Often we are like those first disciples who showed a worldly understanding of life's values; repeatedly Jesus had to reverse those values before his followers could grasp the revolutionary nature of his kingdom. For example, Jesus was filled with the Spirit from his conception, and anointed with the Spirit's power at his baptism. Yet willingly he became as *we* are, though sinless. Often he was vulnerable, he knew the pain of loneli ness and rejection, he suffered mockery and misunderstanding; he learned obedience through suffering, responding with "strong cries and tears"; he was tempted, beaten, and crucified; he was "a man of sorrows and acquainted with grief." We look to the filling of the Spirit, however, to make us like *God:* full of power, authority and glory, overflowing with spiritual gifts, reaching down to the weak and lifting them up. Paul chided the Corinthian Christians, who thought they had "arrived": "Already you are filled! Already you have become rich!... We are fools for Christ's sake, but you are wise in Christ. We are weak, but you are strong. You are held in honor, but we are in disrepute. To the present hour we hunger and thirst, we are ill-clad and buffetted and homeless... We have become, and are now, as the refuse of the world, the offscouring of all things."[9] To follow Jesus means to follow his way of suffering and crucifixion. As the Master was, so must the disciple be.

## Where There's Death, There's Hope

Jesus gave his life for us, both in serving and in dying, for two main reasons. First, he knew that only through the cross could we be forgiven, which was why he came to this world. Second, "for the joy that was set before him [he] endured the cross."[10] He knew that death wasn't the end. Paul accepted the pain of following Jesus for the same two reasons. Although his sufferings could never atone for sin, he saw that "in my flesh I complete what is lacking in Christ's afflictions for the sake of his body... the church."[11] His sufferings were necessary for the sake of others; through his weakness Christ's power would transform many lives. Then, he knew that "the sufferings of this present time are not worth comparing with the glory that is to be revealed to us."[12] He was abounding in hope. In contrast, our unwillingness to pay the cost of discipleship and the price of spiritual renewal shows how fiercely we are clinging to our temporal privileges, how insecure we are in the love of God. We are afraid that if we let go we will have nothing left but God! But Pascal affirmed, "It is a happy time for the church when she is sustained by nothing other than God."[13] We shall never know the security and reality of the Father's love until we dare to depend on him alone.

Today Jesus is looking for those who will follow him, no matter the cost. Thousands are willing to give their lives for political or religious ideals, and Jesus wants his world to be turned upside down by a revolution of love; but he can work effectively only through those who have lost their lives to him and will make his kingdom their highest priority. Today we are in serious danger and tomorrow is a question mark. Now is the time to lose everything for Christ and to hope in God alone. Malcolm Muggeridge said that he longed to see Christians "lash themselves" to the reality of Christ, "as in the old days of sail, sailors would lash themselves to the mast when storms blew up and the seas were rough. For indeed without a doubt, storms and rough seas lie ahead."[14]

### Knowing Christ

The apostle Paul's supreme ambition was *to know Christ*. He knew that only suffering would deepen that knowledge, and counted everything as "refuse... that I may know him and the power of his resurrection, and may share his sufferings, becoming like him in his death..."[15] He realized that when he and others "were so utterly, unbearably crushed that we despaired of life itself," it was "to make us rely not on ourselves but on God who raises the dead," adding, "he delivered us from so deadly a peril, and he will deliver us; on him we have set our hope that he will deliver us again."[16] If we know God only in sunshine, our knowledge will be superficial, but when we trust him in the storms, the relationship will mature. The most distant object we can see in daylight is the sun. But at night we can see myriad stars vastly more distant than the sun—Isaiah's "treasures of darkness."[17]

George Matheson, stricken with blindness and disappointed in love, prayed that he might accept God's will "not with dumb resignation, but with holy joy; not only with the absence of murmur, but with a song of praise." Richard Wurmbrand, who spent fourteen years in communist prisons for his faith in Christ, including three years in solitary confinement thirty feet below ground level, admitted that he was "cold, hungry and in rags." Over the years "they broke four vertebrae in my back, and many other bones, They carved me in a dozen places, They burned and cut eighteen holes in my body." Yet, "alone in my cell... I danced for joy every night ... I had discovered a beauty in Christ which I had not known before."[18] Suffering, though a reflection of evil, does not always mean tragedy.

## Serving Others

The nature of God's love is that he gave his only son for the sake of the world. God's love always gives. We must open our lives to that love and our hearts to one another. Such vulnerability may bring pain, but it will also open a channel for God's love to reach those who are harrassed and helpless. Jürgen Moltmann writes: "A closed human being no longer has any hope. Such a person is full of anxiety. A closed society no longer has any future. It kills the hope for life of those who stand on its periphery, and then it finally destroys itself. Hope is lived, and it comes alive, when we go outside of ourselves and, in joy and pain, take part in the life of others."[19] If Christ lived an open life for others, the body of Christ must do the same today. Sharing our lives with others is always a risky business. Sooner or later it will mean death to ourselves, as our old securities are blown apart. But out of death comes resurrection: "For while we live we are always being given up to death for Jesus' sake, so that the life of Jesus may be manifested in our mortal flesh. So death is at work in us, but life in you."[20] This is both the mystery and the miracle of the gospel, that the resurrection life of Christ is experienced in power.

A living hope in God means that we trust God in all that he is doing in our lives. A chef will pound a steak before he cooks it, to make it tender. Because sin hardens our hearts, God may allow pain to make us tenderhearted and compassionate, like his Son. When our hearts are "tenderized" through suffering, our ministry towards those who suffer will be enriched: "What a wonderful God we have—he is the Father of our Lord Jesus Christ, the source of every mercy, and the one who so wonderfully comforts and strengthens us in our hardships and trials. And why does he do this? So that when others are troubled, needing our sympathy and encouragement, we can pass on to them this same help and comfort God has given us... In our trouble God has comforted us—and this, too, to help you: to show you from our personal experience how God will tenderly comfort you when you undergo these same sufferings. He will give you the strength to endure."[21] Paul was willing to go through incredible hardships, both that the power of Christ might rest upon him,[22] and that others might become "much more bold to speak the word of God without fear."[23] Those who have come through great suffering full of faith and hope have far more authority in their testimony to Christ than those who are simply hoping that God's Word will prove true when the trials come.

## Do Not Lose Heart

The Devil loves to play on our discouragements. In many places Christian work today is extraordinarily tough. Christians are not immune from the depression which increasingly afflicts our society. People everywhere feel the meaninglessness of their existence, without future hope. Our materialistic society is spiritually bankrupt, and a mood of resigned apathy and despair has settled over much of our world, although the affluent minority can afford temporary escapes into the fantasy world of entertainment and travel—two industries that are flourishing in the West.

Paul, in his day, was strongly tempted to discouragement. Twice in 2 Corinthians 4 he wrote, "we do not lose heart," which shows that he was often tempted to do so. He mentioned the discouraging spiritual blindness that kept many from seeing the "light of the gospel of the glory of Christ!" He himself knew the physical and mental exhaustion of the dedicated Christian worker who is "afflicted... perplexed... persecuted... struck down." He discerned the dimensions of the spiritual battle that rages in the world, but he gave two good reasons why he was determined not to lose heart.

First, he was aware of *the privilege of Christian ministry* given to him "by the mercy of God." Not only can we know God for ourselves, but God has called us to be his ambassadors of love and mercy to others. We are entrusted with his Word, the only message in the world that can bring someone forgiveness for the past, a new life in the present, and a glorious hope for the future. And Christ's light has dispelled our heart's darkness.

Second, Paul always had before him *a strong hope of future glory*. "We do not lose heart," he wrote again. "Though our outer nature is wasting away, our inner nature is being renewed every day. For this slight momentary affliction is preparing for us an eternal weight of glory beyond all comparison, because we look not to the things that are seen but to the things that are unseen; for the things that are seen are transient, but the things that are unseen are eternal."[24] It was this confidence about the future that enabled him to endure so much in the present: "We are afflicted in every way, but not crushed; perplexed, but not driven to despair; persecuted, but not forsaken; struck down, but not destroyed; always carrying in the body the death of Jesus, so that the life of Jesus may also be manifest in our bodies." Paul was willing to go through any trial if it would help others ("it is all for your sake") and because he could look beyond it. Paul's "slight momentary affliction" is described in 2 Corinthians 11, where he spoke of beatings, shipwrecks, constant dangers, toil and hardship, many a sleepless night, hunger and thirst, cold and exposure—not to mention the pressure of his daily anxiety for all the churches. Yet he saw all this as nothing compared with the "eternal weight of glory" prepared for every true disciple of Christ.

C. S. Lewis once wrote: "Hope is one of the Theological virtues. This means that a continual looking forward to the eternal world is not (as some modern people think) a form of escapism or wishful thinking, but one of the things a Christian is meant to do. It does not mean that we are to leave this present world as it is. If you read history, you will find that the Christians who did most for the present world were just those who thought most of the next. The Apostles themselves, who set on foot the conversion of the Roman Empire, the great men who built up the Middle Ages, the English Evangelicals who abolished the slave trade, all left their mark on Earth, precisely because their minds were occupied with Heaven. It is since Christians have largely ceased to think of the other world that they have become so ineffective in this. Aim at Heaven and you will get earth 'thrown in'; aim at earth and you will get neither."[25] The old preachers often made the same point: you cannot live well until you can die well. When you are sure of heaven, you can spend yourself in the service of others here on earth. "For living to me means simply 'Christ,' and if I die I should merely gain more of him."[26] The Christian's hope is not a pious dream. It is based on the solid evidence of Christ's own resurrection from the dead, together with his own specific promises.

More than ever today we need to hold fast to this hope. Christ warned his disciples that before the close of the age false teaching would lead many astray. Other cataclysmic events would also precede that day: "There will be signs in sun and moon and stars, and upon the earth distress of nations in perplexity at the roaring of the sea and the waves, men fainting with fear and with foreboding of what is coming on the world; for the powers of the heavens will be shaken. And then they will see the Son of man coming in a cloud with power and great glory. Now when these things begin to take place, look up and raise your heads, because your redemption is drawing near."[27] We cannot say precisely what these words refer to, nor can we interpret dogmatically Peter's description of the Day of the Lord when "the heavens will pass away with a loud noise, and the elements will be dissolved with fire, and the earth and the works that are upon it will be burned up."[28] Such words are not inconsistent with a nuclear holocaust, and the possibility of this frightful form of total human suicide increases every year.

When Third World nations have nuclear weapons, who would prevent their use of them? When the poor have been oppressed and crippled for so long by the greed of affluent countries, it would be understandable if their frustration were unleashed in nuclear vioence. Billy Graham said in 1980 that if God does not judge our Western society, he will have to apologize to Sodom and Gomorrah. This was not a wild statement. The sin of Sodom was not only sexual perversion—though there is plenty of that in our Western world. God declared through Ezekiel: "Behold, this was the guilt of your sister Sodom: she and her daughters had pride, surfeit of food, and prosperous ease, but did not aid the poor and needy. They were haughty, and did abominable things before me; therefore I removed them."[29] Do we imagine that we who have acted with similar neglect and arrogance, shall escape the judgment of God? From every perspective, in human terms, the future seems extraordinarily bleak.

The call to discipleship, however, is also a call to God's promised glory. In view of the urgency of the times, we are to live lives that honor Christ, that heal the wounds within his body, and that hasten the coming of the day of God. This is not a day in which to play religious games. Time is running out fast. Christ looks for disciples who are unashamed of him, bold in their witness, obedient to his Word, united in his love and filled with his Spirit. Joy and woe will be woven fine; tears, pain and sweat will be mingled with radiant love and inexpressible joy. Christ wants disciples who will not only have hope, but give hope. Whatever we receive we are to give away, that others may rise up through the darkness that covers the earth. "Arise, shine; for your light has come, and the glory of the Lord has risen upon you."[30] Like St. Francis of Assisi, we need to pray that where there is hatred, we may give love; where there is injury, pardon, where there is doubt, faith; where there is despair, hope; where there is sadness, joy; where there is darkness, light. "Grant that we may not seek so much to be consoled, as to console; to be understood, as to understand; to be loved, as to love; for in giving we receive, in pardoning, we are pardoned, and dying we are born to eternal life."

The disciple of Christ cannot lose: when he gives all, he gains all; when he loses his life, he finds it. Jim Elliot, martyred as a missionary to the Aucas in South America in 1956, summed it up like this: "He is no fool who gives what he cannot keep, to gain what he cannot lose."

Let us answer God's call with a personal commitment to be his disciples—and change the world!

# AN EVANGELICAL COMMITMENT TO SIMPLE LIFESTYLE

For four days we have been together, 85 Christians from 27 countries, to consider the resolve expressed in the Lausanne Covenant (1974) to "develop a simple lifestyle." We have tried to listen to the voice of God, through the pages of the Bible, through the cries of the hungry poor, and through each other. And we believe that God has spoken to us.

We thank God for his great salvation through Jesus Christ, for his revelation in Scripture which is a light for our path, and for the Holy Spirit's power to make us witnesses and servants in the world.

We are disturbed by the injustices of the world, concerned for its victims, and moved to repentance for our complicity in it. We have also been stirred to fresh resolves, which we express in this Commitment.

## 1. Creation

We worship God as the Creator of all things, and we celebrate the goodness of his creation. In his generosity he has given us everything to enjoy, and we receive it from his hands with humble thanksgiving (1 Tim. 4:4, 6, 17). God's creation is marked by rich abundance and diversity, and he intends its resources to be husbanded and shared for the benefit of all.

We therefore denounce environmental destruction, wastefulness and hoarding. We deplore the misery of the poor who suffer as a result of these evils. We also disagree with the drabness of the ascetic. For all these deny the Creator's goodness and reflect the tragedy of the fall. We recognize our own involvement in them, and we repent.

## 2. Stewardship

When God made man, male and female, in his own image, he gave them dominion over the earth (Gen. 1:26-28). He made them stewards of its resources, and they became responsible to him as Creator, to the earth which they were to develop, and to their fellow human beings with whom they were to share its riches. So fundamental are these truths that authentic human fulfillment depends on a right relationship to God, neighbour, and the earth with all its resources. People's humanity is diminished if they have no just share in those resources.

By unfaithful stewardship, in which we fail to conserve the earth's finite resources, to develop them fully, or to distribute them justly, we both disobey God and alienate people from his purpose for them. We are determined, therefore, to honor God as the owner of all things, to remember that we are stewards and not proprietors of any land or property that we may have, to use them in the service of others, and to seek justice with the poor who are exploited and powerless to defend themselves.

We look forward to "the restoration of all things" at Christ's return (Acts 3:21). At that time our full humanness will be restored; so we must promote human dignity today.

## 3. Poverty and Wealth

We affirm that involuntary poverty is an offense against the goodness of God. It is related in the Bible to powerlessness, for the poor cannot protect themselves. God's call to rulers is to use their power to defend the poor, not to exploit them. The church must stand with God and the poor against injustice, suffer with them, and call on rulers to fulfill their God-appointed role.

We have struggled to open our minds and hearts to the uncomfortable words of Jesus about wealth. "Beware of covetousness" he said, and "a person's life does not consist in the abundance of his possessions" (Luke 12:15). We have listened to his warnings about the danger of riches. For wealth brings worry, vanity and false security, the oppression of the weak, and indifference to the sufferings of the needy. So it is hard for a rich person to enter the kingdom of heaven (Matt. 19:23) and the greedy will be excluded from it. The kingdom is a free gift offered to all, but it is especially good news for the poor because they benefit most from the changes it brings.

We believe that Jesus still calls some people (perhaps even us) to follow him in a lifestyle of total, voluntary poverty. He calls all his followers to an inner freedom from the seduction of riches (for it is impossible to serve God and money) and to sacrificial generosity ("to be rich in good works, to be generous and ready to share" 1 Tim. 6:18). Indeed, the motivation and model for Christian generosity are nothing less than the example of Jesus Christ himself, who, though rich, became poor that through his poverty we might become rich (2 Cor. 8:9). It was a costly, purposeful self-sacrifice; we mean to seek his grace to follow him. We resolve to get to know poor and oppressed people, to learn issues of injustice from them, to seek to relieve their suffering, and to include them regularly in our prayers.

### 4. The New Community

We rejoice that the church is the new community of the new age, whose members enjoy a new life and a new lifestyle. The earliest Christian church, constituted in Jerusalem on the Day of Pentecost, was characterized by a quality of fellowship unknown before. Those Spirit-filled believers loved one another to such an extent that they sold and shared their possessions. Although their selling and giving were voluntary, and some private property was retained (Acts 5:4), it was made subservient to the needs of the community, "None of them said that anything he had was his own" (Acts 4:32). That is, they were free from the selfish assertion of proprietary rights. And as a result of their transformed economic relationships, "there was not a needy person among them" (Acts 4:34).

This principle of generous and sacrificial sharing, expressed in holding ourselves and our goods available for people in need, is an indispensable characteristic of every Spirit-filled church. So those of us who are affluent in any part of the world, are determined to do more to relieve the needs of less privileged believers. Otherwise, we shall be like those rich Christians in Corinth who ate and drank too much while their poor brothers and sisters were left hungry, and we shall deserve the stinging rebuke Paul gave them for despising God's church and desecrating Christ's body (1 Cor. 11:20-24). Instead, we determine to resemble them at a later stage when Paul urged them out of their abundance to give to the impoverished Christians of Judea "that there may be equality" (2 Cor. 8:10-15). It was a beautiful demonstration of caring love and of Gentile-Jewish solidarity in Christ.

In this same spirit, we must seek ways to transact the church's corporate business together with the minimum expenditure on travel, food and accommodation. We call on churches and parachurch agencies in their planning to be acutely aware of the need for integrity in corporate lifestyle and witness.

Christ calls us to be the world's salt and light, in order to hinder its social decay and illumine its darkness. But our light must shine and our salt must retain its saltness. It is when the new community is most obviously distinct from the world —in its values, standards and lifestyle—that it presents the world with a radically attractive alternative and so exercises its greatest influence for Christ. We commit ourselves to pray and work for the renewal of our churches.

### 5. Personal Lifestyle.

Jesus our Lord summons us to holiness, humility, simplicity, and contentment. He also promises us his rest. We confess, however, that we have often allowed unholy desires to disturb our inner tranquility. So without the constant renewal of Christ's peace in our hearts, our emphasis on simple living will be one-sided.

Our Christian obedience demands a simple lifestyle, irrespective of the needs of others. Nevertheless, the facts that 800 million people are destitute and that about 10,000 die of starvation every day make any other lifestyle indefensible.

While some of us have been called to live among the poor, and others to open our homes to the needy, all of us are determined to develop a simpler lifestyle. We intend to re-examine our income and expenditure, in order to manage on less and give away more. We lay down no rules or regulations, for either ourselves or others. Yet we resolve to renounce waste and oppose extravagance in personal living, clothing and housing, travel and church buildings. We also accept the distinction between necessities and luxuries, celebrations and normal routine, and between the service of God and slavery to fashion. Where to draw the line requires conscientious thought and decision by us, together with members of our family. Those of us who belong to the West need the help of our Third World brothers and sisters in evaluating our standards of spending. Those of us who live in the Third World acknowledge that we too are exposed to the temptation of covetousness. So we need each other's understanding, encouragement, and prayers.

## 6. International Development.

We echo the words of the Lausanne Covenant: "We are shocked by the poverty of millions, and disturbed by the injustices which cause it." One quarter of the world's population enjoys unparalleled prosperity, while another quarter endures grinding poverty. This gross disparity is an intolerable injustice; we refuse to acquiesce to it. The call for a New International Economic Order expresses the justified frustration of the Third World.

We have come to understand more clearly the connection between resources, income, and consumption: people often starve because they cannot afford to buy food, and because they have no access to power. We therefore applaud the growing emphasis of Christian agencies on development rather than aid, for the transfer of personnel and appropriate technology can enable people to make good use of their own resources, while at the same time respecting their dignity. We resolve to contribute more generously to human development projects. Where people's lives are at stake, there should never be a shortage of funds.

But the action of governments is essential. Those of us who live in the affluent nations are ashamed that our governments have mostly failed to meet their targets for official development assistance, to maintain emergency food stocks, or to liberalize their trade policy.

We have come to believe that in many cases multinational corporations reduce local initiative in the countries where they work, and tend to oppose any fundamental change in government. We are convinced that they should become more subject to controls and more accountable.

## 7. Justice and Politics.

We are also convinced that the present situation of social injustice is so abhorrent to God that a large measure of change is necessary. Not that we believe in an earthly utopia. But neither are we pessimists. Change can come, although not through commitment to simple lifestyle or human development projects alone.

Poverty and excessive wealth, militarism and the arms industry, and the unjust distribution of capital, land, and resources are issues of power and powerlessness. Without a shift of power through structural change these problems cannot be solved.

The Christian church along with the rest of society, is inevitably involved in politics which is "the art of living in community." Servants of Christ must express his lordship in their political, social, and economic commitments and their love for their neighbors by taking part in the political process. How, then, can we contribute to change?

First, we will pray for peace and justice, as God commands. Secondly, we will seek to educate Christian people in the moral and political issues involved, and so clarify their vision and raise their expectations. Thirdly, we will take action. Some Christians are called to special tasks in government, economics, or development. All Christians must participate in the active struggle to create a just and responsible society. In some situations obedience to God demands resistance to an unjust established order. Fourthly, we must be ready to suffer. As followers of Jesus, the Suffering Servant, we know that service always involves suffering.

While personal commitment to change our lifestyle without political action to change systems of injustice lacks effectiveness, political action without personal commitment lacks integrity.

## 8. Evangelism

We are deeply concerned for the vast millions of unevangelized people in the world. Nothing that has been said about lifestyle or injustice diminishes the urgency of developing evangelistic strategies appropriate to different cultural environments. We must not cease to proclaim Christ as Savior and Lord throughout the world. The church is not yet taking seriously its commission to be witnesses "to the ends of the earth" (Acts 1:8).

So the call to a responsible lifestyle must not be divorced from the call to responsible witness. For the credibility of our message is seriously diminished whenever we contradict it by our lives. It is impossible with integrity to proclaim Christ's salvation if he has evidently not saved us from greed, or his lordship if we are not good stewards of our possessions, or his love if we close our hearts against the needy. When Christians care for each other and for the deprived, Jesus Christ becomes more visibly attractive.

In contrast to this, the affluent lifestyle of some Western evangelists when they visit the Third World is understandably offensive to many.

We believe that simple living by Christians generally would release considerable resources of finance and personnel for evangelism as well as development. So by our commitment to a simple lifestyle we recommit ourselves wholeheartedly to world evangelization.

## 9. The Lord's Return

The Old Testament prophets both denounced the idolatries and injustices of God's people and warned of his coming judgment. Similar denunciations and warnings are found in the New Testament. The Lord Jesus is coming back soon to judge, to save and to reign. His judgment will fall upon the greedy (who are idolaters) and upon all oppressors. For on that day the King will sit upon his throne and separate the saved from the lost. Those who have ministered to him by ministering to one of the least of one of his needy brothers and sisters will be saved, for the reality of saving faith is exhibited in serving love. But those who are persistently indifferent to the plight of the needy, and so to Christ in them, will be irretrievably lost (Matt. 25:31-46). All of us need to hear again this solemn warning of Jesus, and resolve afresh to serve him in the deprived. We therefore call on our fellow Christians everywhere to do the same.

## Our Resolve.

So then, having been freed by the sacrifice of our Lord Jesus Christ, in obedience to his call, in heartfelt compassion for the poor, in concern for evangelism, development and justice, and in solemn anticipation of the Day of Judgment, we humbly commit ourselves to develop a just and simple lifestyle, to support one another in it, and to encourage others to join with us in the commitment.

We know that we shall need time to work out its implications and that the task will not be easy. May Almighty God give us grace to be faithful! Amen.

*"An Evangelical Commitment to Simple Lifestyle" was written and endorsed by the International Consultation on Simple Lifestyle, held at Hoddesdon, England on March 17-21, 1980. The Consultation was sponsored by the World Evangelical Fellowship Theological Commission's Unit on Ethics and Society (Dr. Ronald Sider, chairman) and the Lausanne Committee on World Evangelization's Lausanne Theology and Education Group (Rev. John Stott, chairman).*

*I am grateful to the Administrative Secretary of the Theological Commission of the World Evangelical Fellowship for permission to use this statement.*

# A BASIC
# DISCIPLESHIP COURSE

All these 24 themes are available as 15-minute talks by David Watson on cassette. Each cassette has four talks on it, and comes as a pack with 5 copies of the outline of the talks and questions for study.

Numbers 2, 3 and 4 are available from
    Falcon Audio-Visual Aids,
    Falcon Court, 32 Fleet Street,
    London EC4Y 1DB.
and from
    Christian Foundation Publications,
    45 Appleton Road,
    Hale, Altrincham,
    Cheshire, WA15 9LP.

Number 1 is available from Christian Foundation Publications only.

1. *Live a New Life (1 cassette)*
    How can I know?
    How can I grow?
    How can I show?
    How can I overcome?

2. *Christian Foundations I and II (2 cassettes)*
    *I*
    What can we know about God?
    Who is Jesus Christ?
    Who is the Holy Spirit?
    Is the Bible the Word of God?

*II*
Why the cross?
Prayer
Is there life after death?
The church
3. *Christian Living I and II (2 cassettes)*
   *I*
   Helping others find God
   Common questions
   Giving
   Guidance
   *II*
   Faith
   Suffering
   Forgiveness
   Love
4. *Spiritual Renewal (1 cassette)*
   Worship
   The gifts of the Spirit
   Being filled with the Spirit
   Spiritual warfare

# A FURTHER
# DISCIPLESHIP COURSE

The purpose of this course is to encourage personal study during the week, followed by group work based on the week's study. The following is offered only as a *sample*; other themes could be similarly developed.

## 1. THE POWER OF THE HOLY SPIRIT
Note: Please go through your Readings and Questions during the week before the Group Study.

### A) Daily Bible Readings and Study Questions

*Monday/Acts 1:1-14: "The Promise of the Spirit"*
1. Even after 40 days, when Jesus proved his resurrection and spoke of the kingdom of God, his disciples still had a great need. (see also Luke 24:44-53) What was it? What must they do about it? When would it happen? Why was it necessary?
2. In what ways were their ideas about the future wrong (see 6-8)?
What similar mistakes could we fall into today?
3. How did they prepare themselves for the coming of the Spirit?

*Tuesday/Acts 2:1-36: "The Coming of the Spirit"*
1. How can we be filled with the Spirit today? See Acts 2:38; 5:32; John 7:37-39.
2. How should the filling of the Spirit be worked out in our lives? See v. 4, 11, 17-18, 22ff.
3. What is the place of tongues and other spiritual gifts in connection with the Spirit's fullness (4, 17f)?

**4.** Is the filling (or baptism) of the Spirit always something more after conversion? How can we help (a) young converts; (b) other Christians who feel the need of "something more"?

*Wednesday/Acts 3:1-26: "Witnessing in Jerusalem"*
**1.** Is it ever right to proclaim (or pray for) healing with such confidence as Peter showed (1-10)? What part should healing have in the witness of the church today?
**2.** No doubt there were other sick people listening to Peter, but what was the main thrust of his sermon? What can we learn from this?

*Thursday/Acts 8:1-25: "Witnessing in Judea and Samaria"*
**1.** What 'helped' them to obey Christ's instructions in Acts 1:8? What can we learn from this about the Spirit's prompting?
**2.** What can we learn from Philip's ministry (if time, read also verses 26-40).
**3.** How do you explain the coming of the Holy Spirit after the conversion of these Samaritans (14ff)?

*Friday/Acts 28:16-31: "Witnessing to the end of the earth"*
**1.** Paul had for years wanted to bring the gospel to Rome. What can we learn from this about God's working in our lives in answer to our prayers?
**2.** How did Paul witness to the Jewish leaders about Christ? When might such boldness seem right?

*Saturday and Sunday*
    *Personal*
**1.** How can we be continuously filled with the Spirit? What are your main obstacles or hindrances?
**2.** What are you doing, or could be doing, at present as a witness for Christ, in your area, in the city, and in the world?
    *Corporate*
**1.** What hinders the power of the Spirit in your church?
**2.** How should we expect the Spirit's power to be manifest in and through the church?

**B) Group Study**
**1.** Share briefly some of the answers to your Bible study questions.
**2.** What inadequacies or difficulties do we have when it comes to sharing our faith with unbelievers (see, for example the following list)? What can we do about this?
    I don't know the message.
    I don't have the confidence that Christianity is always "true."
    I can't answer the questions people fire at me.
    I find it hard to talk to people about my personal faith.
    I feel guilty when I "lay" things on other people.
    You lose too many friends when you do this.
    It just doesn't seem all that urgent to me.
    I feel hypocritical talking about new life when I am so messed up myself.
    I don't have a chance to relate to any non-Christians.
    They never ask, so I never tell them.

I'm afraid to speak by myself; I need someone else along.
It's so unnatural for me.
I've never seen it done tastefully; it always seems tactless and offensive.

**C) Optional Reading**
*One in the Spirit* by David Watson (Hodder & Stoughton)
*I Believe in the Holy Spirit* by Michael Green (Eerdmans)

**D) Verses to Learn**
John 7:37-39

## 2. THE BODY OF CHRIST AND THE GIFTS OF THE SPIRIT
Note: Please go through your Readings and Questions during the week before the Group Study.

**A) Daily Bible Readings and Study Questions**

*Monday/1 Corinthians 12:1-11: "Varieties of gifts"*
1. How can we discern between true and counterfeit spiritual gifts (1-3)?
2. Give a brief "definition" of each of the spiritual gifts mentioned in vv. 4-11. In other words, how would you describe them to someone?
3. Do you think this is a complete list of the gifts of the Spirit? If not, what others would you include?

*Tuesday/1 Corinthians 12:12-31: "You are the body of Christ"*
1. How should we recognize and encourage one another's gifts (12-25)?
2. Explain in your own words, verse 26.
3. What are the "higher gifts" that we should earnestly desire (31)?

*Wednesday/Romans 12: "A living sacrifice"*
1. If we are to use God's gifts to his glory, what must we seek to do (1-6)?
2. What further gifts does Paul mention in verses 6-8? Can you explain them simply in your own words?
3. In the practical instructions of verses 9-21, what ones do you personally find to be most relevant or difficult?

*Thursday/Ephesians 4:1-16: "Grow up into Christ"*
1. Why is the "unity of the Spirit" so important (1-6)?
2. What ingredients ensure the building up of the body of Christ into maturity (7-16)?

*Friday/1 Corinthians 3: "Only God gives the growth"*
1. What problems did the Corinthian church face, and what similar dangers could we face today (1-9)?
2. What sort of test are Christians to experience? What does it mean to build with "gold, silver, precious stones" (10-23)?

*Saturday and Sunday*
   *Personal application*
1. What gifts are you using in the fellowship?
2. What gifts are you praying for? How could you develop them?

*Corporate application*
1. Think of specific Christians whose gifts have helped you in the past, and thank God for them.
2. How is the church developing along the lines of Ephesians 4:7-16?

**B) Group Study**
1. Share briefly some of your answers to Bible Study Questions.
2. Discuss how gifts can be developed within the fellowship to edify the body of Christ.

**C) Optional Reading**
(See books for previous study.)

**3. THE GREAT COMMISSION**
Note: Please go through your Readings and Questions during the week before the group study.
**A) Daily Bible Readings and Study Questions**

*Monday/Matthew 28:1-20: "Go... lo..."*
1. What points of evidence do verses 1-15 contribute towards the fact of the resurrection of Christ? (briefly!)
2. What position does Jesus have in the world and in the church, resulting from his crucifixion and exaltation (16-18; see Phil. 2:8-11; Eph. 1:20-23)?
3. What does it mean to "make disciples"?
4. "Baptizing... teaching..." What should be the place of the Word and the sacrament of baptism in "making disciples"?

*Tuesday/Mark 16:9-20* (Not all manuscripts have this 'longer ending' of Mark, but at least it represents the church's tradition, whether part of the true Word of God, or not.)
1. What further evidence is there here for the resurrection? Why were the eleven slow to believe?
2. What place should baptism have in "preaching the gospel"? See also 1 Corinthians 1:13-17.
3. What significance are these signs for today's evangelism (17-20; see also Rom. 15:18f)?

*Wednesday/Luke 24:44-53; 1 Corinthians 15:1-11: "You are witnesses"*
1. What is the essence of the gospel that saves? (See both passages.)
2. What does it mean to be a witness "to Christ" (Acts 1:8) or a witness "of these things"?
3. What is the value of personal testimony (1 Cor. 15:6-11)?

*Thursday/2 Corinthians 5:10-21: Motivation*
1. List at least 5 motives in evangelism in this passage. See, from these verses, what you can learn about them. Write down any common denominator, or any striking factor.

*Friday/1 Corinthians 9:15-27: "By all means save some"*
1. What different ways can you (personally) "preach the gospel" today? Do you have the same urge as Paul expresses it in verses 15-18? If not, why not?
2. Explain the principles in verses 19-23 in your own terms. How does this apply in your situation, for example?
3. What should we guard against, and how, from verses 24-27?

*Saturday and Sunday*
    *Personal*
1. If someone you knew had just become a Christian, how would you follow them up, assuming you were given the responsibility? (Give as much detail as space and time allows!)
    *Corporate*
1. How effective is your local church in "making disciples"?
2. What more could realistically be done—by whom and how?

**B) Group Study**
1. Share some of your answers to Bible study questions.
2. Discuss some of the problems you have in evangelism. How could these be overcome?
3. What evangelistic work are you seeking to do outside your church buildings?

**C) Optional Reading**
*I Believe in Evangelism* by David Watson (Hodder & Stoughton)
*The Christian Persuader* by Leighton Ford (Hodder & Stoughton)

**D) Verses to Learn**
Matthew 28:18-20

**4. SHARING GOOD NEWS**
Note: Please go through your Readings and Questions during the week before the Group Study.
**A) Daily Bible Readings and Study Questions**

*Monday/Luke 19:1-10: Zacchaeus*
1. What were the steps by which Jesus brought "salvation" to his house?
2. What is the meaning of repentance? How far should a person understand the implications of this before he comes to faith in Christ?

*Tuesday/Acts 8:26-40: Philip the evangelist*
1. What lessons can you learn from this passage which indicate that Philip was such a good evangelist?
2. "He told him the good news of Jesus" (35). What steps would you use, with verses, in order to lead a person to Jesus?

*Wednesday/John 3:1-21: Nicodemus*
1. How far is it necessary, from the example of Jesus, to answer a person's questions before leading him to personal faith in Christ?

2. What can we learn about the sovereignty of the Spirit in evangelism? Where do human will and responsibility come in?

3. "He who does not believe is condemned already" (18)—Why? Why do some not believe (19-21)?

*Thursday/1 Corinthians 1:18-2:5: "We preach Christ crucified"*

1. In our message, what is the "power of God"? See 1:18, 23f; 2:2, 5.

2. What is meant by preaching "Christ crucified"?

3. Why can a sense of weakness, inadequacy, and nervousness be an asset in evangelism?

*Friday/Acts 20:17-37: Evangelism and Follow-up*

1. Twice Paul said "I did not shrink" (20, 27), suggesting that sharing good news is not easy. What did he not shrink from?

2. How should we "take heed to ourselves and to all the flock" (28) if the flock refers, at least, to anyone God has given us as a special responsibility?

3. What lessons did Paul teach by his life and example?

*Saturday and Sunday:*

   *Personal application:*

1. Using John 4:1-37, check your position as a witness to Christ. Check the appropriate evaluation:

|  | Developing this area | Weak | New idea |
|---|---|---|---|
| Sensitive to Spirit's leading (4) | | | |
| Willing to share at inopportune times (6) | | | |
| Willing to take the initiative (7) | | | |
| Willing to break social/cultural barriers (7-9) | | | |
| Sensitive to people's real needs (10-15) | | | |
| Frank and honest about personal problems (16-18) | | | |
| Able to avoid red herrings (19-21) | | | |
| Bringing people to a point of decision (25-26) | | | |
| Wanting to share Jesus with others (32) | | | |

After you have checked your position, pray that God will strengthen what is weak in your witness to Christ.

   *Corporate application:*

1. In what ways could your church strengthen its evangelism?

2. In what ways could your church improve its follow-up?

3. How could Christians in your church be better trained and equipped for evangelism and follow-up?

**B) Group Study**

1. Share briefly some of your answers to Bible study questions.

2. Discuss some of the opportunities for evangelism you have in your neighborhood and/or place of work. What are you doing? What difficulties do you have? What more could be done?

**C) Optional Reading**
*How to Give Away Your Faith* by Paul Little (InterVarsity)

**D) Verses to Learn**
Romans 3:23; 6:23; Isaiah 53:6; Mark 8:34; Revelation 3:20

## 5. ANSWERING COMMON QUESTIONS
Note: Please go through your questions during the week before the Group Study. On this occasion you may need a concordance and other aids, although a few verses are suggested as a start!

**A) Daily Study Questions**
What answers (with verses where possible) would you give to the following?
*Monday/ "I don't believe in God."*
(See Rom. 1:18-23; John 14:8-11; John 1:14-18; 1 John 4:12)

*Tuesday/ "I don't feel any need of God."*
(See John 3:3-18; Eph. 2:1-3, 12; Heb. 9:27)

*Wednesday/ "What about suffering?"*
(See Luke 13:1-5; Rom. 8:15-25; 2 Cor. 4:16-18; Ps. 73)

*Thursday/ "What about those who have never heard?"*
(See Luke 12:47-48; Romans 1:18-23; 3:19-24; Acts 10:34f; Gen. 18:25)

*Friday/ "What about other religions?"*
(See John 14:6; Acts 4:12; 1 Tim. 2:5-6; Heb. 1:1-3)

*Saturday/ "I think I'm good enough as I am!"*
(See John 3:3-7; Rom. 2:1-3; 3:9-20; Eph. 2:8-10; Gal. 2:16)

*Sunday/* Write down any other questions, objections, or excuses you have commonly heard; and give, where possible, some passages that speak to them.

**B) Group Study**
1. Share briefly some of your answers to the Study questions.
2. Discuss ways of being equipped with answers, See 1 Peter 2:15.

**C) Optional Reading**
*How to Give Away Your Faith* by Paul Little (InterVarsity)
*Is Anyone There?* by David Watson (Harold Shaw)

**D) Verses to Learn**
Any of the above!

## 6. VISITING AND COUNSELLING
Note: Please go through your questions the week before the Group study.

**A) Daily Study Questions**
*Monday/Evangelistic Visiting*
1. Why is this necessary (Matt. 9:35-10:1; Rom. 10:13-15)?
2. From Luke 10:1-20 what principles can you learn that are relevant for today and in your context?

*When to go:* Choose a likely convenient time. Avoid clashing with the most popular T.V. programs, etc.

*What to do:* Knock (persistently), pray, wait, door opens, smile... !

*What to say:* Announce immediately who you are, where you are from, and what you are doing. Try to get inside the house; develop conversation; don't be in a hurry; listen patiently; record information as quickly as possible afterwards (out of sight!).

*Tuesday/Follow-up Visiting (e.g. after an evangelistic service etc.)*

1. From 1 Thessalonians 2:1-13, what should your attitude and approach be like, over a period of time?

2. From Acts 20:19-35, what should you aim to teach and watch for, over a period of time?

3. Some general points:

Visit as soon as possible after the name has been passed to you—within 24 hours, if possible.

Be friendly, and begin to establish a warm relationship.

Go to someone of the same sex and approximately the same age.

Be interested in him or her as a person.

Read a short passage together, e.g. Psalm 103.

Decide on a regular time to meet, but keep the sessions fairly short.

Lend any useful literature.

*Wednesday/Sick Visiting*

1. From James 5:13-16 what can we learn?

2. General points:

Avoid being either hearty or gloomy.

Sit down, but not always on the bed (pressure might be painful).

If a person is deaf, speak up or write what you want to say.

Don't be hurried, but don't stay too long.

Don't make rash promises about coming again and then fail.

Read some suitable verse(s) and then pray (briefly). Sometimes hold the patient's hand (or lay hands on him or her) while praying.

If a patient is very ill, read a well-known passage, e.g. Psalm 23.

If a patient is unconscious, still read and pray aloud.

Leave suitable literature.

*Thursday/Counselling Those Lacking Assurance*

1. From 1 John 5:13 we are meant to have assurance. How? See 1:1-3, 7; 2:3, 15, 29; 3:9, 14, 21; 4:13; 5:4, 19.

2. Try to discover why those doubts persist: see chapter 8 in *Live a New Life* by David Watson (Hodder & Stoughton).

3. Show the nature of faith from Luke 1:30, 38, 46-49, etc. Help him to rest on the promises in God's Word—see Matthew 7:24-27; 2 Peter 1:3-4, 19.

Pray for him to be filled with the Holy Spirit—see Luke 11:9-13.

*Friday/Counselling Those Who Are Depressed or Defeated.*

1. Read Psalms 42-43 and Romans 8:26-39 as usual material. What can we learn

here about God's answer to our battles?
2. Be very gentle and understanding. Pray ahead of time for the gifts of knowledge and wisdom, so that the real problem may be revealed.
3. In some cases it may be necessary to gently give them time to confess openly (a) every sin, especially sin against others; (b) every way in which they have been hurt by others. It may be right for them to confess the sin of self-pity, and to begin to offer God the sacrifice of praise.

*Saturday/Counselling Those with Wrong Relationships*
1. From Philippians 2:1-5; 4:1-7; Ephesians 4:25-32 and 2 Corinthians 6:14-7:1 what can we learn in general terms? (Most of Paul's letters deal with this vast theme!)

*Sunday/Evaluation*
*Personal:* In which areas are you weak? In which would you appreciate further training? In which do you, in any way (however slight) feel called by God to serve?
*Corporate:* In which areas could your church be strengthened, and how?

**B) Group Study**
1. Discuss some of the answers to your questions.

**C) Optional Reading**
*Live a New Life* by David Watson (Hodder & Stoughton)
*New Life, New Lifestyle* by Michael Green (Hodder & Stoughton)

**D) Verse to Learn**
Isaiah 50:4

**7. PREPARING AND GIVING TALKS**
Note: Please work on this during the week before the group study.
Introduction: Most people are very nervous at the thought of giving a talk, however brief! But most people are quite able to do so. However, a good simple talk does require careful preparation. Mark Twain: "It takes me three weeks to prepare a good impromptu speech!" Preparing a talk is like building a house:

**A) Select the Site**
With the "ground" as the Bible, the "site" will be some verse/passage, etc. 1 Peter 4:11: Our ideas are important; God's Word is vital.
1. Use common sense.
2. Keep a "Jottings Notebook" (especially if speaking fairly regularly).
3. Know the needs of your hearers, as far as possible.
4. *Pray* before beginning any specific preparation.

**B) Lay the Foundations**
Study the verse/passage/theme as thoroughly as you can, until you really know what God is saying in his Word. Without this there will be no conviction about your talk, and it may easily collapse!

**C) Study the Plan** (or work out your message carefully)
Have *one aim:* It is often useful to write out your aim in one short sentence, so that the rest of the talk can be referred back to that. Be ruthless! What is God's message for this occasion?

Note: there are usually many different ways of tackling a passage. Remember Wesley's words, "I offered them Christ."

**D) Erect the Scaffolding**
1. A simple plan: State your point (a heading), Explain, Illustrate, Apply.
2. Work out divisions and headings (usually about 2-3 points in a talk).
(a) Use words from verses, (b) Ask questions (Who? What? Why? etc.) (c) Look for aid from artful alliteration, but don't let it be too forced!

**E) Build the Walls**
Give some substance to your talk. We are to "stimulate," "instruct," "feed," "stir," etc. Most talks will need some doctrine and teaching. Not just "Put your trust in Jesus," but say *why* etc. For this, study more than one translation, have a concordance, and use a well-chosen commentary.

**F) Don't Forget the Windows**—Illustrations are invaluable
Make a note of stories, quotes, topical news, etc. These often allow much light to fall on a path of solid doctrine.

**G) Make It Fit for Living**—This is to be not a museum but a house to live in.
Thus the talk must be relevant, meet the needs of the hearers, and suggest practical action, where possible.

**H) Check Front and Back "Doors"**
The beginning and ending of talks are of special importance. Some useful openings: A question, startling statement, topical news item, story, advertisement, puzzle or problem, etc. Also know when to stop and how to stop!

*Final preparation and delivery:* For most people (though not all) the following is probably wise, at least to start with:
1. Write out the talk in full, and then condense it to shorter notes.
2. Rehearse it—say it aloud (or whisper it!).
3. Be natural in (a) bearing—smile, stand still, avoid mannerisms, (b) voice—"enlarged conversation."
4. Use variety in pace and pitch. Use pauses.
5. At all times *pray* 1 Corinthians 2:1-5.

*Practical work:* Prepare a short talk of not more than five minutes on any verse/theme from the Bible, and give this at the next study group.

# NOTES

Page references in footnotes may refer to the British edition of a title. Wherever possible, an American edition is listed in the bibliography.

## INTRODUCTION
1. From *Evangelical Missions Quarterly*, October 1979, p. 228.

## 1/CALLED TO DISCIPLESHIP
1. John 9:28
2. Mark 2:18
3. Mark 2:18; Luke 11:1
4. John 3:25
5. Matt. 11:2
6. Mark 6:29
7. John 6:60, NEB
8. John 17:9
9. John 15:16
10. 2 Cor. 2:17
11. 2 Cor. 4:1
12. Rom. 1:1, 7
13. 1 Thess. 1:4
14. 1 Cor. 6:19-20
15. Eph. 4:1
16. John 13:34-35
17. John 15:16; cf. Matt. 18:19
18. Luke 5:1-11
19. John 1:44-51
20. Kittel, (Eerdmans, 1964), 4:446.
21. Matt. 7:21
22. Luke 6:46
23. Mark 8:34
24. "More Deadly Than the Male," BBC broadcast on December 4, 1978.
25. *Christ and the Media* (Hodder & Stoughton, 1977), p. 43.
26. *Agenda for Biblical People* (Harper & Row, 1976), p. 23.
27. Heb. 3:13
28. Phil. 1:27b
29. Matt. 10:8
30. Mark 1:17
31. Luke 10:1-20
32. Matt. 20:26-28
33. Luke 18:28-30
34. Luke 6:38
35. Acts 4:32
36. 1 Tim. 6:6-10
37. Phil. 1:29
38. Acts 8:1
39. Matt. 10:17, 21-22
40. 2 Tim. 4:10, 14
41. Rom. 9:2-3
42. Acts 20:31
43. Kittel, 4:452.
44. 1 Cor. 1:26-29

45. John 17:22-24

**2/CALLED INTO GOD'S FAMILY**
1. 1 John 1:3
2. Eph. 2:20
3. John 17:3
4. Acts 2:44; 4:32
5. Ps. 133:1
6. Rom. 8:19-22
7. Heb. 2:8
8. Eph. 3:10
9. *The Community of the King* (InterVarsity, 1977), p. 104.
10. Ibid., p. 125.
11. Mark 10:28-31
12. Ronald J. Sider, *Rich Christians in an Age of Hunger* (InterVarsity, 1977), p. 163.
13. Ibid., p. 164.
14. David J. Bosch, *Witness to the World* (New Foundations Theological Library, 1979), p. 225.
15. Rom. 12:2, *Phillips*
16. Bosch, p. 164.
17. Heb. 4:16
18. John 16:32-33; Luke 21:12, 17; Matt. 24:10, 12
19. *New Covenant Magazine*, November 1978.
20. Ann Ortlund (© 1970 by Singspiration Inc.).

**3/CALLED TO COMMUNITY**
1. *Life Together* (Great Britain: SCM, 1954), pp. 15-17.
2. Mark 7:6
3. *Life Together* (SCM), p. 13.
4. *Why Am I Afraid to Tell You Who I Am?* (Great Britain: Collins, 1969), p. 12.
5. *The Taste of New Wine* (Word Books, 1965), p. 22.
6. 2 Cor. 5:16-17
7. James 5:16
8. Ps. 32:3-4
9. Bonhoeffer, *Life Together* (SCM), p. 90.
10. Ibid., p. 90.
11. 1 John 1:6
12. *More New Testament Words* (SCM, 1948), p. 16. (I am also indebted to William Barclay for his insights on the subject of "Love" in this section.)
13. 1 John 4:7-10
14. 1 Tim. 2:4
15. Rom. 5:8, 10
16. John 3:16; 2 Cor. 5:21
17. Eph. 2:4; Ps. 103:8-10

18. Rom. 8:37
19. Rom. 8:38
20. Heb. 12:6
21. Exod. 20:5
22. Matt. 6:24
23. John 14:15, 21-24
24. 1 John 4:19
25. Gal. 5:22
26. Eph. 5:25-33; 1 Tim. 5:8
27. 1 Tim. 3:1-5, 12; Titus 1:5-8
28. See Eph. 5:8; 5:21-6:4
29. 1 Pet. 2:17; Gal. 6:10
30. Luke 10:27
31. Barclay, p. 21.
32. Matt. 5:44; Luke 6:27
33. Barclay, p. 21.
34. Rom. 12:9; 2 Cor. 6:6; 8:8; 1 Pet. 1:22
35. 2 Cor. 8:24; 1 John 4:11
36. Heb. 6:10; 1 John 3:18
37. Eph. 4:2; Col. 3:12-14
38. Eph. 4:3; Phil. 2:2; Col. 2:2
39. 1 Cor. 13:4-7
40. Rom. 14:15; Gal. 5:13
41. Eph. 4:15; 2 Tim. 2:22-26
42. Rom. 13:10; Col. 3:14; 1 Cor. 13:1 1 Cor. 14:1
43. Barclay, p. 24.
44. *New Covenant Magazine*, Aug. 1977.
45. Eph. 4:12
46. Eph. 4:13
47. Eph. 5:21; 1 Cor. 14:31; Phil. 2:3
48. Eph. 3:18
49. Eph. 2:13-16
50. 1 Cor. 11:27-29

**4/MAKING DISCIPLES**
1. Acts 10:34, 43
2. Matt. 28:19
3. 1 Cor. 11:19
4. February 16, 1976
5. Carl Wilson, *With Christ in the School of Disciple Building* (Zondervan, 1976), p. 25.
6. Acts 20:28
7. 1 Pet. 5:2
8. John 21:15-17
9. Col. 2:20-23
10. Gal. 3:1; 2:12; 5:1
11. 1 Cor. 3:1-4; Heb. 5:11-14
12. Wilson, p. 24.
13. 1 Pet. 5:3
14. 1 Cor. 14:3, 31
15. 1 Cor. 3:5-9, 17
16. Quoted by Michael Harper in *This Is the Day* (Hodder & Stoughton, 1979), p. 156.

17. Quoted in *Fulness*, vol. 24, 47 Copse Road, Cobham, Surrey, England.
18. 2 Tim. 2:2
19. Heb. 13:7, 17
20. Heb. 3:13; 10:24-25
21. Quoted in *Pastoral Renewal*, July 1978.
22. Acts 1:1
23. John 15:27; Luke 22:28; John 13:15
24. *Pastoral Renewal*, July 1978.
25. 1 Tim. 1:2, 18
26. 1 Thess. 2:7-8, 11-12
27. 1 Thess. 1:8
28. Wilson, p. 101.
29. John 20:21
30. Wilson, p. 209.
31. Rom. 8:29; Gal. 4:19
32. John 6:68
33. Acts 20:20, 27
34. 1 Tim. 4:13; 2 Tim. 1:13-14; 4:2; 2:15
35. Matt. 20:25-27
36. 2 Cor. 12:9
37. John 13:15
38. Phil. 4:9
39. 1 Thess. 1:6
40. 1 Tim. 4:12
41. A. W. Tozer ref. not known
42. 3 John 9
43. Acts 6:5, 8
44. Wilson, p. 18.
45. Acts 5:29
46. John 5:30
47. John 6:38
48. John 12:49
49. Luke 7:1-10
50. Eph. 5:18, 21
51. Heb. 13:17
52. Bob Mumford, *New Covenant*, January 1977.
53. *New Covenant*, January 1977.
54. 1 Tim. 3:2-13; Titus 1:5-9.
55. Ps. 75:7
56. Gal. 6:1
57. Rom. 3:16
58. Matt. 7:1-5
59. Col. 1:28
60. 1 Tim. 5:19
61. Rom. 14:19
62. Col. 1:28

## 5/LIFE IN THE SPIRIT

1. John 14:26
2. John 16:8
3. A. E. Taylor, quoted in Stuart B. Babbage, *The Mark of Cain* (Great Britain: Paternoster, 1966), p. 73.

4. 2 Cor. 4:2
5. John 3:6-7
6. From a sermon preached in a London church, February 4, 1968.
7. Rom. 8:15-17
8. 2 Cor. 1:22
9. Rom. 8:18, 39
10. John 16:14
11. 2 Cor. 3:17-18
12. Gal. 5:17, TEV
13. Col. 1:28
14. Heb. 5:8
15. Col. 1:27
16. 2 Cor. 3:18
17. James 5:16
18. John 4:24, TEV
19. Ps. 103:1
20. Eph. 2:18
21. Rom. 5:5; 1 John 4:19
22. Ps. 34:3
23. Acts 2:44-45; 4:32, 35
24. 2 Cor. 8:2
25. John 14:12
26. Acts 7:51
27. Acts 5:39
28. 1 Thess. 5:12-21
29. 2 Tim. 1:7
30. Eph. 4:30-32
31. 1 Cor. 12:1
32. Rom. 12:6
33. 1 Cor. 12:22
34. Hummel, (Great Britain: Mowbrays, 1978), p. 121.
35. 1 Cor. 14:1
36. Luke 11:13
37. Acts 5:32
38. *Thoughts about the Holy Spirit* (New Zealand: Fortuna Press), p. 62.
39. Ibid., p. 6.

## 6/PRAYER

1. Eph. 3:14; Phil. 1:4; Col. 1:9; 1 Thess. 1:2
2. Heb. 4:15
3. Luke 22:40
4. Rom. 3:11
5. Rom. 8:26
6. 1 Cor. 14:14
7. Eph. 6:12, 18
8. 1 John 5:14
9. Rom. 8:15-17
10. Ps. 103:1
11. Ps. 149:2-3; 47:1, 6; 63:4; 1 Cor. 14:15
12. Paul Hinnebusch, *Praise: A Way of Life* (Word of Life, 1976), pp. 2-3.
13. Luke 10:21, TEV

14. Eph. 2:18
15. Matt. 25:14-30
16. Luke 18:15-17
17. Michael Quoist, *Prayers of Life* (Gill, 1963), p. 102.
18. Ps. 73:21-25
19. Ps. 13:1-2
20. Richard J. Foster, *Celebration of Discipline* (Great Britain: Hodder & Stoughton, 1980), p. 35.
21. Heb. 13:3
22. *Prayer Without Pretending* (Great Britain: Scripture Union, 1973), p. 93.
23. 2 Cor. 10:5
24. Ps. 42:5
25. Eph. 3:20
26. Mark 11:24
27. Luke 1:30, 49
28. John 11:41
29. Rom. 4:20-21
30. 1 John 5:14
31. Ps. 103:1
32. Ps. 9:1
33. Mark 7:6
34. Luke 18:1
35. Acts 1:14
36. Acts 6:4
37. Eph. 6:18
38. Matt. 18:20
39. Rev. 12:10
40. Mark 11:25
41. Ps. 66:18
42. Eph. 4:26-27
43. Matt. 18:19
44. 1 Cor. 9:27
45. Luke 6:12-13
46. James 1:5-6
47. Luke 5:15-16
48. Luke 8:46
49. Jer. 2:13
50. Luke 22:31-32
51. Luke 22:40
52. 2 Chron. 5:13-14
53. Eph. 5:20
54. 1 Thess. 5:18
55. Luke 24:53
56. Acts 2:11, 46-47
57. Acts 4:24-31
58. Eph. 5:18-20
59. Quoted in Cardinal Suenens, *A New Pentecost?* (Great Britain: Darton, Longman & Todd, 1975), p. 89.
60. Col. 3:12-17
61. Rev. 5:13
62. Hinnebusch, p. 222.

7/THE WORD OF GOD
1. Matt. 4:3-11, TEV
2. Amos 8:11
3. James S. Stewart, *Preaching*, The Teach Yourself Series (Hodder & Stoughton, 1955), p. 20.
4. Mark 4:19
5. Matt. 4:8-9
6. Foster, *Celebration of Discipline*, p. 13.
7. Mark 8:33, NEB
8. Rom. 1:21-32
9. Rom. 8:15-21; 2 Cor. 3:17
10. 2 Cor. 3:6
11. John 5:39-40
12. Anthony Thistelton, *Obeying Christ in a Changing World*, John Stott, ed. Collins, 1977), p. 99.
13. Heb. 4:12
14. Thistelton, *Obeying Christ*, p. 116.
15. John R. W. Stott, *Your Mind Matters* (InterVarsity, 1972).
16. Rom. 8:6; Gal. 5:25; 1 John 4:1
17. Heb. 1:1-2
18. John 14:9
19. Heb. 1:3
20. Col. 1:15, 19
21. Mark 7:8-13
22. Matt. 22:29-32
23. *Under God's Word* (Marshall, Morgan & Scott, 1980), p. 41.
24. 1 Cor. 14:37-38; cf. Gal. 1:11-12; 2 Pet. 3:15; Rev. 1:1-3
25. Thistelton, *Obeying Christ*, p. 114.
26. Hag. 1:13
27. Acts 11:28
28. Acts 13:2-4
29. 1 Cor. 14:3
30. *I Believe in the Holy Spirit* (Hodder & Stoughton, 1975), p. 173.
31. Eph. 6:17
32. Ed. Colin Brown (Paternoster, 1976).
33. *More New Testament Words*, p. 116.
34. Ibid., p. 460.
35. 2 Tim. 2:15
36. 2 Pet. 1:20-21
37. 1 Cor. 2:11-12
38. Eph. 1:17-18, TEV
39. Col. 1:9f, TEV
40. James 2:26
41. From the Chicago Statement on Biblical Inerrancy, 1978, quoted by J. I. Packer, Op. cit., p. 58.
42. *Customs, Culture and Christianity* (Tyndale, 1963).
43. 1 Cor. 6:9-11

44. 1 Cor. 1:22-24
45. Luke 9:35
46. Ps. 130:5
47. 1 Sam. 3:9
48. 1 Cor. 14:26-31
49. See Richard J. Foster's chapter "The Discipline of Meditation" in *Celebration of Discipline.*
50. Thistelton, *Obeying Christ*, p. 105-06.
51. *Life Together* (SCM, 1954), pp. 59-60.
52. 2 Tim. 2:15
53. Col. 3:16
54. Acts 17:11
55. Acts 2:42
56. James 1:22 TEV
57. Quoted by J. I. Packer, *Presbyterian Journal*, 12 April 1978, pp. 60-61.
58. Rom. 12:1-2 *Phillips*
59. Matt. 4:1-11

**8/SPIRITUAL WARFARE**
1. Rom. 7:15
2. *Screwtape Letters* (Bles, 1942), p. 9.
3. Richard F. Lovelace, *Dynamics of Spiritual Life* (Paternoster, 1979), p. 18.
4. Matt. 4:1
5. Matt. 16:23, NEB
6. Matt. 13:19
7. Matt. 13:39
8. John 8:44
9. John 17:15
10. 2 Cor. 11:14
11. 2 Cor. 2:11
12. Eph. 4:27
13. 1 Tim. 3:7; 2 Tim. 2:26
14. 1 Tim. 4:1
15. Eph. 6:11-12
16. Col. 2:15
17. James 4:7
18. 1 Pet. 5:8-9
19. Edwards, *Thoughts on the Revival*, p. 410.
20. Among many see Michael Harper, *Spiritual Warfare* (Hodder & Stoughton, 1970) and Michael Green, *I Believe in Satan's Downfall* (Eerdmans, 1981).
21. Mark 9:25
22. Lovelace, *Dynamics of Spiritual Life* (Paternoster), p. 256.
23. 1 John 4:1
24. Acts 5:39
25. 2 Cor. 4:4
26. Rev. 12:9
27. 2 Tim. 3:1-5
28. *Dynamics of Spiritual Life* (Paternoster), p. 256.

29. 1 Pet. 5:8-9; 4:12-13
30. C. H. Spurgeon, *Lectures*. vol. 1, p. 167.
31. Rev. 12:10
32. Rom. 2:24
33. 1 Tim. 6:1; Titus 2:5
34. Eph. 6:16
35. 1 Tim. 4:1
36. 2 Cor. 11:15
37. 2 Thess. 2:9
38. 2 Tim. 3:5; Rev. 13:13-14
39. 2 Pet. 2:1
40. 2 Tim. 3:8
41. 1 John 5:19
42. Luke 17:26-27
43. Gal. 6:14
44. Ps. 91:14
45. Rom. 8:21
46. John 8:44; Rev. 9:11
47. Luke 4:33-36
48. Luke 8:26-33
49. Luke 9:37-43
50. Luke 11:24-26
51. Lovelace, *The Dynamics of Spirital Life* (Paternoster), p.140.
52. Col. 1:9, TEV
53. 2 Cor. 2:11
54. Matt. 26:41
55. Jude 17-21
56. 1 John 5:18
57. Eph. 6:10
58. Eph. 1:21-22
59. 1 John 4:4
60. Col. 2:15
61. Rev. 12:10-12
62. Eph. 5:1-20
63. 1 Tim. 1:18
64. Eph. 4:26-27
65. Eccles. 4:9-12
66. Eph. 6:10-20 I have written more fully about this in *How to Win the War* (Harold Shaw Publishers, 1979), chap. 4.
67. Eph. 6:18
68. Ps. 89:15
69. Josh. 6:16, 20
70. 2 Chron. 20
71. Ps. 47
72. Rom. 8:31

**9/EVANGELISM**
1. Matt. 20:28
2. Matt. 9:35
3. Matt. 10:7
4. Luke 10:1-20
5. John 20:21; Acts 1:8
6. Luke 10:3; Mark 16:15; Matt. 28:19

7. Quoted by Bishop John Taylor in *The Winchester Churchman*, July 1979.

8. I have written more extensively about this in *I Believe in Evangelism* (Eerdmans, 1976).

9. John Poulton, The Monthly Letter for May/June 1979 of the WCC Commission on World Mission and Evangelism.

10. Eph. 4:11

11. C. Peter Wagner, *Your Church Can Grow* (Regal, 1976), pp. 72-76.

12. 1 Pet. 3:15 TEV

13. H. Boer, *Pentecost and Missions*, Lutterworth, pp. 122, 128

14. 1 Thess. 1:5

15. Source unknown

16. Acts 5:28

17. Acts 4:20

18. Acts 7; 8:1-5

19. Phil. 1:14

20. *Evangelism-Now and Then* (IVP, 1979), p. 26.

21. *Evangelism in England Today*, a Report by the Church of England's Board for Mission and Unity (Church House Bookshop, Great Smith Street, London SWIP 3BN).

22. *A New Canterbury Tale* (Grove Books, Bramcote, Notts, England).

23. Heb. 1:1-3; 10:10-20

24. Acts 4:12

25. 2 Cor. 5:10

26. Heb. 2:3

27. 2 Cor. 5:20

28. Eph. 1:9-10

29. *Witness to the World* (Marshall, Morgan & Scott), p. 20.

30. Acts 8:6f

31. Poulton, WCC Commission on World Mission and Evangelism, May/June 1979.

32. Acts 2:38

33. Isa. 55:6

34. (Harold Shaw Publishers, 1979), chapter 6.

35. 1 Cor. 2:1-5

36. John 4:1-26

37. *Evangelism and the Sovereignty of God* (InterVarsity Press, 1961), p. 108.

38. 2 Cor. 4:4

39. See *How to Walk with God*, David Winter, Harold Shaw Publishers, 1969.

41. I have written more fully about follow-up in *I Believe in Evangelism* (Eerdmans, 1976), chapter 7. See also Appendix C, pp. 207-216 for further suggestions of a basic teaching course.

**10/SIMPLE LIFESTYLE**

1. 4 February 1980.

2. Phil. 1:18

3. *Enough Is Enough* (SCM, 1975), p. 62.

4. Luke 12:32-33

5. Acts 5:32

6. Acts 5:4

7. Acts 4:34

8. 1 Tim. 5:8

9. 1 Tim. 4:4-5

10. Phil. 4:12

11. Luke 12:34

12. Dietrich Bonhoeffer, *The Cost of Discipleship* (SCM, 1959) pp. 154-157.

13. Matt. 6:22

14. 1 Tim. 6:10

15. Luke 18:22

16. *Rich Christians in an Age of Hunger* (Hodder & Stoughton, 1977), p. 87.

17. Ibid., p. 90

18. See 1 Tim. 6:9-10; James 4:1-2

19. Luke 8:14

20. Matt. 6:34, *Phillips*

21. Matt. 10:7-10

22. Matt. 16:7-8

23. Matt. 17:14-21

24. Luke 10:1-21

25. 1 Tim. 6:10

26. John White, *The Golden Cow* (Marshall, Morgan and Scott, 1979), p. 39, 41-42.

27. Matt. 19:29

28. 2 Cor. 2:17; 4:2; 6:3; 7:2

29. Acts 20:18; 1 Thess. 1:5; 2:9

30. John 8:46

31. John 13:29

32. 1 Tim. 6:8-9

33. Heb. 13:5

34. 2 Pet. 2:14

35. Jude 16

36. 1 Tim. 3:3, 8; Titus 1:7

37. Bonhoeffer, *The Cost of Discipleship* (SCM), pp. 186-87.

38. 1 Cor. 9:19-23

39. Prov. 19:17

40. Matt. 25:35-40

41. Acts 3:6

42. 1 Thess. 2:8

43. Acts 2:44-45, 47

44. Acts 4:32-35

45. 1 John 3:17

46. Acts 11:27-30

47. From an interview in *Third Way*, 13 January 1977.

48. 2 Cor. 6:10

49. *Thoughts about the Holy Spirit*, p. 11.

50. 1 John 3:18. For a sensitive and balanced statement on this whole subject see *An Evangelical Commitment to Simple Lifestyle* in Appendix A, pp. 199-204.

## 11/COST OF DISCIPLESHIP
1. Luke 9:57
2. Heb. 11:1
3. Matt. 7:29, NEB
4. Mark 4:41
5. Matt. 28:18
6. Acts 5:32
7. Preface to *The Young Church in Action* (Bles, 1955), p. vii.
8. Luke 14:26
9. Luke 14:27, 33
10. Heb. 11:8
11. *The Cost of Discipleship* (SCM), pp. 54, 58, 63.
12. John 3:36
13. 2 Thess. 1:8
14. James 1:22
15. Wilson, *With Christ in the School of Disciple Building*, p. 273.
16. Mark 8:31
17. Isa. 53:3
18. John 15:20
19. 2 Tim. 3:12
20. Rom. 6:3-8; Gal. 2:20; 5:24
21. Rom. 6:11-12
22. Heb. 10:18
23. Col. 1:24
24. Heb. 12:3f
25. Phil. 2:5-7
26. 1 Pet. 2:21
27. 1 Pet. 4:12-13
28. Gal. 5
29. 1 John 2:15-16
30. 2 Cor. 5:17, *Phillips*
31. Col. 2:21-23
32. 1 Tim. 4:1-4
33. *The Cost of Discipleship* (SCM), p. 89.
34. Snyder, *Community of the King*, pp. 115-116.
35. Rom. 8:21-25
36. Gal. 6:2
37. *Towards Renewal*, Issue 19, Autumn 1979.
38. John 17:4
39. Rev. 3:16

## 12/ABOUNDING IN HOPE
1. Luke 10:21, *Weymouth*
2. Quoted in *The Church of England Newspaper*, 13 September 1973.
3. 1 Pet. 4:12-14

4. Ps. 126:1-6
5. P. B. Shelley, "Ode to the West Wind."
6. *A New Pentecost?* (Darton, Longman & Todd, 1975), p. 90.
7. Cardinal Suenens
8. John 12:24
9. 1 Cor. 4:8-13
10. Heb. 12:2
11. Col. 1:24
12. Rom. 8:18
13. Suenens, *The Church of England Newsletter* (13 September 1973), p. xi.
14. *Christ and the Media* (Hodder & Stoughton, 1977), p. 43.
15. Phil. 3:8, 10
16. 2 Cor. 1:8, 10
17. Isa. 45:3
18. *Tortured for Christ* (Hodder & Stoughton, 1967), p. 19 and *In God's Underground* (W. H. Allen, 1968), p. 54.
19. *The Open Church* (SCM, 1978), p. 35.
20. 2 Cor. 4:11-12
21. 2 Cor. 1:3-7, TLB
22. 2 Cor. 12:9-10
23. Phil. 1:14
24. 2 Cor. 4:16-18
25. *Mere Christianity* (Collins, 1952), p. 116.
26. Phil. 1:21, *Phillips*
27. Luke 21:25-28
28. 2 Pet. 3:10
29. Ezek. 16:49-50
30. Isa. 60:1

LaVergne, TN USA
09 February 2010

172617LV00001B/152/P